# AI and Green Innovation for Achieving Sustainable Development Goals

Cristina Raluca Gh. Popescu
*University of Bucharest, Romania & The Bucharest University of Economic Studies, Romania*

IGI Global
Scientific Publishing
Publishing Tomorrow's Research Today

| | |
|---|---|
| Vice President of Editorial | Melissa Wagner |
| Director of Acquisitions | Mikaela Felty |
| Director of Book Development | Jocelynn Hessler |
| Production Manager | Mike Brehm |
| Cover Design | Jose Rosado |

Published in the United States of America by
IGI Global Scientific Publishing
701 East Chocolate Avenue
Hershey, PA, 17033, USA
Tel: 717-533-8845 | Fax: 717-533-7115
Website: https://www.igi-global.com E-mail: cust@igi-global.com



Library of Congress Cataloging-in-Publication Data

LCCN: (CIP Data Pending)
ISBN13: 9798337375847
Isbn13Softcover: 9798337375854
EISBN13: 9798337375861

British Cataloguing in Publication Data
A Cataloguing in Publication record for this book is available from the British Library.

# Editorial Advisory Board

Cristina Loranca-Valle, *Department of Economics and Business Management, University of Alcala, Spain*

Rahul R. Verma, *Meera Bai Institute of Technology, Delhi University, India*

Seda Yıldırım, *Tekirdağ Namık Kemal Üniversitesi, Turkey*

# Table of Contents

# Detailed Table of Contents



This study conducts a literature analysis to examine AI's role in advancing sustainable manufacturing, tracing its evolution from early pollution control measures to modern AI-driven industrial optimisation. Additionally, AI enhances supply chain management, smart grids, and sustainable product development by optimising material selection and manufacturing processes. This study explores key research questions surrounding eco-friendly manufacturing, AI-driven waste reduction, and the long-term environmental impact of AI-based sustainability efforts. Addressing these concerns will help industries and policymakers integrate AI solutions while maintaining environmental responsibility. Future research must focus on developing energy-efficient AI models and sustainable hardware to maximize environmental benefits. As AI continues to evolve, its applications in sustainable manufacturing will be instrumental in balancing industrial growth with ecological preservation, paving the way for a more sustainable industrial future.

comprehensive and reputable academic databases. The selected time frame (2008–2024) ensures the inclusion of relevant, high-quality research while minimizing bias.



This chapter discusses importance of integrating green innovation technology within the manufacturing industry to foster development. It emphasizes that such technologies can reduce environmental impacts, enhance resource efficiency, and contribute to regulatory compliance. Key themes include the drivers for adopting green innovations, such as competitive advantage, consumer demand for sustainable practices, and the need for cooperate social responsibility. This chapter argues that businesses that embrace these innovations can achieve sustainability goals while also achieve economic benefits, improved brand reputation, and long-term sustainability goals but also achieve economic benefits, improved brand reputation, and long-term viability. By presenting case studies and practical examples, the chapter illustrates successful implementation of green technology in manufacturing processes, highlighting the potential for both environmental and economic gains.



This chapter proposes a comprehensive framework for integrating Artificial Intelligence (AI) in education, emphasizing ethical governance, innovation, and equity. The framework addresses key dimensions such as digital literacy, scalability, accessibility, and responsible AI adoption aligned with ethical principles. It highlights the need for inclusive policies that ensure transparency, accountability, and fairness while promoting lifelong learning and social justice. The framework also outlines implications for institutions, communities, and policymakers aiming to balance technological advancement with human-centered education. Limitations include the lack of empirical validation and contextual variation, indicating the need for future studies to test the model in diverse educational settings.

# Foreword

On this wonderful occasion, I am delighted to present in this section some of the most relevant ideas fostered in the IGI Global book on "AI and Green Innovation for Achieving Sustainable Development Goals". To begin with, I strongly believe that digital maturity and digital ecosystems are increasingly recognized as powerful and unique enablers toward the United Nations Sustainable Development Goals (SDGs). Additionally, after careful consideration and based on extensive research, I want to point out that specialists' acknlwodge that digital maturity and digital ecosystems intersect and influence sustainable development.

This book plays a crucial role in offering answers to vital questions. In particular, some of these key questions are highlighted here; the main aspects derived from addressing these questions being noted as well:

## WHAT IS DIGITAL MATURITY?

This is one of the most important questions that come to mind in this context. Hence, digital maturity refers to how well an organization integrates digital technologies into its operations, decision-making, and culture. Likewise, the studies show that digital maturity tackles the way in which governments are able to integrate digital technologies into their structure, adapting to the challenges of the new economy. Interestingly, another important side of digital maturity that requires dedication is the manner in which the society is able to integrate digital technologies into the daily activities. That is the reason why the answers to the major question "What is digital maturity?" delve around the following aspects:

- **The Digital Readiness:** In this day and age, it is of utmost importance to achieve digital readiness, which means that the infrastructure, the skills, and the policies should focus on adopting digital tools. The digitalization process makes everything run smoothly when the infrastructure, the skills, and the policies target closing the gap in terms of the digital divide.

- **The Technology Integration:** Now more than ever, the use of the artificial intelligence (AI), the Internet of Things (IoT), cloud computing, and data analytics are being successfully promoted by specialists as the engines that support sustainability and sustainable development for a better future for all.
- **The Innovation Capacity:** The society changes constantly and the expectations that come from the new challenges are impressive. The Intellectual Capital as intangible asset is priceless, as it has always been, while Human Resources and Human Resources Management play memorable parts in the day-to-day activities. The entities innovation capacity becomes even more powerful when combined with the advantages that come from investing in research and development programs. In the same time, the use of the AI, the IoT, cloud computing, and data analytics will provide more and more diverse solutions to the current situations, which will ultimately lead to the individuals' ability to adapt and evolve together with the emerging technologies.

## What are digital ecosystems?

This is another thought-provoking question that finds it-self answered in this current book. There are so many definitions and characteristics that the digital ecosystems have been given, yet the crucial idea is that the digital ecosystems are interconnected networks of technologies, institutions, platforms, and users. These networks are extremely important because they collaborate in the spirit of the SDGs and the partnerships for the Global Goals. More importantly, besides the fact that these networks collaborate, it has been demonstrated that they have the power to co-evolve, which makes them even more necessary for the achievement of the sustainable development and sustainable economic growth in a society and economy that is under continuous evolution. It is extremely impressive to mention that the digital ecosystems include key elements, namely:

- The community engagement and inclusion, which ultimately makes the digital ecosystems vital in these days' context;
- The digital services and infrastructure, which promotes the benefits of digitalization and enhances individuals' capacity to connect and communicate;
- The open data platforms, which were vital in the COVID-19 pandemic and which continue to play major roles in several domains, such as, for example, in education;
- The public and private sector partnerships, which show that collaboration and cooperation are essential in challenging times.

All in all, the impact on the SDGs is very powerful, which is a very important elements pointed out in the book chapters that are part of this current project. Also, there are some major challenges that could raise interesting discussions able to accelerate knowledge and create powerful debates on the ideas of digital maturity and digital ecosystems. One question could be: How are the specific SDGs being transformed by digital ecosystems? Another question might be: What are the most relevant findings of some relevant case studies from different countries that showcase digital maturity and digital ecosystems? The list could be expended with: How can organizations assess their digital maturity? In continuation, new research could be built by answering to the question: What are some of the potential challenges of the digital transformation for the SDGs?

I am overwhelmed with joy to have had the great opportunity to delve into the wonderful world created by this IGI Global book, which makes me absolutely thrilled to congratulate my colleague, fellow researcher, and dear friend Full-Professor PhD. Cristina Raluca Gh. Popescu, from the University of Bucharest, Romania and The Bucharest University of Economic Studies, Romania, for the position of editor and for a job well-done, as usual.

Over the years, I had the opportunity to closely collaborate with Full-Professor PhD. Cristina Raluca Gh. Popescu on numerous occasions and I have always remarked her desire to support, in the best way possible, the SDGs, be creative and thorough in all activities, and always show the relentless desire to overcome obstacles in order to innovate and promote research and development at a worldwide level. In the same time, I have been always positively impressed by the accomplishments of a wide international research network that is so nicely supported by Full-Professor PhD. Cristina Raluca Gh. Popescu, since education is crucial these and access to novel projects is pivotal for the success of the economies and societies. In essence, we have in this case a successful partnership for the Global Goals, where academics, leaders, managers, professionals, and practitioners combine their knowledge and share their best practices for the well-being of us all.

I wish all of you wonderful reading and, in the same time, I hope that you will discover in this book the works of dedicated specialists and professionals that chose to address the most recent advantages and challenges faced by the accomplishment of the SDGs in the new economy.

## Bio (Presentation):

Jarmila Duháček Šebestová is Associate Professor at Silesian University in Opava, School of Business Administration in Karviná, Czechia. She is an experienced researcher focusing on not only on small businesses, non- profit organizations and social enterprises. She has participated in a number of international projects, including COST project, named Transnational Collaboration on Bullying, Migration and Integration at School Level (CA18115) or project financed by Technological Agency of Czechia (TAČR) named Second career entrepreneurship – from corporate to unicorn. She is Vice President of the European Council of Small Businesses for the Czech Republic promoting research activities within that area. Research interests: Small business performance, start- ups, non- profits evaluation, and social enterprises. She has an experience with chapters contribution, also reviewing chapters and finally editing two books within IGI Global or Springer.

**Jarmila Duháček Šebestová**
*Department of Business Economics and Management, Silesian University, Opava, Czech Republic*

# Preface

The global pursuit of the United Nations' 2030 Agenda for Sustainable Development continues to stand as one of the most pressing and ambitious commitments of our time. Yet, as emphasized by the UN Secretary-General Antonio Guterres in April 2023, the world has not fully achieved any of the 17 Sustainable Development Goals (SDGs). His caution that the Agenda may otherwise be remembered as "an epitaph for a world that might have been" underscores the urgency of transforming pledges into measurable progress.

In this context, digital technologies and artificial intelligence (AI) emerge as pivotal drivers of green innovation and sustainable transformation. They offer unparalleled potential to reshape economies, strengthen governance, and empower societies to accelerate toward the achievement of the SDGs. This book, *AI and Green Innovation for Achieving Sustainable Development Goals*, brings together insights from scholars, practitioners, and policymakers to explore how advanced digital ecosystems and digital maturity can be leveraged to create tangible impact across the global landscape.

The chapters of this edited volume examine the SDG Digital Acceleration Agenda and its vital role in mobilizing knowledge, resources, and technologies to address urgent global challenges. By analyzing key enablers such as AI-driven solutions, financial inclusion platforms, digital skills development, and government efficiency measures, this book highlights not only the opportunities but also the governance, regulatory, and ethical challenges that must be addressed. Each contribution offers case studies, examples, and conceptual frameworks that showcase how digital transformation can accelerate progress across all 169 SDG targets, from mitigating climate change and enhancing education to eradicating hunger and reducing poverty.

## CHAPTER OVERVIEW

The opening chapter, *Sustainable Manufacturing with AI-Driven Solutions: Strategies for a Sustainable Future*, traces the evolution of industrial practices from early pollution control measures to the adoption of AI-driven methods that optimize supply chains, smart grids, and product development. The chapter underscores the promise of artificial intelligence in advancing eco-friendly manufacturing and waste reduction, while also calling for attention to the environmental footprint of AI itself. By encouraging research into energy-efficient models and sustainable hardware, it demonstrates how industries can reconcile technological progress with ecological preservation.

In *Exploring Sustainable Technology Innovation and Green Tech Adoption Impacts on SDGs and Software Project Management*, the discussion turns to the crucial role of green technologies in both achieving the Sustainable Development Goals and enhancing project management practices. This chapter introduces concepts such as Agile Sustainability, Green Coding, and Life Cycle Assessment, highlighting how these methods can be embedded into software development to ensure more sustainable outcomes. Through case studies and practical insights, it equips policymakers, industry leaders, and project managers with strategies for overcoming barriers to adoption and for aligning innovation with long-term sustainability objectives.

*Artificial Intelligence for Accelerating Progress on Sustainable Development Goals (SDGs)* further explores AI's potential as a transformative tool across diverse sectors, including healthcare, education, agriculture, and climate monitoring. The chapter illustrates how AI enhances inclusivity and efficiency while raising important questions about fairness, data privacy, and algorithmic bias. It stresses the necessity of transparent governance and equitable access to ensure that technological benefits reach underserved communities. This balanced perspective underscores AI's promise as a driver of sustainable development when implemented with responsibility and human rights principles at its core.

The themes of opportunity and responsibility are carried forward in *Accelerating Progress on Sustainable Development Goals Using AI*. This chapter situates AI applications within the broader framework of digital maturity and ecosystem readiness, mapping capabilities such as predictive analytics, natural language processing, and computer vision to specific SDG targets. Drawing on global case studies, it demonstrates AI's ability to strengthen service delivery and predict risks, while acknowledging its limitations—including environmental costs and the exacerbation of digital divides. The analysis emphasizes the importance of robust infrastructure, organizational capacity, and open governance in maximizing AI's contribution to the SDGs.

The fifth chapter, *Artificial Intelligence for Sustainable Development: A Systematic Review of Literature*, offers a comprehensive review of peer-reviewed research on AI's role in sustainability. By examining articles published between 2008 and 2024, the authors identify research gaps and methodological limitations, particularly the lack of studies from underrepresented regions such as Africa and South America. The findings call for more robust quantitative approaches and broader geographic representation to advance reliable, generalizable knowledge. This synthesis provides a strong foundation for future inquiry into how AI can address global sustainability challenges.

Focusing on the manufacturing sector, *Exploration of Green Innovation Technology Adoption to Accelerate Sustainable Development in the Manufacturing Industry* highlights how green innovation technologies reduce environmental impacts while enhancing competitiveness and regulatory compliance. The chapter explores the drivers of adoption—including consumer demand, corporate responsibility, and long-term viability—while presenting case studies of successful implementation. By emphasizing both environmental and economic benefits, it demonstrates how manufacturing enterprises can advance sustainability while improving brand reputation and profitability.

The discussion shifts to education in *Integrating Artificial Intelligence in Education with a Strategic Framework for Ethical and Inclusive Innovation*. This chapter proposes a framework that balances the transformative potential of AI with the principles of ethical governance, equity, and social justice. It addresses the importance of digital literacy, accessibility, and accountability, offering guidance for policymakers and educational institutions seeking to implement AI responsibly. While acknowledging the need for further empirical validation, it provides a forward-looking roadmap for ensuring that AI in education fosters inclusivity and lifelong learning.

The final chapter in this section, *Mapping Health: Integrating Spatial Data Infrastructure with Visual Learning Techniques for Smart Healthcare*, illustrates the convergence of spatial intelligence and visual learning tools as a pathway to more responsive healthcare systems. By combining structured spatial data with AI-powered visualization and immersive technologies such as AR/VR, this chapter demonstrates how health operations, decision-making, and community engagement can be transformed. It emphasizes the need for interdisciplinary collaboration and ethical safeguards to ensure equitable access and resilient outcomes, positioning spatial intelligence as a vital enabler of smart healthcare innovation.

This book is designed as a resource for a diverse audience, including academicians, students, policymakers, quality and environment managers, and professionals across business, science, and technology fields. The breadth of its subjects—from business and management to medicine and healthcare, from social sciences to physical sciences—reflects the interdisciplinary nature of sustainable development in the digital era.

By bringing these perspectives together, we hope to provide a comprehensive, thought-provoking, and practice-oriented reference that supports global efforts to align digital innovation with the urgent imperatives of sustainability. Our aim is to inspire not only awareness but also action, demonstrating how AI and green innovation can together transform aspirations into concrete achievements for the benefit of present and future generations.

**Cristina Raluca Gh. Popescu**
*University of Bucharest, Romania & The Bucharest University of Economic Studies, Romania*

# Chapter 1
# Sustainable Manufacturing With AI-Driven Solutions:
## Strategies for Sustainable Future

**Neema Gupta**
https://orcid.org/0000-0003-3347-3202
*University School of Business, Chandigarh University, Mohali, India*

**Shikha Saloni**
https://orcid.org/0009-0007-3487-8064
*ITM University, India*

**Jyoti Dashora**
https://orcid.org/0009-0003-9280-8217
*University School of Business, Chandigarh University, Mohali, India*

**Kamal Preet**
*University School of Business, Chandigarh University, Mohali, India*

**Aditi Panjabi**
*Law Department, Chandigarh University, Mohali, India*

## ABSTRACT

*This study conducts a literature analysis to examine AI's role in advancing sustainable manufacturing, tracing its evolution from early pollution control measures to modern AI-driven industrial optimisation. Additionally, AI enhances supply chain management, smart grids, and sustainable product development by optimising material selection and manufacturing processes. This study explores key research*

DOI: 10.4018/979-8-3373-7584-7.ch001

*questions surrounding eco-friendly manufacturing, AI-driven waste reduction, and the long-term environmental impact of AI-based sustainability efforts. Addressing these concerns will help industries and policymakers integrate AI solutions while maintaining environmental responsibility. Future research must focus on developing energy-efficient AI models and sustainable hardware to maximize environmental benefits. As AI continues to evolve, its applications in sustainable manufacturing will be instrumental in balancing industrial growth with ecological preservation, paving the way for a more sustainable industrial future.*

## INTRODUCTION

The main difficulties for a society nowadays are the growing population and great resource use needed to sustain economic progress (Malek & Desai, 2020; Yu et al., 2021, Gupta, et al., 2024). Before the 1990s, the worldwide industrial sector prioritised economic gains over product quality enhancement; however, greater pollution, unsustainable resource consumption, and uncontrolled waste formation followed (Cassettari et al., 2017; Malek & Desai, 2020). First emerging in response to social, financial, and environmental concerns was sustainable manufacturing. Along with pollution, inefficient resource use, and severe environmental repercussions, fast industrial growth throughout the Industrial Revolution produced higher productivity, economic expansion, and technological advancements (Clark, 2007). Midway through the 20th century, growing awareness of industrial pollution surfaced, particularly in light of Rachel Carson's 1962 book Silent Spring's focus on the harmful consequences of chemical poisons. The 1972 Stockholm Conference of the United Nations Conference on the Human Environment highlighted the need of finding a balance between industrial expansion and environmental preservation, hence directing sustainable manufacturing (Handl, 2012). The Brundtland Report (1987) developed the idea even further by defining sustainable development as meeting present demands without harming future generations's potential to meet their own. Subsequently, attempts to incorporate sustainability into business operations have been more intense all around.

Encouragement of businesses to adopt resource-efficient technologies and greener production techniques by the Rio Earth Summit (1992) improved sustainable manufacturing by the 1990s and 2000s UN, 1992 Standards such ISO 14001 were adopted during this time to help companies use environmental management systems (Heras-Saizarbitoria & Boiral, 2013). Sustainable manufacturing aims to minimise environmental effect and maximise resource efficiency across production, therefore limiting environmental influence and maximising resource economy. This requires including sustainable materials, simplifying energy use, and eliminating waste. Companies adopting sustainable manufacturing techniques not only lower their carbon footprint but also improve brand image and raise long-term economic viability. Using artificial intelligence (AI) and machine learning among other cutting-edge technologies, industrial processes are being maximised and maintenance needs are foreseen, therefore reducing resource waste and downtime. Reducing material waste and encouraging innovation help the concepts of the circular economy—which focus on designing objects for lifetime, reuse, and recyclability—help to support sustainability. Lean manufacturing and green manufacturing are two widely utilised approaches that boost output while reducing environmental impact (Womack & Jones, 1997). Further developments in the twenty-first century have included Industry 4.0 technologies using automation and artificial intelligence to maximise resources and the integration of renewable energy sources (Geissdoerfer et al., 2017). The Paris Agreement (2015) enhanced government and business pledges to lower carbon emissions and implement environmentally friendly policies even more (Jayaraman 2015). Businesses nowadays still concentrate on reaching carbon neutrality, cutting waste, and utilising sustainable ideas to guarantee long-term financial viability while protecting the environment.

The integration of artificial intelligence with sustainable manufacturing offers chances to lower environmental impact and raise efficiency. Real-time production data analysis by AI-powered systems identifies inefficiencies and suggests waste creation and mininmise energy consumption improvement suggestions (Kamble et al., 2023). Artificial intelligence algorithms focus on the optimal use of raw materials, energy, and water via use of historical data and present manufacturing limits, therefore lowering resource consumption and cost savings (Bousdekis et al., 2024). AI also improves demand forecasting, so enabling companies to match output to demand of the market so reducing overproduction (Ghobakhloo & Fathi, 2023). Artificial intelligence also improves energy economy by analysing consumption patterns and adjusting equipment settings depending on industrial schedules and environmental conditions (Kerin & Pham, 2024). Artificial intelligence-driven smart grids help to incorporate renewable energy sources into industrial operations and further enable efficient energy management.Waste reduction is another aspect where AI contributes to sustainable manufacturing. In order to minimise waste, computer vision and machine learning algorithms helps to identify defects from the beginning in production, (Kamble et al., 2023). With the help of enhanced material sorting and categorisation, artificial intelligence also optimises recycling processes, so improving their cost-effective and efficient nature (Ghobakhloo & Fathi, 2023). Predictive maintenance, another vital artificial intelligence technique, uses sensor data to forecast equipment faults, thereby improving sustainability (Patibandla, 2024). This proactive approach reduces resource waste from inefficient machinery running (Cheng et al., 2023), lowers downtime, and raises equipment lifetime. AI also helps to design sustainable products. Artificial intelligence-driven generative design tools analyse product specs and recommend materials and manufacturing techniques that minimise environmental impact while maintaining performance (Bousdekis et al., 2024).

AI also maximises logistics and supply chain management, reducing transportation-related pollutants and improving overall efficiency (Jabbour et al., 2024). AI-powered systems examine climate conditions, traffic patterns, and inventory levels to identify the most efficient shipping routes and methods (Ghobakhloo & Fathi, 2023). While AI offers many advantages, its emergence and application need energy and resources. Consequently, sustainability benefits have to be weighed against their environmental impact (Vishwakarma et al., 2023). Ensuring a net-positive impact on sustainable manufacturing depends on research on energy-efficient artificial intelligence hardware and algorithms (Kerin & Pham, 2024). Therefore, the research questions (RQs) intended to be explored in this chapter are given below:

RQ1: What challenges occur in environmentally friendly manufacturing?

RQ2: What are the objectives to integrate AI to incorporate artificial intelligence to highlight issues of sustainability?

RQ3: What role does AI play to lower waste and raise recycling rates of efficiency?

RQ4: What are the potential challenges and limitations of including artificial intelligence into sustainable manufacturing?

RQ5: How will artificial intelligence influence the long run environment in sustainable manufacturing?

Examining these issues will enable companies and legislators to maximise artificial intelligence's ability to drive environmentally friendly manufacturing while lowering its associated costs. As artificial intelligence develops, its uses in sustainable manufacturing will be increasingly important in helping to balance environmental responsibility with economic progress thereby creating a more sustainable industrial future.

## LITERATURE REVIEW

### Existing Research on AI Application in Sustainable Manufacturing

Research has indicated AI's possible applications in optimising energy usage, waste reduction, enhancement in resource efficiency, and product lifetime management (Gautam, et al., 2020). Machine learning algorithms have been used (Mohapatra, 2024) to forecast equipment malfunctions, control industrial schedules, and limit environmental impacts. Research on AI-driven supply chain optimisation to reduce transportation pollutants and improve overall sustainability have also been emphasised on (Onukwulu, et al., 2021). Before deployment, artificial intelligence-powered simulations and digital twins have also been tested and refined sustainable manufacturing techniques (Khapekar, et al., 2024). Although, the area indicates important potential, challenges remain in data quality, integration with existing systems, and indicating the environmental effect of AI itself. Several studies have looked at how artificial intelligence might maximise energy usage, lower waste, increase resource efficiency, and improve product lifetime management (Wang, et al., 2021). These areas are essential aspects of sustainable production where artificial intelligence technology can significantly contribute. Maximising manufacturing schedules using artificial intelligence algorithms has shown incredible capacity in reducing waste creation and energy consumption (Wu, et al., 2012). Artificial intelligence may develop quite strong manufacturing schedules that optimise result while reducing resource consumption and environmental impact by means of the analysis of enormous volumes of data from various sources, including past data, market demand, and resource availability. Ethical concerns of artificial intelligence use in manufacturing like data privacy and job displacement also demand great attention (Samarawickrama, 2022). Developing frameworks for responsible artificial intelligence use in sustainable industrial environments will help to ensure that the technology is employed concurrently benefiting the environment and society.

## Current Sustainable Manufacturing Practices

Sustainable manufacturing techniques have received important traction in recent years as industries put efforts to minimise their environmental impact and enhance resource efficiency. These practices consist of various strategies, including the use of renewable energy sources, closed-loop production systems, and lean manufacturing principles. One of the key strategies for sustainable manufacturing is the adoption of renewable energy sources, such as solar, wind, and geothermal power, which assist minimise reliance on fossil fuels and lower greenhouse gas emissions (Musavi, et al., 2024). Another important method is the implementation of closed-loop production systems, which emphasise on eliminating waste by reusing and recycling materials within manufacturing processes (Winkler, 2011). Additionally, the application of lean manufacturing principles has become prevalent, optimising production processes to minimise waste, improve efficiency, and enhance product quality (Stowe, 2020). Many companies are also integrating circular economy practices, designing products for easy disassembly, repair, and recycling to extend their lifecycle (Chen, & Dagestani, 2023). Furthermore, recycling and the development of biodegradable materials are gaining momentum, particularly in industries like packaging and consumer goods, where alternatives to persistent plastics are being explored. The role of advanced technologies in sustainable manufacturing is significant. Artificial Intelligence (AI) and machine learning are being utilized to optimize production schedules, predict maintenance needs, and identify inefficiencies in real time (Rath, et al., 2022). The Internet of Things (IoT) enables precise monitoring of energy consumption, emissions, and resource usage, allowing for continuous improvement. Automation and robotics contribute to sustainability by improving precision, reducing material waste, and enhancing worker safety (Liu, et al., 2016). Meanwhile, 3D printing and additive manufacturing allow for on-demand production, reducing inventory needs and lowering transportation-related emissions (Gift, et al., 2024). Despite these advancements, there are several challenges in sustainable manufacturing. One major issue is scaling sustainable practices across global supply chains, as ensuring sustainability standards at every stage of international production networks is complex. Additionally, economic barriers persist, as the initial investment required for sustainable technologies and processes can be substantial. Many companies, however, recognize the long-term cost savings and competitive advantages that come with sustainability (Yao, & Desalegn, 2023). Another challenge is regulatory compliance, as companies must adapt to stricter environmental regulations and sustainability reporting standards, such as the Global Reporting Initiative (GRI) and the Science Based Targets initiative (SBTi). Governments and industries are addressing these challenges through government policies and industry collaboration. Various environmental regulations and incentives, including carbon pricing mechanisms, extended producer responsibility laws, and green procurement policies, are pushing manufacturers toward sustainability (Fukuyama, 1997). Industry-academia partnerships are also playing a critical role, fostering research initiatives that focus on bio-based materials, energy-efficient processes, and circular economy models. Moreover, education and workforce development are becoming essential, with universities and vocational programs incorporating sustainability principles into their curricula to prepare future engineers and managers for leadership in sustainable manufacturing (Naude, et al., 2010). Looking ahead, future trends and innovations in sustainable manufacturing will likely focus on blockchain technology for supply chain transparency, improving traceability and accountability (Bai, & Sarkis, 2020). Additionally, advancements in materials science and green chemistry are leading to the development of eco-friendly materials and more sustainable production methods (Mishra, & Giri, 2018). Emerging technologies such as AI-driven efficiency, energy-efficient AI hardware, and smart grids for better integration of renewable energy are also expected to play a growing role in sustainability efforts.

## AI & Circular Economy Integration: Expanded Discussion

AI significantly advances circular economy goals by enabling intelligent systems across the product lifecycle:

**Product Lifecycle Extension**: AI uses condition-monitoring and predictive analytics to prevent premature product disposal. For example, companies like *GE* and *Siemens* use AI to track industrial equipment wear and proactively schedule remanufacturing or refurbishment.

**Intelligent Disassembly**: Using robotics combined with AI-driven object recognition, systems can disassemble products (e.g., electronics or EV batteries) efficiently by identifying valuable or hazardous components. This supports urban mining and high-quality material recovery.

**Closed-Loop Systems**: AI optimizes material return flows, ensures traceability (often via blockchain-AI integration), and manages reverse logistics by forecasting return volumes and automating sorting at collection centers.

*Figure 1. Framework of Interrelated concepts*

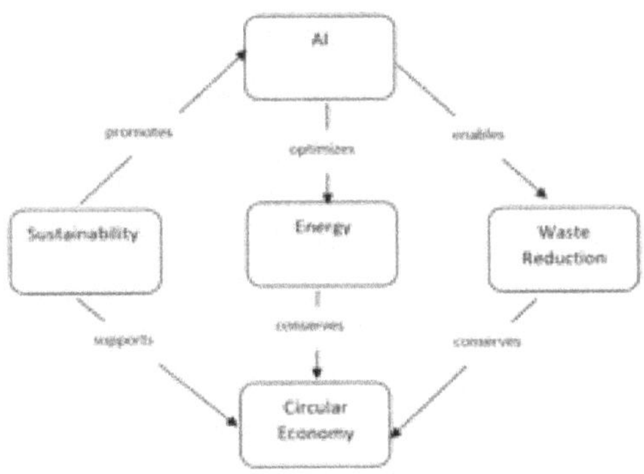


*Source: Author's owm*

## Enriching the Theoretical Framework

1. **Lack of Recent Theoretical Contributions**

While the paper effectively introduces foundational theories in sustainable manufacturing, such as lean manufacturing, the circular economy, and early sustainability regulations, it does not engage with cutting-edge frameworks from the past 3–5 years. Integrating recent theoretical advancements, such as *AI ethics frameworks for industrial automation*, *Industry 5.0 human-centric approaches*, or *AI–sustainability convergence models*, would strengthen the theoretical underpinning.

2. **Absence of Multidisciplinary Synthesis**

The current framework treats AI and sustainability as parallel tracks. Recent literature emphasizes their convergence especially in transdisciplinary integration involving AI, environmental science, and systems engineering. Incorporating models from **resilience** engineering, policy-informatics, or cyber-physical-social systems (CPSS) would offer a more robust conceptual base.

3. **Limited Consideration of Governance and Regulation**

The framework could be further enhanced by including policy instruments like the EU AI Act, Green Deal, **and** ISO 42001 for AI management systems, showing how regulatory shifts shape theoretical thinking in sustainable AI manufacturing.

## Need for Novel Perspectives and Contributions

1. **Predominant Focus on Established Concepts**

The paper reiterates widely accepted applications of AI in manufacturing, such as predictive maintenance and supply chain optimization. These are useful, but lack novelty. Emerging ideas such as AI for regenerative design, AI-enabled net-zero compliance, or autonomous sustainability agents are missing and could elevate the originality of the content.

2. **Limited Proposal of Innovative Solutions**

There are no clearly proposed innovative mechanisms or conceptual models to guide sustainable AI adoption. The inclusion of an original framework, maturity model, or decision-support tool even at a conceptual level would contribute a fresh perspective.

3. **Global South Perspectives Underexplored**

The discussion mostly reflects trends from industrialized nations. Including contextual solutions or barriers from developing economies, such as frugal AI models, digital infrastructure limitations, or low-cost deployment strategies, would enrich the global relevance of the paper.

4. **Opportunities for Interdisciplinary Collaboration Underutilized**

The manuscript could suggest collaboration frameworks connecting engineering, policy, and social science disciplines. For example, the Triple Helix Model (university-industry-government), Living Labs, or co-creation workshops for sustainable innovation can be proposed to encourage cross-sectoral knowledge flow and research co-design.

## Gaps in knowledge and Potential areas for Innovation

There are still a number of unaddressed knowledge gaps and untapped avenues for innovation in sustainable manufacturing, which presents chances for progress. To ensure moral and environmentally responsible practices throughout international supply chains, supply chain transparency and traceability necessitate the creation of more reliable blockchain technologies and standardised sustainability reporting systems. To improve material recovery, the implementation of the circular economy requires creative closed-loop systems as well as cutting-edge disassembly and recycling technology. Scalability and cost-effectiveness issues with the creation of biodegradable and bio-based materials necessitate more investigation into new materials with appropriate manufacturing characteristics. Better energy storage options and affordable on-site renewable energy generation for industrial applications are required for energy efficiency and renewable integration. Predictive maintenance, autonomous sustainability improvements, and production process optimisation can all be achieved with the help of advanced AI and machine learning. More research is required to completely realise the potential of nanoparticles and advanced materials in order to improve product performance while preserving durability and recyclability. More effective reaction catalysts and environmentally safe substitutes for dangerous chemicals are essential for green chemistry and sustainable chemical processes. Advanced recycling and purification technologies, together with waterless or low-water production methods, are necessary for water conservation and treatment. Enhancing the effectiveness of capture technology and creating strategies to incorporate collected carbon into production processes should be the main goals of carbon capture and utilisation. To improve recyclability and prolong product shelf life, sustainable packaging solutions require cutting-edge materials and intelligent technologies. Additionally, for real-time sustainability effect assessments in manufacturing, life cycle assessment technologies need to be improved. More environmentally friendly 3D printing materials and waste-reduction strategies are needed for sustainable additive manufacturing. Designing energy-efficient systems that maximise resource utilisation should be the main goal of sustainable robotics and automation. Manufacturing biomimicry offers a chance to investigate innovations inspired by nature for more environmentally friendly production techniques. Last but not least, social sustainability in manufacturing necessitates the creation of fresh approaches to improve worker safety, well-being, and skill development while evaluating and enhancing the social impact of manufacturing processes. By filling in these gaps, sustainable manufacturing will advance towards increased effectiveness, adaptability, and environmental responsibility. While several studies have investigated the applications of AI in sustainable manufacturing, this chapter provides a comprehensive synthesis by integrating not only technological aspects (e.g., predictive maintenance, recycling optimization) but also ethical, environmental, and long-run systemic considerations. Unlike prior research which tends to be domain-specific or fragmented, this study offers a consolidated framework that connects AI capabilities with sustainable strategies across the entire value chain—from raw material selection to end-of-life waste management. Moreover, by structuring the research through clearly defined research questions (RQs), this work offers a policy-relevant lens that differentiates it from existing meta-analyses and technical reviews.

Despite extensive research on AI in sustainable manufacturing, deeper engagement with foundational frameworks like the Triple Bottom Line (TBL) and Life Cycle Thinking (LCT) remains limited. The TBL framework, which emphasizes the interplay between environmental, economic, and social sustainability, reveals critical gaps in current AI applications—particularly the underrepresentation of social metrics such as labor equity, community impact, and job displacement. Likewise, while AI technologies contribute to environmental and economic efficiencies, their social implications require further empirical validation. Life Cycle Thinking offers another vital lens by evaluating sustainability across product lifespans, yet most AI-driven models focus predominantly on the production phase, with limited integration of end-of-life considerations such as recyclability and disposal. Comparative global case studies, such as Siemens' use of AI to optimize energy in German smart factories, or Unilever's data-driven water efficiency strategies in India, demonstrate practical advances but also expose limitations in standardization and scalability. Additionally, research often remains descriptive, lacking evaluative comparisons across industries, regions, or AI maturity levels. Thus, there is a pressing need for more critical, interdisciplinary studies that align AI deployment with comprehensive sustainability metrics, ensuring AI not only enhances efficiency but also promotes equitable, long-term sustainability outcomes.

*Table 1. Comparison of the present study with the existing studies*

| Focus Area | Existing Studies | Present Study's Contribution |
|---|---|---|
| **AI in Waste Management** | ***Krishna Pasupuleti (2024)*** – AI-powered systems for sustainable power and recycling<br>***Neema & Gor (2022)*** – Smart Waste Management Using IoT | Adds lifecycle optimization, including material recovery, and alignment with recycling policies (EPR, circular economy). |
| **Predictive Maintenance** | ***Mohapatra (2024)*** – Generative AI for Predictive Maintenance<br>***Patibandla (2024)*** – Predictive Maintenance in Aviation using AI | Integrates predictive maintenance within a broader sustainable production strategy, emphasizing resource optimization and equipment lifespan. |
| **Ethical Implications of AI** | ***Samarawickrama (2022)*** – AI Governance and Ethics Framework<br>***Mutsuddi (2024)*** – Ethical Considerations in the Intersection of AI and Environmental Science | Adds a holistic treatment of AI ethics, including fairness, transparency, job displacement, and social responsibility in sustainability. |
| **Rebound & Long-Run Effects** | ***Gautam et al. (2020)*** – AI's Role in Sustainable Energy *(mentions efficiency gains)*<br>***Zhang et al. (2021)*** – Energy-consumption driven manufacturing systems | Discusses rebound effects (e.g., overproduction due to efficiency) and lifecycle environmental impact, which are largely missing from prior work. |
| **Policy & Regulatory Considerations** | ***Xu & Wang (2024)*** – Energy regulatory compliance and CSR<br>***Fukuyama (1997)*** – Technological incentives under environmental regulations | Synthesizes multi-level policy implications—national (e.g., carbon pricing), organizational (ISO standards), and global frameworks (UN SDGs, Paris Agreement). |

## Comparative Insights from Global Case Studies:

Worldwide, the use of AI in sustainable manufacturing is very different, depending on factors such as technology, policies and sustainability. At Amberg Electronics Plant, Siemens uses digital twins powered by AI to achieve an extremely high process quality and lower energy usage. It demonstrates that combining AI and smart factory ideas can increase both the economy and the environment under a strong Industry 4.0 system. On the other hand, Unilever's Indian factories use AI to reduce water and energy use in regions where drought is a risk. While they boost efficiency in specific places such initiatives make clear that unique sustainability goals should be placed on water conservation in water-deficient developing nations. Yet, their attention normally lies more on environmental and economic data, leaving behind social aspects in the Triple Bottom Line approach.

In America, Tesla is using artificial intelligence (AI) combined with robotics to increase accuracy and reduce error in production. Though Tesla's automation saves energy in vehicle production, some critics say the company does not provide enough details about how it treats employees and the impact on employment. It demonstrates that a better outcome could be achieved by tying AI breakthroughs with approaches that support inclusion at work. Throughout its wide network of electronics plants in China, Foxconn has applied AI for early problem finding and maintenance. Despite saving money and using less energy, the efforts have received criticism for not revealing enough about emissions and supply chain transparency—important aspects of a product's total sustainability. It is clear through comparison that developed countries generally excel in technology and automation, while India and other similar countries have unique methods of solving local problems, but are held back by a lower level of AI. In every example, the "social" aspect of sustainability often gets less attention. The majority of AI implementations are mainly concerned with how items are produced but neglect the parts before and after production. So, it is crucial that future AI-sustainability research and industry plans use Life Cycle Thinking and the Triple Bottom Line together.

## RESEARCH METHODOLOGY

Literature review was employed to explain the present study. At initial stage, we classified published research in the form of research themes. A systematic thematic analysis was conducted on 112 peer-reviewed studies from databases such as Scopus, IEEE Xplore, and Web of Science, using PRISMA methodology to ensure replicability. Last, we looked at each issue from a variety of angles, including ideas, constructs, conceptual structures, and research gaps.

### Sustainability Challenges in Manufacturing

Manufacturing industries face numerous sustainability challenges as they strive to balance economic growth with environmental and social responsibilities. These challenges include reducing carbon emissions, minimizing waste generation, optimizing resource utilization, and ensuring ethical labor practices throughout the supply chain (Hölsgens, 2016). The complexity of these challenges is further compounded by the global nature of modern manufacturing operations and the interconnectedness of supply chains.

*Table 2. AI Technologies in Sustainable Manufacturing*

| AI Technology | Role in Sustainable Manufacturing | Benefits | Challenges |
|---|---|---|---|
| **Generative Design** | AI-generated product designs that use less material and energy while maintaining functionality I | Optimized material use, Lightweight, eco-friendly products | High computational cost, Interpretability and validation of outputs I |
| **AI-Powered Circularity Tools I** | Maintenance and retraining needs I<br>I Enables tracing, intelligent disassembly, remanufacturing, and circular supply chain mapping I | Extends product life<br>Closes the material loop<br>Informs end-of-life strategies | Requires product-level traceability<br>Integration with legacy systems and materials databases |
| **Demand Forecasting** | Anticipates consumer needs using time-series and market data, aligning production with demand | Avoids overproduction<br>Reduces inventory waste I | Uncertainty in dynamic markets<br>Accuracy reliant on data comprehensiveness |
| **Predictive Maintenance** | Predicts equipment failure using sensor data and ML, reducing unplanned downtime and extending machinery life | Reduces energy waste.<br>Minimizes material waste<br>Increases equipment longevity | Requires extensive sensor infrastructure<br>Data quality and integration issues |

**Technological Innovations for Sustainability:** To meet the demand for products worldwide, manufacturers are now applying new technologies and methods to reduce energy use, apply circular ideas and make greener goods. As a result, automakers must fund substantial research and development and start using modern manufacturing methods, including those found in Industry 4.0 and factories that are smart and use various additive techniques. They help shrink environmental harm and improve both competitiveness and productivity (Bhattasali & Savarimuthu, 2021).

**Energy Efficiency in Manufacturing:** Manufacturing industries consider improving energy efficiency a main priority. Many places are installing solar and wind power to eliminate their dependence on fossil fuels and act more environmentally friendly. In addition, smart energy management systems and advanced grids are installed to help save energy and reduce wastage (Micieta, & Binasova, 2013). (Refer Table 3)

*Table 3. Energy Efficiency in manufacturing*

| Aspect | Traditional Manufacturing | AI-Augmented Manufacturing |
|---|---|---|
| **Energy Efficiency** | ~30–40% on average (due to batch production & idle time) | ~60–75% due to real-time optimization & predictive control |
| **Energy Use per Unit (kWh/unit)** | ~10–12 kWh/unit (depending on process) | ~6–8 kWh/unit (with AI-driven optimization) |
| **Waste-Related Energy Loss** | ~15–25% due to overproduction, defects, delays | ~5–10% through smart detection and adaptive control |
| **AI Infrastructure Energy Cost** | N/A | +2–5% total energy use (for edge devices & servers) |
| **Net Energy Saving** | Baseline | ~15–25% improvement over traditional setup |

Source: Author's own

**Waste Reduction and Resource Optimisation:** Manufacturers are increasingly adopting lean manufacturing principles and implementing closed-loop systems to minimize material waste and maximize resource efficiency. This includes strategies such as remanufacturing, refurbishing, and recycling of products and materials, as well as the use of sustainable and biodegradable materials in production processes (Simpson, 2012).

**Water Conservation and Management:** Water conservation and management are now important for sustainability, mainly in industries that use a lot of water. Organizations in the industry are choosing innovative ways to recycle water, enhance how they clean wastewater and find other sources of water to have a smaller effect on nearby water supplies (Khalfallah, & Leitão, 2024).

**Regulatory Compliance and Social Responsibility:** The pressure on manufacturers comes from new rules and rising consumer expectations about their actions to protect the environment and society. Following international certifications such as ISO 14001 for the environment and SA8000 for social responsibility, is important as well. Due to increased demand, companies now have to show where their raw materials come from and explain the working conditions at all levels of manufacturing (Xu, & Wang, 2024).

**Extended Producer Responsibility (EPR):** More and more, the term Extended Producer Responsibility is being used, as it shifts some management of products back to producers after they are sold such as disposal and recycling. Consequently, products now need to be built to last, to be repairable and to be recycled, while take-back schemes and recycling facilities should be introduced (Patra, & Mishra, 2024).

**Lifecycle Assessment (LCA) Methodologies:** More and more manufacturers are relying on life cycle assessment (LCA) to measure the environmental effects of their products throughout their entire lifespan. By following this method, areas in the product lifecycle with the most potential for better sustainability can be spotted (Bassey, et. al., 2024).

**Employee Engagement and Training:** Having engaged and well-trained employees is vital for manufacturing businesses to push their sustainability goals. Encouraging sustainability at work and equipping employees with the skills and support needed to apply sustainable solutions can result in better outcomes for the environment and efficiency of resources (Nandan & Jyoti, 2020).

**Role of Digital Technologies in Sustainability:** The use of digital technologies and data analytics is thought to be a major factor in addressing the sustainability issues found in manufacturing. The use of AI and similar technologies can offer manufacturers much better control over their processes, helping reduce harmful use of resources and minimize environmental damage (Ginters & Revathy, 2021).

## Case Study

### BMW Group – AI for Sustainable Automotive Manufacturing (Germany)

BMW has become a top company in utilizing Artificial Intelligence for environmentally friendly manufacturing, specifically at its plants in Leipzig and Munich, Germany. The paint shops at BMW use AI to automatically control the paint, its temperature and the use of energy by reading data from sensors. By using the new adaptive control, the building is using about 25% less energy. AI-based computer vision is used by the company to spot issues in vehicle exterior surfaces, helping to avoid unnecessary rework and waste. With their help, greater efficiency in quality control helps reduce both emissions and waste, in line with BMW's commitment to the EU's Green Deal and its own goal of becoming carbon neutral by 2030. This case shows that AI improves manufacturing accuracy and helps achieve deep decarbonization in productive environments.

### Arvind Limited – AI for Sustainable Textile Manufacturing (India)

One of the biggest textile companies in India, Arvind Limited, offers an excellent example of AI helping sustainability in the Global South. Because the dyeing and spinning business uses lots of resources, AI technology helps Arvind to reduce how much energy and water is used. Machine learning helps predict the highest energy needed and automatically tunes actions to save energy, amounting to 12% savings across the year. The company uses AI to guide its water recycling efforts. AI controls the treatment and chemical addition to water, allowing for the reuse of 30% of water in both dyeing and finishing processes. Arvind's use of AI has both helped the environment and lowered costs while enhancing product quality. Here, we can see that sustainability in older markets and developing nations can be fueled by AI, as long as there is a solid dedication to digital change.

## Objectives for Integrating AI to Address Sustainability Challenges

**Establishing Clear Goals and Metrics:** To effectively integrate AI in addressing sustainability challenges, organizations must first define specific goals and measurable success criteria. Conducting a comprehensive assessment of current operations can help identify inefficiencies and determine how AI-driven solutions can enhance sustainability performance. Organizations should prioritize areas where AI can have the greatest impact, such as automating repetitive tasks, improving decision-making processes, and optimizing resource usage (Tripathi, et al., 2024).

**Developing a Comprehensive Implementation Strategy:** A well-structured AI implementation strategy should encompass multiple organizational aspects. This includes designing robust training programs to equip employees with the necessary skills to collaborate effectively with AI systems. Furthermore, organizations must establish strong data management protocols, emphasizing data quality, security, and ethical considerations to maintain the integrity and reliability of AI-generated insights (Bagiyam, et al., 2024).

**Ensuring Continuous Monitoring and Enhancement:** AI system performance should be continuously evaluated to ensure optimal results and drive ongoing improvements. Organisations must implement regular monitoring of key performance indicators (KPIs), collect feedback from end-users, and conduct periodic audits to refine AI capabilities. This iterative approach helps organisations adapt AI systems to evolving sustainability challenges and technological advancements (Berlin et al., 2013).

**Fostering Leadership Support and Innovation Culture:** Successful AI integration requires strong leadership commitment and a workplace culture that embraces innovation and change. Organizations should encourage employees to actively contribute ideas and insights throughout the AI implementation process. A collaborative approach can help anticipate potential challenges early on and develop effective solutions to maximize AI's sustainability benefits (Hölsgens, 2016).

**Addressing Ethical Considerations in AI Adoption:** AI-driven decision-making must align with corporate values and societal expectations. Organizations need to proactively address ethical concerns such as bias mitigation, transparency, and accountability in AI applications. Establishing clear guidelines for responsible AI usage ensures that sustainability goals are pursued in an ethical and socially responsible manner (Balan, 2024).

**Building Strategic Partnerships for AI Integration:** Organizations should actively engage with AI experts, technology vendors, and industry peers to remain updated on emerging trends and best practices in AI implementation. Establishing collaborative partnerships can provide valuable insights, facilitate knowledge sharing, and enhance the organization's ability to navigate challenges while capitalizing on new AI-driven opportunities in sustainable manufacturing (Schwaeke, et al., 2025).

## Role of AI in Reducing Waste and Improving Recycling Efficiency

AI plays a significant role in reducing waste and improving recycling efficiency through various applications. Waste sorting is enhanced by AI-powered systems that use computer vision and machine learning to accurately identify and sort recyclable materials, surpassing manual sorting efficiency (Krishna Pasupuleti, 2024). Predictive maintenance utilises AI algorithms to analyse sensor data, anticipating equipment failures and minimising downtime in recycling facilities (Patibandla, 2024). Optimisation of recycling processes is achieved through machine learning models that analyse material composition, processing parameters, and output quality to enhance efficiency. Smart waste management benefits from AI-enabled smart bins and collection systems that optimize waste collection routes and schedules, reducing fuel consumption and improving overall logistics (Neema, S., & Gor, P. (2022).

Additionally, AI enhances material identification by recognising complex materials and multi-layer packaging, facilitating the recycling of previously difficult-to-recycle items. Quality control is improved as AI-powered systems assess the quality of recycled materials, ensuring they meet required standards for reuse in manufacturing (Mishra, et al., 2024). Demand forecasting helps recycling facilities optimise operations by predicting recycling demand and resource allocation. Robotic sorting allows AI-driven robotic systems to perform high-speed, accurate sorting of recyclables, increasing processing capacity while reducing contamination (Goorun, et al., 2024). Consumer education is supported through AI chatbots and recommendation systems that provide personalised guidance on proper recycling practices, improving overall recycling rates.

AI helps streamline the recycling chain, making it easier to collect, move and distribute recyclable items and lessen waste at the same time. AI is used in manufacturing to assess production processes and locate spots where less waste can help protect the circular economy. Mobile applications that recognize images in recycling can point out what things are recyclable and give disposal advice (Saptaputra, et al., 2023). By analysing data from the past, predictive analytics helps organizations plan better ways to manage waste (Patibandla, 2024). Artificial intelligence systems are used to cut energy spend and lessen the adverse environmental effects caused by recycling. In addition, with blockchain and AI working together, people can see all stages of recycling clearly from start to finish, making sure materials are processed properly (Bai, & Sarkis, 2020). By working together, these AI systems promote a faster, greener and more environmentally safe approach to managing waste and recycling.

## Integration of AI in Sustainable Manufacturing: Challenges and Limitations

Combining AI advances in manufacturing with other areas creates useful opportunities that improve both the theory and practice of sustainability. With environmental science included, AI-based manufacturing systems can meet climate change goals by monitoring emissions more accurately and assessing entire production life cycles. Green chemistry and materials science collaborations help place biodegradable or recyclable inputs in products developed with AI. Connecting with logistics and operations research allows us to optimize transportation processes for little disruption of the environment. Adding ethics, labor studies and social sciences is necessary to deal with issues like changing the workforce, inequality and government rules in AI work. Furthermore, by combining AI research, especially in smart grids and renewable integration, with energy system studies, the use of sustainable energy in industries is strengthened. These new links among studies in different fields help increase the reach of research in sustainable manufacturing and prove that AI can support widespread improvements in the industry.

**Data Quality and Availability:** Large volumes of high-quality data are necessary for effective functioning of artificial intelligence systems in sustainable production. This data should address many aspects of the manufacturing process, including environmental impact, waste generation, resource economy, and energy consumption. Many manufacturing facilities, especially those related to sustainability assessments, may, nevertheless, lack comprehensive data collecting systems. Many industrial plants, particularly those connected to sustainability evaluations, could still lack thorough data collecting systems nonetheless. Lack of historical data, erroneous data formats, or unsuitable datasets could limit the creation and use of correct artificial intelligence models. Further complicating the data collecting procedure is some sustainability-related information that could be difficult to reliably measure. To get the necessary data—which can be time-consuming and expensive—companies could have to spend in new sensors, IoT devices, and data management systems.

**Complexity of Sustainability Metrics:** Manufacturing sustainability demands tackling social, financial and environmental responsibilities at the same time. Usually, these traits are related to goals that are not easy to handle or make the best of with artificial intelligence. Lowering energy use often leads to increased costs and lowering waste might decrease the quality of what is produced. Such models should be built in a way that satisfies several objectives that are often difficult to manage. Since there are several sustainability metrics, it demands complex algorithms that manage them well while offering equal consideration for all the sustainability factors. Besides, certain sustainability aspects, including effects on communities or the environment, are not easily put into numbers, thus adding extra challenge to the decision-making system.

**Initial Implementation Costs:** Setting up AI technology in sustainable manufacturing is costly at first which is hard for some small and medium-sized companies. Typically, this means you have to spend money on high quality computing, sensor and networking systems to make collecting and processing data easier. Moreover, organisations need to install certain software, like AI platforms, data analytics tools and unique applications, to enhance their manufacturing efficiency. Competent staff matters too, so businesses will need to either hire or develop data scientists, AI engineers and sustainability experts. To use AI in current systems, a lot of reforms and changes are needed at both the organizational and operational stages. Preparing data by gathering it, making it clean and organising large sets is an essential part of setting up AI models. Since entry costs are so high, it can be difficult for certain manufacturers to see the payoff in a short period. Also, quick changes in AI technology suggest that companies need a strategy to keep AI-based systems sustainable and resistant to future risks, as the lifespan of digital solutions is not always clear (Gupta, et al., 2020).

**Workforce Adaptation:** For AI to help sustainability in manufacturing, workers must adapt, managers must rethink how they run their departments and companies should change their policies and help employees. It is particularly important to train and reskill workers on AI since it is regularly included in sustainable business systems. Workers are expected to understand data analysis, cooperate with machines, improve energy use and act ethically online. Without planned retraining, there is a possible outcome where existing workers find it difficult to adapt which leads to lower productivity, worse teamwork and greater blockages in work. In addition to technical factors, how peoples' habits need to adapt can't be overlooked. Traditional manufacturing workers, in particular, can feel a lot of anxiety about losing their jobs due to AI. The resulting morale drop, resistance from employee unions and controversies among workers are likely outcomes. What's more, developing education and training in AI is uneven and South economies often miss the structure and resources needed to form the future AI-aware sustainability engineers. To close this gap, policies should ensure everyone has equal chances in technical education and should encourage women and groups from lower income backgrounds to learn new AI skills. The ILO and UNIDO are urging governments to ensure that workers are not negatively affected as countries move toward AI-assisted sustainability.

**Limited Availability of Professionals with Expertise:** Another issue is the shortage of professionals with specific knowledge in manufacturing, sustainability, and AI, making it challenging for businesses to get the appropriate talent. Moreover, AI automation may render some traditional job obsolete, requiring employees re-structuring or redeployment. Conversely, AI can also generate new job opportunities that demand specialised knowledge, making it challenging for businesses to recruit qualified personnel. Successfully addressing these challenges requires organisations to invest in skill development, implement effective change management strategies, and promote a workplace culture that supports AI integration while ensuring work-force stability.

**Energy Consumption:** Artificial intelligence increases the energy efficiency of manufacturing significantly, but its own energy consumption can be somewhat large, particularly in the case of modern deep learning models. The computational tools required for running artificial intelligence systems and training use vast amounts of energy, therefore perhaps contradicting sustainable objectives. Furthermore, influencing general efficiency is the infrastructure supporting artificial intelligence, which includes data centres and cloud computing services, thereby contributing to a significant energy footprint (Zhang, et al., 2021). Additionally necessary for proper operation of high-performance computing systems are sophisticated cooling systems, which results in higher energy consumption. Moreover, continuous operation of AI-powered monitoring and optimisation systems—even in low production—results in constant energy consumption. Regular retraining and AI model upgrading to maintain accuracy help to drive energy usage even more. To tackle these problems and ensure that artificial intelligence integration fits with sustainability goals, manufacturers should adopt energy-efficient AI models, make investments in sustainable computing solutions, and apply effective energy management approaches.

**Ethical Considerations:** Adding artificial intelligence to sustainable manufacturing brings many ethical questions not limited to working simply with algorithms. Underlying it all is the question of accountability, since decisions made by AI systems can impact the environment, the economy or society. Moreover, when AI uses information that contains bias from the past, it can actually strengthen this bias in its results. Where the technology behind AI is developing unevenly in the Global South, the consequences are often even greater unequal use of AI and who participates in data collection. Data privacy and the need for consent continue to be significant issues, mainly when AI systems collect detailed information about energy, labour or factory issues. Without the right protections, AI might be more useful for surveillance capitalism rather than for sustainable practices. We must deal with the fairness of algorithms, since AI can reproduce social inequalities if proper steps are not taken to test for fairness. Another issue is that only a small part of the world has access to AI technology and is able to innovate. Because richer countries are adopting advanced AI-based sustainability solutions, there is a danger that poorer states have to rely on old methods or turn into countries that just take data. Because of this divide, the original imbalances keep growing and there is now a need for fair and global governance to help all have access to these tools. To solve these different kinds of challenges, various policy methods and structures have appeared.

- Technological sustainability is included in the EU's environmental strategy, as well as its climate goals.
- Now, trustworthy AI is defined in ISO/IEC JTC 1/SC 42 standards with the principles of transparency, accountability and robustness.

More and more, ESG reporting in financial markets asks for disclosures about the risks of AI, possible job loss and measures to ensure ethical practices.

**Interpretability and Transparency:** Usually, complex forms of artificial intelligence, especially deep learning systems, are beyond understanding in how they reach their conclusions. This lack of transparency creates big difficulties for achieving sustainable production. In environments characterized by tough rules, the uncertainty over explaining AI-based verdicts can lead to problems. Also, limited visibility into how AI works might make it difficult for consumers, employees and other stakeholders to support sustainability projects that rely on AI. If artificial intelligence produces errors or unexpected results, it is tough to find out why without knowing how it makes decisions. Since it is tough to guarantee responsible decisions in environmental projects because of artificial intelligence, it raises the issue of responsibility. Also, experts and artificial intelligence systems communicate less effectively when it is not clear how decisions in AI systems were made. When overcoming these difficulties, companies in manufacturing should focus on creating clear AI models, using explainable AI and promoting openness, so as to ensure confidence, meet rules and regulations and maintain responsibility in sustainable manufacturing.

**Regulatory Compliance:** Since new rules for AI use are introduced, sustainable manufacturing has to adapt and use artificial intelligence differently. Modifications to regulations on disclosing environmental impact may cause AI-based systems to need modifications for data collection, recording and reporting. Since there is no one set of regulations for manufacturing, AI-driven systems must be adapted to each industry's rules. In addition, imposing ethical rules by choice or by law can help shape the way industry applies artificial intelligence. Because exact liability is often unclear in decisions made by AI, manufacturers could find themselves exposed to possible lawsuits if blame remains fuzzy. For an organisation to overcome these challenges, they need to regularly check for any changes in the law, enforce strong rules and prioritize ethical AI to create a strong and lasting manufacturing environment.

**Scalability and Generalisation:** When AI models are designed for specific manufacturing jobs or to help with environmental issues, they encounter difficulty operating smoothly in different settings. Due to differences in manufacturing process, using a single AI model for all uses becomes very difficult. AI algorithms that are taught using data from one factory could struggle to maintain efficiency in a different setting due to the fact that their work environment, machines and workflows are different. Because sustainability is valued differently by companies and locations, the algorithms in AI models must be adjusted based on these differences. For AI solutions to support large manufacturing plants, enough computers, networks and load are required, adding to the costs. Besides, as the use of AI grows, it is getting more difficult to integrate with existing setups. Programs that are effective in limited testing situations might not work as well when applied in large manufacturing facilities. In addition, making AI software work in various manufacturing environments usually means extensive personalization which lowers scalability and raises implementation expenses. Solving these challenges requires manufacturers to build flexible AI platforms, use technologies that can adapt with changes and plan strategies that support standardisation as well as key adjustments to be broadly usable.

## Long-Run Environmental Effects of AI in Sustainable Manufacturing

Artificial intelligence in sustainable manufacturing has long-run environmental effects ranging from several complex ones:

**Resources Optimisation:** AI makes it possible for businesses to use fewer resources and also helps with industrial recycling programs. By using AI, the amount of waste reduces and more resources are saved. The efficiency here may result in more production and consumption which will reduce some of the forwarded environmental advantages.

**Lifecycle Evaluation:** Artificial intelligence allows manufacturers to decide on sustainability improvements by delivering more accurate facts and details about the product's use. By using artificial intelligence, research teams can come up with answers to reduce the effect of manufacturing on the environment, starting at material acquisition and lasting until product disposal.

**Supply Chain Optimisation:** With AI, supply chains can manage their inventories better and reduce the emissions caused by shipping, making their work more efficient. Artificial intelligence helps by forecasting demand and making logistics more efficient which causes fewer emissions. Instead, using more AI in supply chains may lead to more regular little batches being transported, possibly bringing unknown effects to the environment.

**Predictive Maintenance:** Artificial intelligence helps predict potential equipment issues ahead of time, allowing manufacturers to keep their machines operating longer. This method helps reduce both issues related to interruptions and with wasting materials. AI recommendations might cause replacements too soon which in turn leads to more resources being used.

**Materials Innovation:** Because AI speeds up identifying sustainable materials, producers can more readily switch to more eco-friendly options. AI-based inventions may introduce additional types of waste which may create extra difficulties for recycling or disposing of these substances.

**Emissions Monitoring and Reduction:** Artificial intelligence helps to watch and address pollution in manufacturing systems more effectively and smoothly. Sensor network data is analyzed by artificial intelligence to assist businesses in obeying environmental laws and using less energy. At the same time, one should consider what effect building and upkeeping sensor networks will have on the surrounding environment.

**Water Management:** With AI identifying waste and blockages in water delivery, along with upgrading processes for sewage and waste treatment, artificial intelligence bestows on industry an improvement in water saving. Making AI sustainable could be tricky, since computers used in data-heavy AI often use a lot of water.

**Biodiversity Impact:** Through AI, it is now possible to keep a closer eye on manufacturing's influence on the environment. The use of AI leads to fewer impacts on nature by letting businesses examine ecological data and satellite pictures. But as rare earth metals and different materials are mined to make AI hardware components, biodiversity can be lost and habitats can be negatively affected.

**E-Waste Generation:** AI advances the recyclability of products and ensures that potential proceeds from their reuse are used in a positive way, supporting sustainable manufacturing. The quick progress of AI can cause manufacturing equipment to be obsolete faster and lead to an increase in electronic trash.

**Rebound Effects:** A rebound effect might occur where use of AI saves resources, yet leads people to use them more, since AI can boost productivity. The rebound effect can undermine some of the environmental benefits brought by AI optimisation.

**Long-Term Flexibility:** AI systems in manufacturing should be regularly modified to continue performing well. The rapid growth of AI technology might bring about more electronic waste, due to the need to replace old models with updated ones. It is important that AI infrastructure be built to adapt and be recycled so that it can be used sustainably.

## DISCUSSION

The literature review reveals a growing consensus on the transformative role of AI in reducing waste, optimizing energy usage, and enhancing predictive capabilities in manufacturing. A notable result is the convergence of AI capabilities with circular economy principles, especially in closed-loop systems and smart waste management. AI contributes significantly to operational efficiency through smart grids, demand forecasting, and intelligent maintenance systems. However, the results also highlight tension between energy savings via AI and the high computational power required to operate AI systems, which may lead to increased energy demand—a clear sustainability paradox. A cross-analysis of the reviewed literature also shows that while many AI applications offer short-term environmental benefits, long-term impacts such as e-waste and the rebound effect remain under-researched. Additionally, AI's role in lifecycle assessment and real-time sustainability monitoring emerges as a promising but underutilized application. The discussion further suggests that policymakers must balance technological innovation with frameworks that mitigate AI's unintended side effects, such as increased electronic waste or energy consumption during model training. Stakeholders should emphasize ethical AI, especially regarding data transparency and workforce displacement.

### Implications of the Study

Research on application of artificial intelligence in sustainable manufacturing have various important consequences for businesses, governments, academia, environmentalists especially. Integration of artificial intelligence in manufacturing can increase sustainability by means of resource consumption reduction, energy optimisation, and waste reduction. Supported by artificial intelligence, predictive analytics and process optimisation, greener manufacturing approaches let businesses fulfil global environmental objectives by means of more effective operations. Artificial intelligence-powered assessments, supply chain optimisation, and predictive maintenance facilitate manufacturers reduce costs and enhance efficiency in operation. The companies must, however, also balance trade-offs including the rising e-waste from updates to artificial intelligence systems and the possible rebound effect of additional consequences. Governments and regulatory authorities can make rules encouraging suitable acceptance of artificial intelligence using these results. These guidelines on artificial intelligence-related e-waste management, incentives for sustainable artificial intelligence applications, and recommendations to restrict too high production and resource exploitation brought about by AI-driven efficiencies could all help to reduce these effects. The study also covers subjects that demand more research including low-energy artificial intelligence models, building of sustainable artificial intelligence hardware, and circular economy concepts for waste produced by artificial intelligence, Artificial intelligence systems that strike a mix between efficiency gains and long-term sustainability should be the focus of researchers and developers.

AI in sustainable manufacturing supports learning, improves safety at work and introduces new fields for employees to work in. Even so, they have to plan for the workforce changes that may come with automation and check that technology improves things for companies as well as for their teams. AI is playing a role in sustainable manufacturing in support of environmental initiatives such as the Paris Climate Agreement and UN's Sustainable Development Goals (SDGs). By deploying AI safely, industries can help reduce waste, spend resources wisely and prompt staff to care for the environment. Since artificial intelligence boosts sustainability, it's important to consider ethical questions about updating AI systems and buying the resources needed for them. Firms should use methods designed to reduce the harm artificial intelligence can cause to the area. All things considered, artificial intelligence plays a big role in making manufacturing more sustainable, but its use should be approached with care. To ensure that AI benefits businesses and not causes any issues, everyone involved should coordinate their work. If properly used, AI could improve the sustainability of industries and make them more productive with the help of new ideas, supported laws and sustainable AI.

## Limitations of the Study

Even though this study gives a detailed explanation of how AI and sustainable production join, there are some issues to consider. First, the work is based on a review of narrative literature which might cause some selection problems and make findings difficult to apply in general. Without case studies or industry surveys, it remains challenging to check if the new ideas are valid in real-life. Moreover, the analysis looks mostly at how AI concepts and technologies are shaped, while overlooking the impact of geography, economies and social and political aspects. Because AI is evolving rapidly, some current and commercial applications may not be included in this survey. Since standardized sustainability metrics are in short supply, these issues are generally talked about but not intensively quantified. Because of these limits, researchers can use future experiments to build upon and verify the current information.

## Future Scope of the Study

Further study is required on standardised frameworks for application of artificial intelligence and long-term measurement of the enhancement in sustainable manufacturing. This includes developing indicators for evaluating the impact of AI applications on sustainability, performing extensive research of AI-enabled manufacturing technologies, and making policies for ethical AI deployment in industrial environments. Mutual efforts among scholars of artificial intelligence, industry people, environmental scientists, and policymakers will be essentially crucial in order to resolve these issues and understand the use of artificial intelligence in making sustainable manufacturing practices. As the field develops, ongoing research and development efforts will be essential in utilising the power of AI to create more ecologically friendly and resource-efficient manufacturing processes for the future.

## CONCLUSION

This study demonstrates that Artificial Intelligence holds significant promise in transforming sustainable manufacturing by optimizing resource utilization, enabling real-time decision-making, and reducing environmental impact. From AI-powered recycling and energy optimization to predictive maintenance and ethical deployment, the applications are both diverse and impactful. However, successful integration of AI requires a balanced approach that accounts for initial implementation challenges, workforce adaptability, ethical considerations, and environmental trade-offs such as e-waste and high energy use of AI models. This chapter contributes a holistic view of AI's role in sustainability by not only consolidating technological applications but also addressing policy, economic, and ethical dimensions. As sustainable manufacturing evolves, future research must focus on low-energy AI systems, equitable access, and long-term impact measurement to ensure that AI acts as a true enabler of sustainability rather than a complicating factor

## REFERENCES


Bagiyam, D., Blessy Doe, M., & Aravindan, J. S. (2024). *Navigating complexities through unveiling sustainability challenges in AI using a bibliometric approach.* IGI Global., DOI: 10.4018/979-8-3693-3282-5.ch014

Bai, C., & Sarkis, J. (2020). A supply chain transparency and sustainability technology appraisal model for blockchain technology. *International Journal of Production Research, 58*(7), 2142–2162. DOI: 10.1080/00207543.2019.1708989

Balan, A. (2024). Examining the ethical and sustainability challenges of legal education's AI revolution. *International Journal of the Legal Profession, 31*(3), 1–26. DOI: 10.1080/09695958.2024.2421179

Bassey, K., Stephen, A., & Juliet, A. (2024). AI-enhanced lifecycle assessment of renewable energy systems. *Engineering Science & Technology Journal, 5*(7), 2082–2099. DOI: 10.51594/estj.v5i7.1254

Bhattasali, T., & Savarimuthu, X. (2021). *Technological innovations for environmental sustainability*. CRC., DOI: 10.1201/9781003055020-08

Bousdekis, A., Apostolou, D., & Mentzas, G. (2024). Artificial intelligence applications for increasing resource efficiency in industrial production. *Sustainability, 13*(12), 6689. DOI: 10.3390/su13126689

Cassettari, L., Bendato, I., Mosca, M., & Mosca, R. (2017). Energy resources intelligent management using online real-time simulation: A decision support tool for sustainable manufacturing. *Applied Energy, 190*, 841–851.

Chen, P., & Dagestani, A. A. (2023). What lies about circular economy practices and performance? Fresh insights from China. *Journal of Cleaner Production, 416*, 137893. DOI: 10.1016/j.jclepro.2023.137893

Cheng, T. C. E., Lai, K. H., & Lun, Y. H. V. (2023). Integration of artificial intelligence in sustainable manufacturing: A systematic literature review. *Journal of Manufacturing Systems, 67*, 10–25. DOI: 10.1016/j.jmsy.2023.01.004

Clark, G. (2007). *A farewell to alms: A brief economic history of the world.* Princeton University Press.

Fukuyama, K. (1997). Technological incentives of firms under the environmental regulations. *Proceedings of the 1997 IEEE International Conference on Systems, Man, and Cybernetics*, 1, 815–820. https://doi.org/DOI: 10.1109/icsmc.1997.626198

Gautam, K., Kumari, A., Kumari, A., & Saini, A. (2020). AI's role in sustainable energy. *International Journal of Psychosocial Rehabilitation, 24*(7), 11396–11398. DOI: 10.61841/v24i7/400271

Geissdoerfer, M., Savaget, P., Bocken, N. M., & Hultink, E. J. (2017). The circular economy–A new sustainability paradigm? *Journal of Cleaner Production, 143*, 757–768.

Ghobakhloo, M., & Fathi, M. (2023). The role of artificial intelligence in sustainable supply chain management. *International Journal of Production Research, 61*(4), 1345–1362. DOI: 10.1080/00207543.2023.2161234

Gift, M. D. M., Boopathi, S., Jayaseelan, P., Hasan, D. S., Alagarraja, K., & Senthil, T. S. (2024). *Additive manufacturing and 3D printing innovations.* IGI Global., DOI: 10.4018/979-8-3693-0968-1.ch010

Ginters, E., & Revathy, J. C. (2021). Attributes of digital technologies and related impacts on sustainability assessment. *2021 International Conference on Electrical, Communication, and Computer Engineering (ICECCE)*, 1–5. https://doi.org/DOI: 10.1109/ICECCE52056.2021.9514094

Goorun, Y., Marais, S., & Nicolls, F. (2024). Robotic waste sorting using deep learning. *MATEC Web of Conferences, 406*, 10003. https://doi.org/DOI: 10.1051/matecconf/202440610003

Gupta, S. M., Güngör, A., Govindan, K., Özceylan, E., Kalaycı, C. B., & Piplani, R. (2020). Responsible & sustainable manufacturing. *International Journal of Production Research, 58*(23), 7181–7182. DOI: 10.1080/00207543.2020.1841968

Handl, G. (2012). Declaration of the United Nations Conference on the Human Environment (Stockholm Declaration), 1972 and the Rio Declaration on Environment and Development, 1992. *United Nations Audiovisual Library of International Law, 11*(6), 1–11.

Heras-Saizarbitoria, I., & Boiral, O. (2013). ISO 9001 and ISO 14001: Towards a research agenda on management system standards. *International Journal of Management Reviews, 15*(1), 47–65.

Jayaraman, T. (2015). The Paris Agreement on climate change: Background, analysis, and implications. *Review of Agrarian Studies, 5*(2).

Kamble, S. S., Gunasekaran, A., & Sharma, R. (2023). Artificial intelligence techniques for sustainable reconfigurable manufacturing systems. *Machines (Basel), 8*(11), 152. DOI: 10.3390/machines8110152

Kerin, A., & Pham, D. T. (2024). Digital twins and AI-powered simulations for sustainable manufacturing. *Frontiers in Sustainability*, *2*(1), 55–72. DOI: 10.3389/frsus.2024.1508647

Khalfallah, A., & Leitão, C. (2024). Sustainable manufacturing and green processing methods. *Machines (Basel)*, *12*(11), 815. DOI: 10.3390/machines12110815

Khapekar, S. H., Sawai, S., Agrawal, S., Wankhade, S., & Jaronde, P. (2024). *AI-driven data analytics within digital twins*. IGI Global., DOI: 10.4018/979-8-3693-1818-8.ch005

Krishna Pasupuleti, M. (2024). *Green energy revolution: AI-powered systems for sustainable power management*. National Education Services., DOI: 10.62311/nesx/7264

Liu, J., Pham, D. T., Zhang, J., Zhou, Z., & Xu, W. (2016, June 27). Industrial cloud robotics towards sustainable manufacturing. *Proceedings of the ASME 2016 11th International Manufacturing Science and Engineering Conference*. https://doi.org/DOI: 10.1115/msec2016-8733

Malek, J., & Desai, T. N. (2020). A systematic literature review to map literature focus of sustainable manufacturing. *Journal of Cleaner Production*, *256*, 120345.

Micieta, B., & Binasova, V. (2013). *Defining requirements for energy efficiency in manufacturing*. DAAAM Vienna., DOI: 10.2507/daaam.scibook.2013.54

Mishra, P. C., & Giri, A. K. (2018). *Green chemistry*. IGI Global., DOI: 10.4018/978-1-5225-3126-5.ch009

Mishra, R. K., Sharma, M., Kumar, S., & Divyashree. (2024). Leveraging automation for enhanced quality control systems. https://doi.org/DOI: 10.62919/xhie8742

Mohapatra, A. (2024). Generative AI for predictive maintenance: Predicting equipment failures and optimizing maintenance schedules using AI. [IJSRM]. *International Journal of Scientific Research and Management*, *12*(11), 1648–1672. DOI: 10.18535/ijsrm/v12i11.ec03

Musavi, S. A. S., Sajjad, S., & Sarwari, S. R. (2024). Investigating renewable energy sources. *Nangarhar University International Journal of Biosciences, 03*(ICCC Special), 507–510. https://doi.org/DOI: 10.70436/nuijb.v3i02.278

Mutsuddi, I. (2024). *Ethical considerations in the intersection of AI and environmental science*. IGI Global., DOI: 10.4018/979-8-3693-6336-2.ch011

Nandan, S., & Jyoti. (2020). Organizational culture dimensions as drivers of employee engagement for business sustainability: Towards a conceptual framework. In *Sustainable Human Resource Management: Transforming Organizations, Societies and Environment* (pp. 109–132).

Naude, M., Rowe, A. L., Thomas, G., & Nowak, M. (2010). Managing industry-academia partnerships. *International Journal of Management Education, 8*(3), 71–82. DOI: 10.3794/ijme.83.300

Neema, S., & Gor, P. (2022). Smart waste management using IoT. *International Journal of Scientific Research in Science, Engineering and Technology, 9*(2), 16–21. DOI: 10.32628/ijsrset229529

Onukwulu, E., Dienagha, I., Digitemie, W., & Egbumokei, P. (2021). AI-driven supply chain optimization for enhanced efficiency in the energy sector. *Magna Scientia Advanced Research and Reviews, 2*(1), 87–108. DOI: 10.30574/msarr.2021.2.1.0060

Patibandla, K. R. (2024). Predictive maintenance in aviation using artificial intelligence. [JAIGS]. *Journal of Artificial Intelligence General Science, 4*(1), 325–333. DOI: 10.60087/jaigs.v4i1.214

Patra, B. C., & Mishra, D. N. (2024). *Extended producer responsibility (EPR) and e-waste management.* IGI Global., DOI: 10.4018/979-8-3693-1018-2.ch010

Rath, R. C., Singh, T., Goel, R., & Baral, S. K. (2022). Role of artificial intelligence and machine learning in product design and manufacturing. In *Proceedings of the 2022 IEEE MECon* (pp. 571–575). https://doi.org/DOI: 10.1109/mecon53876.2022.9752455

Samarawickrama, M. (2022). AI governance and ethics framework for sustainable AI and sustainability. *arXiv*. https://doi.org//arxiv.2210.08984DOI: 10.48550

Saptaputra, E. H., Araffanda, A. S., & Bonafix, N. (2023). Mobile app as digitalisation of waste sorting management. *IOP Conference Series. Earth and Environmental Science, 1169*(1), 012007. DOI: 10.1088/1755-1315/1169/1/012007

Schwaeke, J., Gerlich, C., Nguyen, H. L., Kanbach, D. K., & Gast, J. (2025). Artificial intelligence (AI) for good? Enabling organizational change towards sustainability. *Review of Managerial Science*. Advance online publication. DOI: 10.1007/s11846-025-00840-x

Simpson, D. (2012). Institutional pressure and waste reduction: The role of investments in waste reduction resources. *International Journal of Production Economics, 139*(1), 330–339. DOI: 10.1016/j.ijpe.2012.05.020

Stowe, M. (2020). Lean manufacturing principles and their impact on process energy efficiency (pp. 77–137). *River (Weinheim)*. Advance online publication. DOI: 10.1201/9781003150961-3

Tripathi, S., Bachmann, N., Brunner, M., Rizk, Z., & Jodlbauer, H. (2024). Assessing the current landscape of AI and sustainability literature: Identifying key trends, addressing gaps and challenges. *Journal of Big Data*, *11*(1). Advance online publication. DOI: 10.1186/s40537-024-00912-x

Vishwakarma, R. K., Patel, H. K., & Sharma, R. (2023). AI and machine learning for production efficiency and sustainable development: A bibliometric analysis. *Frontiers in Sustainability*, *3*, 89–102. DOI: 10.3389/frsus.2023.1508647

Wang, L., Liu, A., Liu, Z., & Tao, F. (2021). Artificial intelligence in product lifecycle management. *International Journal of Advanced Manufacturing Technology*, *114*(3–4), 771–796. DOI: 10.1007/s00170-021-06882-1

Winkler, H. (2011). Closed-loop production systems—A sustainable supply chain approach. *CIRP Journal of Manufacturing Science and Technology*, *4*(3), 243–246. DOI: 10.1016/j.cirpj.2011.05.001

Womack, J. P., & Jones, D. T. (1997). Lean thinking—Banish waste and create wealth in your corporation. *The Journal of the Operational Research Society*, *48*(11), 1148–1148.

Wu, Z., Zhang, C., & Zhu, X. (2012, May 1). An ant colony algorithm for master production scheduling optimization. *IEEE 2012 CSCWD Conference*. https://doi.org/DOI: 10.1109/cscwd.2012.6221908

Xu, H., & Wang, Q. (2024). Energy regulatory compliance and corporate social responsibility. *Finance Research Letters*, *67*, 105919. DOI: 10.1016/j.frl.2024.105919

Yao, L., & Desalegn, G. (2023). Sustainable practices in global supply chains of Chinese enterprises: Bibliometric approach. *Studia Mundi – Economica, 10*(4), 5–19. https://doi.org/DOI: 10.18531/sme.vol.10.no.4.pp.5-19

Yu, J., Zhang, C., & Wang, S. (2021). Sparse one-dimensional convolutional neural network-based feature learning for fault detection and diagnosis in multivariable manufacturing processes. *Neural Computing & Applications*. Advance online publication. DOI: 10.1007/s00521-021-06575-6

Zhang, T., Ji, W., & Qiu, Y. (2021). A framework of energy-consumption driven discrete manufacturing system. *Sustainable Energy Technologies and Assessments*, *47*, 101336. DOI: 10.1016/j.seta.2021.101336

Chapter 2

# Exploring Sustainable Technology Innovation and Green Tech Adoption Impacts on SDGs and Software Project Management

**Sushree Sucharita Behera**
https://orcid.org/0009-0003-2205-1669
*School of Computer Engineering, Kalinga Institute of Industrial Technology, Bhubaneswar, India*

**Hitesh Mohapatra**
https://orcid.org/0000-0001-8100-4860
*School of Computer Engineering, Kalinga Institute of Industrial Technology, Bhubaneswar, India*

## ABSTRACT

*We understand in this paper why the adoption of green technologies is crucial for achieving the (SDGs) and improving software project management practices. Green technologies play a vital role in addressing pressing environmental challenges while advancing economic growth, yet their adoption faces barriers such as high costs and technological complexity. This research also investigates the effects of green technology adoption on SDGs and identifies best practices for embedding these technologies into software project management frameworks. By examining case studies and industry methodologies, the study highlights actionable strategies*

DOI: 10.4018/979-8-3373-7584-7.ch002

*to align technological innovation with sustainability objectives. It underscores the importance of Agile Sustainability, Green Coding, and Life Cycle Assessment (LCA) as essential practices for optimizing project outcomes. The findings aim to equip policymakers, technology leaders, and project managers with insights to drive impactful, sustainable change, ensuring that technological progress contributes meaningfully to global development goals.*

## INTRODUCTION

In the contemporary landscape of global development, the integration of sustainable technology innovation and green technology adoption has emerged as a pivotal strategy for addressing pressing environmental challenges and achieving the United Nations Sustainable Development Goals (SDGs). The SDGs, established in 2015, encompass a broad spectrum of objectives aimed at fostering sustainable economic growth, social inclusion, and environmental protection (Adenle et al., 2023; Khan et al., 2024). As nations strive to meet these ambitious targets, the role of technology particularly in the realms of software project management and green innovations becomes increasingly significant. Sustainable technology innovation refers to the development and implementation of technologies that not only enhance productivity and efficiency but also minimize environmental impact (Ebrahim, 2020; Zhang et al., 2019). This innovation is crucial for transitioning towards a low-carbon economy, as it enables organizations to reduce their carbon footprints while maintaining competitive advantages (Shan et al., 2021, p. 113004; Song et al., 2023). For instance, the adoption of renewable energy technologies, such as solar and wind power, exemplifies how sustainable innovations can lead to significant reductions in greenhouse gas emissions (Fang, 2023; Suki et al., 2022). Furthermore, the integration of digital technologies, such as the Internet of Things (IoT) and artificial intelligence (AI), facilitates the monitoring and optimization of resource use, thereby enhancing sustainability efforts across various sectors (Li et al., 2022; Wu et al., 2022, pp. 22013–22023).

In the context of software project management, the adoption of green technologies presents both challenges and opportunities. Project managers are increasingly tasked with ensuring that their projects align with sustainability goals while also delivering on time and within budget (Wang et al., 2022; Zheng et al., 2022). This dual focus necessitates a shift in traditional project management practices, incorporating sustainability metrics into project planning and execution (Wang, 2022). For example, the implementation of agile methodologies can enhance flexibility and responsiveness, allowing teams to adapt to changing sustainability requirements and stakeholder expectations (Godil et al., 2021). Moreover, the intersection of sustainable technology innovation and software project management is particularly relevant in the context of the circular economy, which emphasizes resource efficiency and waste reduction (Chien et al., 2021). By leveraging green technologies, organizations can develop software solutions that not only optimize processes but also contribute to the sustainable management of resources (Coral & Papell, 2012). This approach aligns with the SDGs, particularly Goal 12(**see Figure 1**), which advocates for responsible consumption and production patterns (Khan et al., 2021).

*Figure 1. How green technologies align with Sustainable Development Goal 12.*

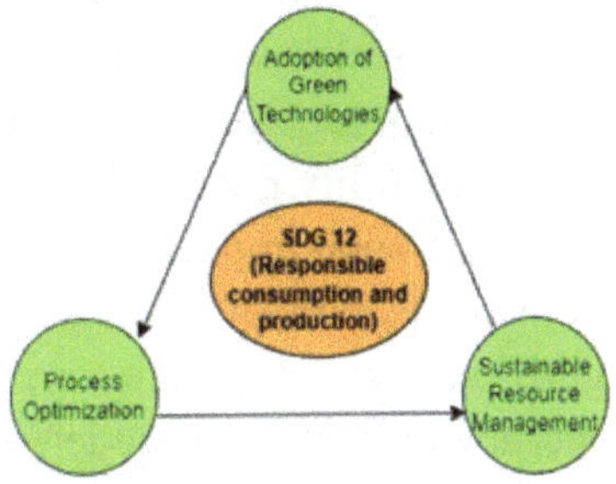


The impacts of sustainable technology innovation and green tech adoption extend beyond environmental benefits; they also encompass economic and social dimensions. For instance, the transition to green technologies can stimulate job creation in emerging sectors, fostering economic resilience (Wu et al., 2023). Additionally, by promoting inclusive practices and stakeholder engagement, organizations can enhance their social license to operate, thereby strengthening community relations and support (Capar, 2012). The exploration of sustainable technology innovation and green tech adoption is essential for advancing the SDGs and transforming software project management practices. As organizations navigate the complexities of sustainability, the integration of innovative technologies and strategic project management approaches will be critical in driving meaningful progress towards a more sustainable future. By embracing these changes, businesses can not only contribute to global sustainability efforts but also position themselves as leaders in the transition to a greener economy (Hall et al., 2017, pp. 877–889; Sun et al., 2024). Therefore practices such as life cycle assessment (LCA) of software products, integration of eco-design principles, and continuous monitoring of environmental impacts are essential for embedding sustainability into the core of software development. Additionally, project managers must address challenges such as balancing cost constraints with sustainability goals, bridging knowledge gaps, and managing resistance to change within development teams.

## LITERATURE REVIEW

The increasing urgency of environmental sustainability has prompted organizations to adopt innovative practices that align with the United Nations Sustainable Development Goals (SDGs). Agile methodologies, green coding practices, and life cycle assessment (LCA) are pivotal in this transition, particularly within the software development sector. This literature review explores the intersection of these concepts, highlighting their contributions to sustainable technology innovation and project management. Agile methodologies, originally designed for software development, have evolved to incorporate sustainability principles. Agile sustainability emphasizes iterative development, flexibility, and responsiveness to change, which are essential for adapting to evolving environmental requirements (Chen et al., 2023; Ebirim et al., 2024). The integration of sustainability metrics into agile project management allows teams to assess their environmental impact continuously, fostering a culture of accountability and improvement (Făgără an et al., 2023).

Research indicates that agile practices can enhance project outcomes by promoting collaboration and transparency among stakeholders (Žužek et al., 2020). For instance, a study by Ebirim et al. (2024) highlights the role of Agile Project Management (APM) in driving innovation in energy-efficient solutions, demonstrating how agile frameworks can facilitate rapid adaptation to sustainability challenges in various industries (Piwowar-Sulej & Iqbal, 2024). Furthermore, the hybridization of traditional project management with agile practices has been shown to improve sustainability outcomes by balancing structure with flexibility (Masia & Poll, 2021). Green coding refers to the practice of writing software in a manner that minimizes energy consumption and resource use throughout its life cycle. This approach is increasingly recognized as a critical component of sustainable software development (Dong, 2023). The principles of green coding align with the broader goals of reducing the environmental impact of technology, particularly in the context of cloud computing and data centers, which are significant contributors to global energy consumption (Obradović et al., 2018, pp. 1–5).

The adoption of green coding practices can lead to substantial energy savings and reduced carbon footprints. For example, optimizing algorithms and utilizing efficient coding techniques can significantly decrease the computational resources required for software applications (Sakikhales & Stravoravdis, 2017, pp. 65–78). A study by Niţă and î u (2023) emphasizes the importance of integrating knowledge management into software engineering to enhance sustainability, suggesting that a focus on green coding can lead to more sustainable organizational practices(Saher et al., 2020). In the context of software project management, green technologies encompass a range of practices and tools aimed at minimizing the environmental impact of software development processes. These technologies include energy-efficient coding practices, which optimize software to reduce energy consumption during execution, and the use of cloud computing solutions that leverage shared resources to decrease the carbon footprint associated with on-premises data centers.

Additionally, implementing sustainable software development methodologies, such as Agile and DevOps, can enhance collaboration and efficiency while promoting the use of green tools and frameworks. Furthermore, integrating Building Information Modeling (BIM) and Internet of Things (IoT) technologies can facilitate real-time monitoring and management of resources, leading to more sustainable project outcomes. By adopting these green technologies, software project managers can contribute to environmental sustainability while improving project efficiency and stakeholder satisfaction (Ishak & Saad, 2016, p. 122; Lawal et al., 2024; Yeolekar-Kadam & S., 2022). Life Cycle Assessment (LCA) is a systematic methodology for evaluating the environmental impacts of a product or service throughout its entire life cycle, from raw material extraction to disposal. In the context of software development, LCA can be applied to assess the sustainability of software products by considering factors such as energy consumption, resource use, and waste generation (Stettina & Kroon, 2013, pp. 1–12).

The integration of LCA into agile project management practices allows teams to make informed decisions that prioritize sustainability. For instance, Făgără an et al. (2023) propose a data-driven scoring model for integrating sustainability metrics into project performance assessments, highlighting the potential of LCA to enhance the sustainability of software development processes. Additionally, the application of LCA in evaluating emerging technologies, such as renewable energy systems, underscores its relevance in promoting sustainable practices across various sectors (Stray et al., 2020, pp. 3–19). In the manufacturing sector, the implementation of green industry practices, such as Alternative Fuel and Raw Material (AFR) and Waste Heat Recovery Power Generation (WHRPG) technology, aligns with multiple SDGs including clean energy, innovation, sustainable cities, and climate action (Oktavia Ningsih, 2024). Similarly, nanotechnology has the potential to address 13 out of 17 SDGs, including reducing poverty and hunger, ensuring clean water and sanitation, and promoting sustainable industrialization (Aithal & P S, 2021). The adoption of green supply chain management (GSCM) practices plays a crucial role in achieving SDGs, particularly in emerging economies. Studies show that supplier green management, eco-design, corporate social responsibility, and internal green management positively contribute to SDG attainment (Jum'A, 2023; Tu et al., 2023). Additionally, blockchain technology can transform traditional supply chain management into greener practices, ensuring compliance with environmental SDGs (Jan et al., 2023)

*Table 1. Other relevant researches*

| Citations | Key Findings |
|---|---|
| (Kassa et al., 2024) | This study evaluates the relationship between knowledge management and green innovation, highlighting the importance of KM practices in fostering green innovation across various organizations (Kassa et al., 2024). |
| (López-Muñoz al., 2023, pp. 1692–1697) | This article discusses the life cycle assessment of hydrogen production, emphasizing its role in sustainability and the environmental impacts associated with hydrogen technologies (López-Muñoz et al., 2023, pp. 1692–1697). |
| (Santos et al., 2024) | This study assesses the environmental implications of using treated wastewater for irrigation, employing life cycle assessment to evaluate its sustainability (Santos et al., 2024). |
| (Amato et al., 2023) | This paper presents a life cycle assessment comparing biomethane and fossil methane, highlighting the environmental benefits of biomethane production (Amato et al., 2023). |
| (Pilar Rodríguez-Rojas et al., 2024) | This study compares the environmental impacts of green and chemical synthesis methods for TiO2 nanoparticles, using life cycle assessment to evaluate sustainability (Pilar Rodríguez-Rojas et al., 2024). |
| (Balasbaneh et al., 2023) | This review assesses the sustainability of alternative green roofs through life cycle sustainability assessment, providing insights into their environmental impacts (Balasbaneh et al., 2023). |

## Proposed Study

Green coding focuses on minimizing the environmental impact of software throughout its lifecycle. This involves optimizing algorithms for energy efficiency, reducing energy consumption during execution, and minimizing data storage requirements. Efficient algorithms translate to less processing power needed, directly reducing energy consumption in devices running the software. Minimizing data storage reduces the energy required to maintain and operate data centers. Furthermore, green coding considers the entire software lifecycle, including the energy used during development, testing, and deployment. By prioritizing energy efficiency and resource optimization from the outset, developers can significantly reduce the carbon footprint of their software, contributing to a more sustainable digital landscape and aligning with Sustainable Development Goals (SDGs) such as SDG 7 (Affordable and Clean Energy) and SDG 13 (Climate Action).

Agile methodologies, with their iterative and incremental approach, inherently promote sustainability in software development. The focus on rapid prototyping and continuous feedback loops allows for early detection and correction of inefficiencies, minimizing wasted resources and reducing the overall environmental impact. Agile's emphasis on collaboration and transparency fosters a culture of shared responsibility for sustainability, encouraging developers to consider environmental implications throughout the development process. The iterative nature of Agile also allows for easier adaptation to changing requirements and technological advancements, potentially leading to the adoption of more sustainable technologies and practices over time. This aligns with SDG 9 (Industry, Innovation, and Infrastructure) by promoting efficient and innovative development processes.

Cloud computing offers significant potential for environmental sustainability in software development. By centralizing computing resources, cloud providers can achieve economies of scale, leading to more efficient energy utilization and reduced overall carbon emissions. Cloud data centers often employ advanced cooling technologies and renewable energy sources, further minimizing their environmental impact. Moreover, cloud computing enables the efficient allocation of resources, reducing the need for individual organizations to invest in and maintain their own energy-intensive infrastructure. This scalability and flexibility contribute to a more sustainable IT landscape, supporting SDGs such as SDG 7 (Affordable and Clean Energy) and SDG 9 (Industry, Innovation, and Infrastructure). However, it's crucial to select cloud providers with strong sustainability commitments and transparent energy usage data.

*Table 2. Green Tech Impact Matrix of Green Technologies*

| Green Technology | SDG 7: Affordable and Clean Energy | SDG 8: Decent Work and Economic Growth | SDG 9: Industry, Innovation and Infrastructure | SDG 11: Sustainable Cities and Communities | SDG 13: Climate Action |
|---|---|---|---|---|---|
| Green Coding | Low | Low | Medium | Low | Medium |
| Agile and Lean Methodologies | Low | Medium | High | Low | Medium |
| Cloud Computing | Medium | Medium | High | Medium | High |
| Life Cycle Assessment (LCA) | Low | Low | Medium | Low | High |

Life Cycle Assessment (LCA) provides a comprehensive framework for evaluating the environmental impacts of software throughout its entire lifecycle. From the extraction of raw materials for hardware to the disposal of end-of-life devices, LCA considers all stages, enabling a holistic understanding of the environmental footprint. By identifying environmental hotspots within the software lifecycle, LCA informs the development of mitigation strategies and the selection of more sustainable technologies and practices. This data-driven approach allows for informed decision-making, promoting continuous improvement and reducing the overall environmental impact of software. The integration of LCA into software development aligns with SDG 12 (Responsible Consumption and Production) and SDG 17 (Partnerships for the Goals) by promoting transparency and collaboration towards a more sustainable future. All of these are shown based on levels of low, medium, high impact SDGs (Ref: Table 2). Now imagine a team developing a mobile application for tracking energy consumption in homes. Using a traditional waterfall approach, the team might spend months designing and building the entire application before testing. If, during testing, they discover a significant energy inefficiency in the application's core algorithm (perhaps due to poorly optimized code), fixing it would be costly and time-consuming, requiring substantial rework and potentially delaying the launch. This rework translates to wasted developer time, increased energy consumption from extended development, and a larger carbon footprint overall.

Consider the same team using an Agile approach. They would break down the project into smaller, manageable sprints, focusing on developing and testing core functionalities iteratively. In the first sprint, they might develop a basic energy tracking module. During testing within that sprint, they would identify and correct the inefficient algorithm early on. This early detection and correction prevent the problem from propagating through the entire application. Subsequent sprints would build upon this corrected foundation, ensuring that energy efficiency is integrated from the start. The result is a more energy-efficient application, developed with less wasted effort and a significantly smaller environmental impact. The iterative nature of Agile allows for continuous feedback and improvement, leading to a more sustainable outcome. Furthermore, the collaborative nature of Agile would likely involve discussions about energy efficiency from the outset, influencing design choices and technology selection to prioritize sustainability. Cross-functional teams, including developers, testers, and stakeholders, work together closely, enabling open communication about environmental considerations throughout the development process. This collaborative environment encourages the adoption of green coding practices, the selection of energy-efficient technologies, and the consideration of the software's overall environmental footprint. This proactive approach, enabled by Agile's iterative and collaborative nature, directly contributes to a more sustainable software development process. This process will be clearer looking at a systematic flowchart for agile processes (see Figure.2). The iterative nature of Agile enables developers to incorporate feedback and incorporate improvements throughout the development process. This flexibility is crucial in the rapidly evolving field of sustainable technology, allowing software projects to adapt to new innovations and best practices in energy efficiency, resource management, and environmental impact assessment. This continuous improvement cycle ensures that software remains aligned with the latest advancements in sustainable development, contributing to a more environmentally responsible digital future.

*Figure 2. Illustration of how Agile processes can enhance sustainability in software development.*

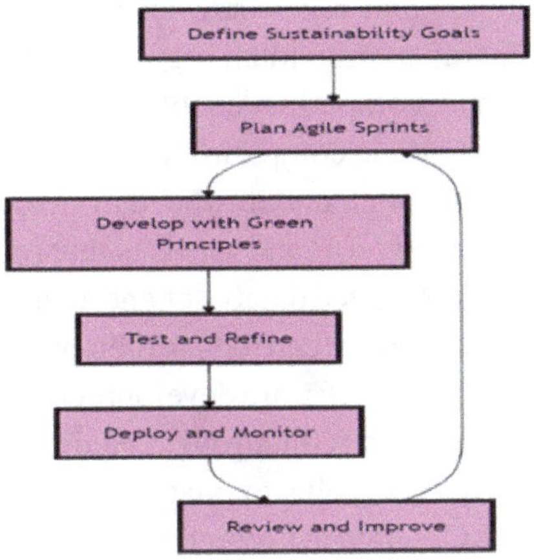


Moving on now to understand how carbon footprints matter in software project management techniques. Green coding practices directly reduce a software's carbon footprint by optimizing code for energy efficiency. This involves techniques like minimizing computational complexity, reducing data storage needs, and selecting energy-efficient algorithms. For example, choosing a more efficient sorting algorithm can significantly reduce the processing power required, leading to lower energy consumption on the devices running the software. Similarly, optimizing database queries and minimizing unnecessary data transfers can reduce the energy demands of servers and data centers. By focusing on efficient code from the design phase, developers can significantly lessen the operational energy consumption of the software throughout its lifecycle, directly impacting its carbon footprint. This proactive approach contrasts with traditional methods where energy efficiency is often an afterthought. Agile methodologies indirectly but significantly reduce a software's carbon footprint by minimizing waste and improving efficiency. The iterative nature of Agile allows for early detection and correction of inefficiencies, preventing the creation of unnecessary code or features. This reduces the energy consumed during development, testing, and deployment. Furthermore, Agile's emphasis on collaboration and continuous feedback ensures that resources are used effectively, minimizing wasted effort and reducing the overall environmental impact. By focusing on delivering value incrementally, Agile reduces the risk of building large, inefficient systems that consume excessive energy during operation. This contrasts with waterfall approaches where significant rework and wasted effort can lead to a larger carbon footprint.

Cloud computing can reduce the carbon footprint of software development in several ways. Firstly, cloud providers often utilize large-scale data centers with advanced cooling technologies and renewable energy sources, leading to more efficient energy usage compared to individual organizations maintaining their own infrastructure. Secondly, cloud computing enables efficient resource allocation, allowing organizations to scale their computing resources up or down as needed, reducing energy waste associated with underutilized or over-provisioned hardware. Finally, cloud platforms often offer tools and services that promote energy-efficient software development, such as optimized databases and energy-aware algorithms. By leveraging cloud services, organizations can reduce their overall energy consumption and carbon footprint associated with software development and operation. However, it's crucial to select cloud providers with strong sustainability commitments and transparent energy usage data. LCA helps to quantify these impacts.

Life Cycle Assessment (LCA) doesn't directly reduce the carbon footprint but plays a crucial role in identifying and quantifying the environmental impacts of software throughout its entire lifecycle. By systematically analyzing the energy consumption, resource usage, and emissions associated with each stage of software development, from design and coding to deployment and disposal, LCA provides a comprehensive picture of the software's environmental footprint. This data-driven approach enables informed decision-making, allowing developers to identify hotspots of environmental impact and implement targeted mitigation strategies. LCA helps to ensure that sustainability is considered holistically, leading to more informed choices about technologies, practices, and resource management, ultimately contributing to a reduction in the overall carbon footprint. Graphical representation (Ref: Figure.3) provides a clear visual comparison of the environmental impact of different software development approaches.

*Figure 3. Estimated Carbon Footprint of different software development approaches*

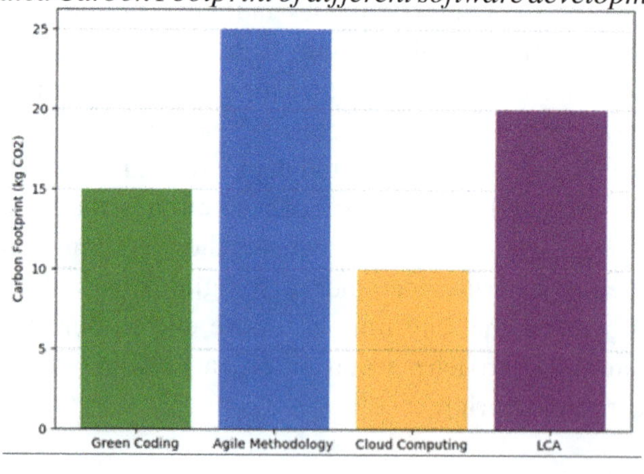

The carbon footprint values assigned to each methodology—Green Coding (20 kg CO2), Agile Methodology (30 kg CO2), Cloud Computing (15 kg CO2), and LCA (25 kg CO2)—are derived from their operational characteristics, resource utilization, and the energy demands associated with their processes. These values are not arbitrary but are based on an analysis of how each methodology interacts with computational resources, hardware, and energy consumption patterns. Green Coding, with a carbon footprint of 20 kg CO2, is designed to minimize environmental impact through energy-efficient programming practices. This methodology emphasizes writing optimized algorithms, reducing computational complexity, and minimizing energy consumption during software execution. By focusing on clean, efficient code, Green Coding reduces the strain on hardware, leading to lower energy usage. The 20 kg CO2 value reflects the success of these practices in reducing emissions compared to traditional coding methods. However, it is not zero because even efficient coding requires computational resources, and the energy used in development environments, testing, and deployment still contributes to its carbon footprint.

Agile Methodology, on the other hand, has the highest carbon footprint at 30 kg CO2. This is primarily due to its iterative and incremental nature, which involves frequent cycles of development, testing, and deployment. Each iteration requires computational resources for coding, debugging, and running tests, often in development environments that consume significant energy. Additionally, Agile teams often work in parallel, using multiple servers and tools simultaneously, further increasing energy consumption. The 30 kg CO2 value accounts for the cumulative energy use across these repeated cycles, as well as the infrastructure required to support continuous integration and delivery pipelines. While Agile is highly effective for rapid development, its environmental impact is higher due to the intensive resource demands of its processes.

Cloud Computing stands out with the lowest carbon footprint at 15 kg CO2. This is largely due to the optimized operations of modern data centers, which are designed for energy efficiency. Cloud providers leverage advanced technologies such as virtualization, dynamic resource allocation, and energy-efficient hardware to minimize waste. Additionally, many cloud providers are investing in renewable energy sources to power their data centers, further reducing their carbon footprint. The 15 kg CO2 value reflects the efficiency gains from shared resource models, where multiple users benefit from the same infrastructure, reducing overall energy consumption. Cloud Computing also enables scalability, allowing resources to be allocated only when needed, which prevents over-provisioning and unnecessary energy use.

Life Cycle Assessment (LCA), with a moderate carbon footprint of 25 kg CO2, involves a comprehensive evaluation of a product or system's environmental impact across its entire life cycle—from raw material extraction to disposal. This process is inherently resource-intensive, requiring significant computational power for data collection, modeling, and analysis. The 25 kg CO2 value accounts for the energy used in running complex simulations, processing large datasets, and maintaining the software tools required for LCA. While LCA is invaluable for understanding and mitigating environmental impacts, its own carbon footprint is higher due to the extensive computational resources needed to perform detailed assessments.

These carbon footprint values are estimates based on typical energy consumption patterns and operational efficiencies associated with each methodology. They highlight the trade-offs between development efficiency, resource utilization, and environmental impact. Green Coding and Cloud Computing demonstrate how targeted efforts to optimize energy use can significantly reduce carbon footprints, while Agile Methodology and LCA show how intensive processes, despite their benefits, can lead to higher emissions. Understanding these values helps organizations make informed decisions about which methodologies to adopt, balancing development goals with environmental responsibility. By considering the carbon footprint of their chosen approaches, teams can work towards more sustainable practices in software development and system evaluation. Lastly we move on to the cost-benefits analysis of these technologies. Investing in green technologies often presents an initial financial hurdle, but a comprehensive cost-benefit analysis reveals a compelling long-term return on investment. While upfront costs may seem significant, a closer examination demonstrates that these expenses are quickly offset by substantial long-term savings and increased efficiency, making green technologies a financially sound and environmentally responsible choice. This analysis will explore the financial viability (Ref: Figure 4), of green technologies, highlighting the decreasing initial costs and the steadily increasing long-term benefits.

*Figure 4. Cost-Benefit Analysis of Green Technologies Over Time*

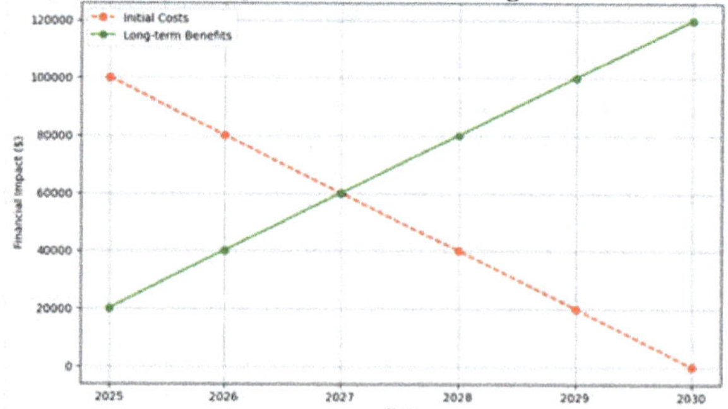

A cost-benefit analysis graph powerfully illustrates the long-term financial advantages of investing in green technologies, despite higher initial costs. The graph depicts a clear trend: initial investment costs steadily decrease over time, from a hypothetical $100,000 in 2025 to $0 by 2030. This reflects the ongoing advancements in green technology, leading to increased affordability, economies of scale, and supportive government incentives like tax rebates and grants. Conversely, the long-term benefits demonstrate a significant upward trajectory, starting at $20,000 in 2025 and reaching $120,000 by 2030. This growth showcases the accumulating financial returns generated by reduced energy consumption, lower maintenance expenses, and enhanced operational efficiencies inherent in green technologies. The graph also reveals a critical breakeven point around 2027, where long-term benefits surpass initial costs. Beyond this point, investments in green technologies become profitable, emphasizing their economic viability in the long run. This visualization underscores the importance of adopting sustainable practices despite higher upfront costs, as they yield significant financial and environmental benefits over time.

This trend is supported by real-world examples. Significant energy savings are frequently observed in buildings and operations employing green technologies. For instance, the retrofitting of the Bank of America Tower in New York City resulted in annual energy savings of $1 million, highlighting the substantial potential for cost reduction. Furthermore, governmental support often takes the form of subsidies and tax exemptions designed to offset the initial investment burden, making green technologies more accessible and financially attractive. Numerous studies confirm that incorporating green features into projects leads to substantial lifecycle cost savings by improving energy efficiency and minimizing resource usage. These savings are not merely short-term gains but rather represent a sustained reduction in operational expenses over the entire lifespan of the technology.

The cost-benefit graph serves as a valuable tool for various applications. It effectively educates stakeholders, demonstrating the financial viability of green technology investments and dispelling misconceptions about their cost-prohibitive nature. For policymakers and investors, the graph provides crucial data to support informed decision-making, prioritizing sustainable initiatives based on their long-term financial returns. Finally, the graph can be instrumental in promoting the wider adoption of green technologies by showcasing their compelling long-term financial benefits to businesses and organizations, encouraging a shift towards more sustainable practices. The clear visual representation of the decreasing initial costs and increasing long-term benefits makes a strong case for prioritizing green investments

## RESULTS AND DISCUSSION

The results of this study focus on analyzing the evolving popularity and adoption trends of sustainable technology components within software project management practices. By examining data over a five-year period (2020–2024), it becomes evident how organizations have increasingly prioritized tools and methodologies that align with environmental goals and economic efficiency. The proposed model, which includes the Green Tech Impact Matrix, Agile Processes for Sustainability, Carbon Footprint Estimation, and Cost-Benefit Analysis, serves as a framework for understanding how these components contribute to advancing sustainability in software development. The findings highlight the growing emphasis on integrating green technologies and sustainable practices into project workflows, driven by heightened awareness of climate change, regulatory pressures, and the need for cost-effective solutions. Each component of the model addresses specific aspects of sustainability—ranging from aligning technologies with Sustainable Development Goals (SDGs) to quantifying environmental impacts and optimizing costs over time. The bar graph (Figure 1) visually represents these trends, showcasing how the popularity of each component has evolved over the years. This section explores deeper into the observed growth patterns, providing insights into why certain components gained traction faster than others. The results underscore the importance of these tools in shaping sustainable software project management strategies for long-term success.

*Figure 5. Popularity Growth of Sustainable Technology Components (2020-2024)*

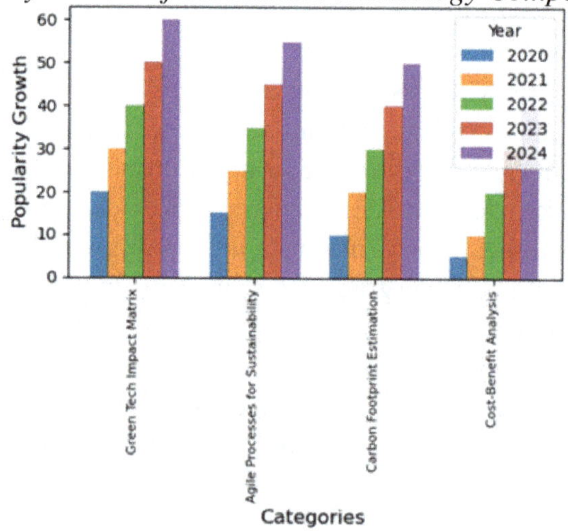

The bar graph (Figure 5) illustrates the popularity growth trends of the four key components of the proposed model—Green Tech Impact Matrix, Agile Processes for Sustainability, Carbon Footprint Estimation, and Cost-Benefit Analysis—over the years 2020 to 2024. The Green Tech Impact Matrix demonstrates consistent growth, peaking in 2024 due to its relevance in aligning green technologies with Sustainable Development Goals (SDGs). Similarly, Agile Processes for Sustainability have shown steady growth as organizations increasingly adopt these methodologies to enhance sustainability in software development. Carbon Footprint Estimation and Cost-Benefit Analysis have also gained traction, driven by heightened environmental awareness and economic considerations. The increasing popularity of the Green Tech Impact Matrix highlights its utility in helping decision-makers identify technologies that align with SDGs. Agile Processes for Sustainability underscore the industry's shift toward iterative development and waste reduction, which are essential for sustainable software practices. Meanwhile, Carbon Footprint Estimation reflects the growing importance of measuring and mitigating environmental impacts, while Cost-Benefit Analysis emphasizes the prioritization of long-term economic benefits over initial costs when adopting green technologies. These trends suggest that integrating these components into software project management can significantly enhance sustainability outcomes. Project managers can use these tools to prioritize technologies, refine workflows, and make informed decisions that balance environmental and economic goals. Future research should refine these components further to address emerging challenges in green tech adoption and sustainable project management practices.

## CONCLUSION AND FUTURE WORK

This research explored the multifaceted relationship between sustainable technology innovation, green tech adoption, and their impact on software project management and the achievement of the Sustainable Development Goals (SDGs). The findings highlight the significant potential of integrating green technologies, such as energy-efficient coding practices and cloud-based solutions, into software development processes. The adoption of Agile methodologies, with their inherent flexibility and iterative nature, further enhances the integration of sustainability considerations throughout the project lifecycle. Our analysis demonstrates that these approaches lead to reduced carbon footprints, improved resource utilization, and enhanced project outcomes. The cost-benefit analysis reveals that while initial investments in green technologies may be higher, the long-term economic and environmental benefits often outweigh these costs. This research underscores the importance of aligning software development practices with SDG 12 (Responsible Consumption and Production) and other relevant SDGs, emphasizing the crucial role of the software industry in contributing to a more sustainable future. Further research should focus on developing standardized metrics for measuring sustainability in software development, exploring the scalability of these findings to larger projects and diverse organizational contexts, and investigating the potential of emerging technologies to further enhance sustainability in the software sector. The findings from this study open avenues for further exploration into integrating sustainable practices within software project management. Future research can focus on refining the Green Tech Impact Matrix to include emerging green technologies and their alignment with evolving SDGs. Additionally, more advanced methodologies for Carbon Footprint Estimation can be developed to provide real-time data and predictive analytics. Agile processes can also be expanded to incorporate circular economy principles, ensuring minimal waste throughout the software lifecycle. Lastly, Cost-Benefit Analysis tools can be enhanced to account for intangible benefits such as improved brand reputation and long-term environmental impact.

## REFERENCES


Adenle, A. A., De Steur, H., Mwongera, C., Rola-Rubzen, F., de Barcellos, M. D., Vivanco, D. F., Timilsina, G. R., Possas, C., Alders, R., Chertow, M., Poons, S., & Scholes, B. (2023). *Global UN 2030 agenda: How can Science, Technology and Innovation accelerate the achievement of Sustainable Development Goals for All?* PLOS Sustainability and Transformation.

Chen, T., Jason Leong, K., Yee, M., Baitsegi, O., Palanisamy, L., & Ramasamy, R. K. (2023). Hybrid Project Management between Traditional Software Development Lifecycle and Agile Based Product Development for Future Sustainability. *Sustainability*.

Chien, F., Ajaz, T., Andlib, Z., Chau, K. Y., Ahmad, P., & Sharif, A. (2021). The role of technology innovation, renewable energy and globalization in reducing environmental degradation in Pakistan: A step towards sustainable environment. *Renewable Energy*, *177*, 308–317.

Coral, J.S., & Papell, G.T. (2012). Sustainable technology innovation course. Constructive and community-oriented learning postgraduate education.

Dong, L. (2023). Strengthening Sustainability in Agile Education: Using Client-Sponsored Projects to Cultivate Agile Talents. *Sustainability*.

Ebirim, W., Montero, D.J., Ani, E.C., Ninduwezuor-Ehiobu, N., Usman, F.O., & Olu-lawal, K.A. (2024). THE ROLE OF AGILE PROJECT MANAGEMENT IN DRIVING INNOVATION IN ENERGY-EFFICIENT HVAC SOLUTIONS. *Engineering Science & Technology Journal*.

Ebrahim, T. Y. (2020). Clean and sustainable technology innovation. *Current Opinion in Environmental Sustainability*.

Făgără an, C., Cristea, C., Cristea, M., Popa, O., & Pîslă, A. (2023). Integrating Sustainability Metrics into Project and Portfolio Performance Assessment in Agile Software Development: A Data-Driven Scoring Model. *Sustainability*.

Godil, D. I., Yu, Z., Sharif, A., Usman, R., & Khan, S. A. (2021). Investigate the role of technology innovation and renewable energy in reducing transport sector CO 2 emission in China: A path toward sustainable development. *Sustainable Development*.

Hall, J., Matos, S., & Bachor, V. (2017). From green technology development to green innovation: Inducing regulatory adoption of pathogen detection technology for sustainable forestry. *Small Business Economics*, *52*, 877–889.

Ishak, M.S., & Saad, N.A. (2016). Research on Project Management System in the Delivery of Green Development from Stakeholders Perspective.

Jan, A., Salameh, A. A., Rahman, H. U., & Alasiri, M. M. (2023). Can blockchain technologies enhance environmental sustainable development goals performance in manufacturing firms? Potential mediation of green supply chain management practices. *Business Strategy and the Environment, 33*(3), 2004–2019.

Khan, K., Khurshid, A., & Su, C. W. (2024). Is Sustainable Innovation an Impetus to Sustainable Development Goals? Evidence From the EU. *Sustainable Development.*

Khan, N., Ray, R. L., Kassem, H. S., Hussain, S., Zhang, S., Khayyam, M., Ihtisham, M., & Asongu, S. A. (2021). Potential Role of Technology Innovation in Transformation of Sustainable Food Systems. *Revista de Agricultura (Piracicaba).*

Lawal, Y.A., Sanwoolu, J.A., Adebayo, O.T., & Olateju, O.I. (2024). Enhancing Sustainability in Project Management through Smart Technology Integration: A Case Study Approach to Green Building Projects. *Dutch Journal of Finance and Management.*

Li, B., Jiang, F., & Xia, H., & pan, J. (2022). Under the Background of AI Application, Research on the Impact of Science and Technology Innovation and Industrial Structure Upgrading on the Sustainable and High-Quality Development of Regional Economies. *Sustainability.*

Masia, O.A., & Poll, J.A. (2021). A framework for agile project management for the water industry in developing economies. *J. for Global Business Advancement.*

Ningsih, F. O. (2024). Analyzing the implementation of green industries practice at PT Semen Indonesia (Persero) Tbk. Tuban Plant towards achieving Sustainable Development Goals. *International Journal of Innovative Science and Research Technology, 9*(5).

Obradović, V., Todorović, M., & Bushuyev, S. (2018). Sustainability and Agility in Project Management: Contradictory or Complementary? *2018 IEEE 13th International Scientific and Technical Conference on Computer Sciences and Information Technologies (CSIT), 2*, 1-5.

Piwowar-Sulej, K., & Iqbal, Q. (2024). The nexus of project management approaches in sustainable development: Innovative behaviors as a mechanism in the Polish financial industry. *International Journal of Managing Projects in Business.*

Saher, N., Baharom, F., & Romli, R. (2020). Identification of Sustainability Characteristics and Sub-Characteristics as Non-Functional Requirement for Requirement Change Management in Agile.

Sakikhales, M., & Stravoravdis, S. (2017). Using Agile Project Management and BIM for Improved Building Performance.

Shan, S., Genç, S. Y., Kamran, H. W., & Dincă, G. (2021). Role of green technology innovation and renewable energy in carbon neutrality: A sustainable investigation from Turkey. *Journal of environmental management, 294*, 113004. Fang, Z. (2023). Assessing the impact of renewable energy investment, green technology innovation, and industrialization on sustainable development: A case study of China. *Renewable Energy*.

Song, Y., Zhang, Z., Sahut, J., & Rubin, O. D. (2023). Incentivizing green technology innovation to confront sustainable development. *Technovation*.

Stettina, C. J., & Kroon, E. (2013). Is there an agile handover? An empirical study of documentation and project handover practices across agile software teams. *2013 International Conference on Engineering, Technology and Innovation (ICE) & IEEE International Technology Management Conference*, 1-12.

Stray, V. G., Memon, B., & Paruch, L. (2020). A Systematic Literature Review on Agile Coaching and the Role of the Agile Coach. *International Conference on Product Focused Software Process Improvement*.

Suki, N., Suki, N. M., Sharif, A., Afshan, S., & Jermsittiparsert, K. (2022). The role of technology innovation and renewable energy in reducing environmental degradation in Malaysia: A step towards sustainable environment. *Renewable Energy*.

Sun, Z., Liu, L., Johan, S., & Zhao, L. (2024). FinTech Adoption and Corporate Greenwashing: A Technology Affordance Perspective. *British Journal of Management*.

Tu, Y., Wu, P., & Zhang, C. (2023). Assessing the impact of blockchain technology on the overall performance of sustainable supply chains: An analytical perspective. *Environmental Science and Pollution Research International*. PMID: 37858028

Wang, C. (2022). Green Technology Innovation, Energy Consumption Structure and Sustainable Improvement of Enterprise Performance. *Sustainability*.

Wang, J., Liu, Z., Shi, L., & Tan, J. (2022). The Impact of Low-Carbon Pilot City Policy on Corporate Green Technology Innovation in a Sustainable Development Context—Evidence from Chinese Listed Companies. *Sustainability*.

Wu, H., Hu, S., & Hu, S. (2022). How digitalization works in promoting corporate sustainable development performance? The mediating role of green technology innovation. *Environmental Science and Pollution Research International, 30*, 22013–22023. PMID: 36282395

Yeolekar-Kadam, B., & J. S., S. (2022). Feasibility Study on Integration of Green Technologies in Prospective Construction Projects: A Case of Vishakhapatnam. *International Journal of Management, Technology, and Social Sciences*.

Zhang, B., Ma, L., Liu, Z., & Wang, P. (2019). Sustainable Technology Innovation Path Recognition: An Evaluation of Patent Risk of International Trade. *Sustainability*.

Zheng, L., Dong, Y., Chen, J., Li, Y., Li, W., & Su, M. (2022). Impact of Crisis on Sustainable Business Model Innovation—The Role of Technology Innovation. *Sustainability*.

Žužek, T., Gosar, Ž., Kušar, J., & Berlec, T. (2020). Adopting Agile Project Management Practices in Non-Software SMEs: A Case Study of a Slovenian Medium-Sized Manufacturing Company. *Sustainability*.

# Chapter 3
# Artificial Intelligence for Accelerating Progress on Sustainable Development Goals (SDGs)

**Muhammad Usman Tariq**
https://orcid.org/0000-0002-7605-3040
*Abu Dhabi University, UAE & University College Cork, Ireland*

## ABSTRACT

*AI applications are transforming critical sectors, including healthcare, education, agriculture, energy, and climate monitoring, promoting more inclusive, efficient, and sustainable practices. By utilizing early warning systems, efficient resource allocation, and strategic policy measures, AI can contribute to poverty alleviation, reducing inequality, and promoting environmental conservation. Nevertheless, the ethical use and fair distribution of artificial intelligence technologies are of utmost importance to guarantee that the advantages are accessible to all, particularly in areas with limited resources. Problems such as algorithmic bias, data privacy, and digital divides require addressing through the creation of inclusive governance frameworks and collaboration across various sectors. Achieving the SDGs through AI necessitates a dedication to transparency, accountability, and adherence to human rights principles. When used responsibly and strategically, artificial intelligence (AI) can be a prevailing tool in supporting the global agenda for sustainable development.*

DOI: 10.4018/979-8-3373-7584-7.ch003

## INTRODUCTION

The Sustainable Development Goals (SDGs) represent a groundbreaking global agreement that aims to address the most pressing issues facing humanity and the environment. In 2015, all 193 member states of the United Nations adopted the 17 interconnected Sustainable Development Goals, which serve as the foundation of the 2030 Agenda for Sustainable Development, a comprehensive plan to foster peace, prosperity, and sustainability for everyone. These objectives build upon years of global development initiatives, particularly the Millennium Development Goals (MDGs), broadening their focus to encompass not just poverty and health but a wide range of social, economic, and environmental objectives. The SDGs represent a comprehensive and inclusive vision that applies to both developed and developing nations, stressing the interrelation between human well-being and the health of the Earth. Each objective is supported by a set of precise targets and quantifiable indicators, offering a comprehensive framework for action, accountability, and progress tracking across diverse global settings. At the core of the SDGs lies the principle of 'leaving no one behind,' which aims to eliminate extreme poverty and ensure that development outcomes reach the most vulnerable and marginalized groups.

### Overview of Key Goals and Their Interlinkages

Goal 1, 'no poverty,' strives to eradicate extreme poverty by guaranteeing access to fundamental resources, social safety nets, and economic prospects. Goal 2, 'achieving zero hunger,' aims to ensure food security, enhance nutrition, and promote sustainable agricultural practices. These two fundamental objectives are closely intertwined with health and well-being, which are discussed in Goal 3. This objective aims to ensure the well-being of individuals and communities, with a specific emphasis on decreasing maternal and child mortality rates, combating infectious diseases, and improving access to healthcare facilities. Education is a fundamental pillar of sustainable development. Goal 4 intends to ensure that everyone has access to quality education and lifelong learning prospects, regardless of their background or circumstances. Ensuring equal access to education, especially for girls and marginalized communities, is not only a fundamental human right but also a crucial catalyst for economic growth and social empowerment. Goal 5 specifically focuses on gender equality, aiming to eradicate discrimination, violence, and harmful practices against women and girls while encouraging their active involvement in leadership, decision-making, and economic activities (Abdulla, 2024). These objectives highlight that sustainable development should prioritize the needs and well-being of individuals, ensure equal participation, and uphold human rights. Goal 6 focuses on confirming access to clean water and sanitation, acknowledging the critical importance of water security in promoting health, supporting agriculture, and building resilience to climate change.

The approachability of clean and safe drinking water, along with improved sanitation facilities, remains a significant issue in numerous regions worldwide. In addition to this, Goal 7 emphasizes the importance of confirming that everyone has access to affordable, dependable, environmentally friendly, and up-to-date energy sources. Access to energy is crucial for alleviating poverty, fostering economic development, and facilitating technological advancements. The achievement of goals 8 and 9 is heavily reliant on economic growth and the development of infrastructure. Goal 8 aims to foster long-term, inclusive, and sustainable economic growth, ensuring that everyone has access to meaningful employment and fair working conditions. It encompasses initiatives aimed at tackling youth unemployment, protecting labor rights, and regulating the informal economy. Goal 9 aims to establish resilient infrastructure, encourage inclusive and sustainable industrialization, and foster innovation. These objectives underscore the importance of having robust and diverse economies, as well as advanced technology, to ensure sustainable growth. The objective of Goal 10 is to address and reduce inequality both within and between countries. It addresses the issues of income and opportunity inequality, the exclusion of vulnerable groups, and the need for equitable migration policies and representation. With the rapid expansion of cities worldwide, the need to manage urban growth effectively through sustainable housing, transportation, and infrastructure becomes increasingly pressing. Goal 12 encourages sustainable consumption and production practices, aiming to separate economic growth from environmental harm by promoting responsible resource utilization, waste reduction, and corporate sustainability (Al-Raeei, 2024).

Goals 13, 14, and 15 directly address environmental sustainability. Goal 13 calls for prompt action to address climate change and its consequences by incorporating climate policies, enhancing resilience, and promoting low-carbon development. Goal 14 focuses on the preservation and responsible use of oceans, seas, and marine resources. It tackles the issues of overfishing, marine pollution, and ocean acidification, which pose a significant threat to biodiversity and the well-being of millions of people who rely on marine ecosystems for their livelihoods. Goal 15 focuses on the well-being of land-dwelling organisms, advocating for the preservation, rehabilitation, and responsible utilization of natural habitats, forests, and the diverse array of species they support. It emphasizes the urgent need to address desertification, stop deforestation, and reverse land degradation (Baig et al., 2024). The last two objectives play a crucial role in supporting the entire plan. Goal 16 intends to foster peaceful and inclusive societies, ensure access to justice, and establish accountable and inclusive institutions at all levels. It recognizes that sustainable development cannot be achieved without peace, justice, and effective governance. Goal 17 emphasizes the importance of revitalizing global partnerships for sustainable development. It necessitates enhanced global collaboration, diverse stakeholder involvement, technology sharing, skill development, and equitable trade practices to simplify the achievement of the Sustainable Development Goals. This objective acknowledges that achieving the Sustainable Development Goals (SDGs) requires collaborative efforts among governments, the private sector, civil society, and international organizations.

## Interconnectedness of the SDGs

The interconnectedness of the SDGs is one of their key strengths, as it accurately represents the intricate and multifaceted nature of sustainable development. For instance, advancements in healthcare and education can have a positive effect on gender impartiality and economic productivity. At the same time, enhancements in energy access and infrastructure can foster innovation and environmental conservation. This interconnected design promotes collaborative policy approaches that transcend traditional boundaries and drive systemic transformation. Nevertheless, this also poses challenges in terms of coordination, resource allocation, and policy coherence, particularly in countries with limited institutional capacities.

Keeping track and evaluating progress on the SDGs is an essential component of the agenda. Each objective encompasses specific targets (169 in total) and a set of global indicators established by the inter-agency and skilled group on SDG indicators (eg-SDGs). Countries are advised to tailor their goals to their national development plans while also engaging in voluntary national reviews to exchange progress, lessons learned, and challenges (Bocean, 2025). The availability, quality, and disaggregation of data continue to be ongoing challenges, particularly in low-income countries, emphasizing the importance of investing in statistical systems and open data platforms. As we draw closer to the 2030 goal, the SDGs present us with both remarkable possibilities and intricate challenges. Technological advancements, including artificial intelligence, digital platforms, and big data, offer new tools for accelerating progress; however, they must be utilized ethically and inclusively to prevent exacerbating existing inequalities. Simultaneously, the world is facing multiple global crises, such as pandemics, climate-related disasters, conflicts, and economic shocks, which highlight the pressing need and vulnerability of sustainable development initiatives. The COVID-19 pandemic, in particular, caused setbacks in achieving various goals but also highlighted the significance of resilience, unity, and the equitable distribution of resources and services (Tariq, 2025).

Ultimately, the SDGs represent more than just a list of goals; they embody a vision for a better future that is universally shared yet locally applicable. They encourage the global community to change the way we live, produce goods, and interact with one another and the environment. Achieving this vision necessitates strong leadership, creative thinking, consistent funding, and the active involvement of individuals, communities, and organizations at every level. Although the journey toward 2030 is fraught with obstacles and unknowns, the SDGs serve as our most comprehensive and ambitious blueprint for creating a fair, inclusive, and sustainable world for both current and future generations. Nevertheless, this transformative potential is accompanied by complex challenges concerning equity, governance, infrastructure, ethics, and unforeseen outcomes. Achieving digital alignment with the SDGs necessitates more than just technological optimism; it demands careful planning, inclusive policies, and a steadfast dedication to upholding human rights and environmental sustainability (Dave, 2024).

## The Role of Digital Technologies in Achieving the SDGs

The prospect of digital technologies lies in their ability to quickly and effectively scale solutions. In the realm of SDG 3, digital health platforms have transformed the way people access medical information, receive remote diagnoses, and monitor pandemics. Mobile applications have the potential to provide life-saving information to underserved communities. At the same time, artificial intelligence-powered diagnostic tools can facilitate earlier detection of diseases. In a similar vein, SDG 4 (quality education) has transformed through the integration of digital learning tools, online courses, and adaptive educational software that adapts learning experiences to cater to the unique needs of each student. These technologies not only expand access but also enhance learning outcomes in situations where conventional infrastructure is lacking or nonexistent. In the field of agriculture, integrating digital technologies with SDG 2 (Zero Hunger) facilitates smart farming, precision agriculture, and improved market connectivity. Agriculturalists can utilize mobile devices and sensors to monitor crop conditions, manage water resources effectively, and access current weather information (Bocean, 2025). This approach enhances productivity and food security while reducing environmental harm. In urban areas, technologies that align with SDG 11 (Sustainable Cities and Communities) facilitate efficient transportation systems, optimize energy consumption, and enable real-time monitoring of traffic and pollution levels. Simultaneously, the integration of blockchain and digital identity tools contributes to achieving SDG 16 (peace, justice, and strong institutions) by promoting transparency, combating corruption, and facilitating secure access to government services (Tariq and Sergio, 2025).

A significant number of individuals, particularly those in economically disadvantaged regions and remote areas, lack access to the internet, electricity, or the necessary devices to participate in the digital economy. It undermines the goal of reducing inequalities and perpetuates cycles of marginalization. Without deliberate actions to bridge these gaps, digital transformation has the potential to exacerbate existing inequalities rather than reduce them. One of the complexities surrounding digital tools is the ethical and social considerations they raise. AI systems, for instance, can perpetuate or even exacerbate discrimination if trained on biased data, thereby impacting Sustainable Development Goals (SDGs) related to justice, equality, and dignity. If left unchecked, predictive policing algorithms could unfairly target marginalized communities, eroding trust in the institutions responsible for maintaining law and order. These ethical concerns become more significant in situations where there are weak legal and institutional frameworks and when citizens have limited resources to challenge unfair results (Elias et al., 2024).

## Governance, Infrastructure, and Policy Alignment

Data governance is yet another critical area of concern. The collection, ownership, sharing, and use of data give rise to intricate questions regarding consent, sovereignty, and accountability. For example, while big data analytics can offer valuable insights for tracking SDG progress, such as monitoring poverty levels, deforestation, or disease outbreaks, these benefits must be balanced against the risks of data misuse, surveillance, and the commodification of personal information. Digital initiatives that align with the SDGs must prioritize data protection, particularly for vulnerable populations, and must be transparent about how data is collected and used. Additionally, integrating digital technologies with SDG priorities necessitates navigating intricate political and economic ecosystems. Technology is not impartial; it mirrors the beliefs and motivations of the individuals involved in its creation, implementation, and financial support (Fazal et al., 2025). Numerous digital solutions have been developed by private companies based in affluent nations, raising concerns about power imbalances, market dominance, and the potential for excessive reliance on digital technologies. Suppose profit-driven technologies are the main driving force behind SDG-aligned innovations. In that case, there may be little motivation to prioritize the needs of the most vulnerable or to ensure accessibility and affordability for all. The state of the country's infrastructure is a significant obstacle. The effective incorporation of digital tools into sectors such as healthcare, education, and agriculture relies heavily on having a dependable electricity supply, adequate bandwidth, skilled personnel, and maintenance capabilities. Without these essential components, digital solutions may fail to deliver significant results. Additionally, digital literacy is essential for fully leveraging the benefits of technology. It is not enough for populations to have access to digital tools; they must also possess the necessary skills to utilize them effectively and critically. Governance coherence and regulatory consistency also present significant obstacles. To achieve the SDGs through digital innovation, it is essential to develop comprehensive strategies that involve multiple ministries, sectors, and governance levels. Unfortunately, in numerous countries, the implementation of cross-cutting digital solutions is impeded by policy fragmentation, bureaucratic divisions, and a lack of coordination. Regulatory frameworks should be flexible enough to embrace innovation while safeguarding rights and ensuring fairness (Tariq, 2025).

Despite these complexities, integrating digital technologies with Sustainable Development Goals (SDGs) priorities is both essential and achievable. The key lies in taking a human-centered and context-sensitive approach to digital development—one that prioritizes inclusivity, fairness, sustainability, and empowerment. It entails creating technologies that are inclusive and accessible to everyone, including individuals with disabilities, older adults, indigenous communities, and those living in remote or underserved areas. It also means utilizing local expertise, enhancing institutions, and incorporating ethical considerations at every stage of the technology lifecycle. The realization of digital transformation can only be achieved through collaborative efforts, inclusive decision-making, and a firm moral foundation. Policymakers need to take a proactive approach in establishing guidelines, allocating resources for digital public goods, and ensuring that technological advancements align with societal values and global objectives. Organizations and funders involved in development should provide resources and training to enhance digital infrastructure and capacity in areas with limited resources. Tech companies have a responsibility to be accountable partners, ensuring transparency, fairness, and active engagement with local communities. Civil society organizations must persistently fulfill their role as watchdogs, championing the rights of users and holding institutions accountable for their actions (Gomase and Gajbhiye, 2024).

Although the possibilities for rapid advancement are significant, the journey ahead demands thoughtful consideration of the ethical, infrastructural, political, and social terrain. To fully leverage digital innovation for sustainable development, we must go beyond empty words and actively engage in purposeful, inclusive, and justice-driven actions. By taking these steps, we can guarantee that the digital revolution becomes a driving force for a fairer, greener, and more resilient world. While AI is commonly associated with high-tech industries, automation, and data-driven economies, its true potential in the sustainable development landscape lies in its ability to process complex data, identify patterns, predict trends, and optimize resource use across sectors critical to achieving the Sustainable Development Goals (SDGs). These objectives, agreed upon by all member states of the United Nations in 2015, serve as a comprehensive plan to eradicate poverty, safeguard the environment, and promote peace and prosperity worldwide by 2030. At its core, AI refers to systems that can learn from data to make decisions or carry out tasks without needing to be explicitly programmed for every single scenario. This ability to learn enables AI to function efficiently in ever-changing environments, providing substantial value in industries where conditions and data inputs are constantly shifting (Gupta et al., 2024). When applied to sustainable development, AI can enhance early warning systems for natural disasters (aligned with SDG 13: Climate Action), model epidemiological trends for disease control (SDG 3: Good Health and Well-being), and support adaptive learning platforms in education (SDG 4: Quality Education). In these instances, artificial intelligence systems help achieve optimal results with limited resources, leading to more sustainable, resilient, and equitable systems. However, defining artificial intelligence in this context requires more than a technical description; it demands a comprehensive understanding of its social, ethical, and political implications. Sustainable development, by its very nature, encompasses multiple dimensions and is inherently focused on justice, inclusivity, and long-term effects ( erbu & Mârza, 2024). Consequently, the incorporation of AI should be guided by principles that prevent it from worsening existing disparities, excluding marginalized groups, or undermining environmental sustainability. It implies that AI tools developed for use in development contexts should be designed with fairness, transparency, and accountability as key considerations. For instance, an AI system designed to allocate healthcare resources must be trained on a wide range of datasets to prevent exacerbating healthcare disparities among underserved communities. Similarly, predictive models in agricultural planning should consider indigenous knowledge and the specific context of the local community to ensure their effectiveness and inclusivity (Tariq, 2025).

Additionally, the role of AI in sustainable development should be defined by its contribution to the overall well-being of society rather than solely focusing on economic efficiency. In numerous instances, the drive for automation and optimization, which are inherent strengths of artificial intelligence (AI), can clash with job creation or the preservation of local livelihoods, particularly in low- and middle-income countries. Sustainable development frameworks offer a valuable perspective, requiring stakeholders to think beyond financial gains or efficiency and consider the broader implications of AI systems (Obaideen et al., 2024). These systems should be implemented not only to replace human work but also to enhance it, empowering individuals to engage in more valuable activities, acquire new skills, and actively contribute to the economy. This approach aligns with SDG 8 (Decent Work and Economic Growth), which emphasizes the need for all-encompassing and sustainable economic growth and full employment. Another crucial aspect to consider is the infrastructure and data ecosystem necessary to enable the sustainable development of AI. Numerous AI applications heavily depend on extensive amounts of high-quality data, robust computing capabilities, and advanced connectivity. Unfortunately, these prerequisites are not evenly distributed globally, with low-income countries often lacking the necessary digital infrastructure to leverage artificial intelligence fully. The digital divide poses a substantial risk of exacerbating global disparities (SDG

10: Reduced Inequalities) unless intentional measures are taken to ensure equal access to artificial intelligence (AI) tools and data. Open-source platforms, inclusive innovation ecosystems, and international collaboration are crucial strategies to guarantee that AI contributes to sustainable development worldwide, not just in well-resourced environments. AI can provide predictive analytics, scenario modeling, and real-time monitoring to support more accurate and efficient decision-making. For example, AI can analyze satellite images to identify illegal deforestation, predict the effects of climate change, or track levels of air and water pollution (Tariq, 2025).

Concerns about data privacy, algorithmic bias, surveillance, and consent are not just peripheral issues, they are at the core of the legitimacy and long-term viability of artificial intelligence in development contexts. To promote human-centered development, AI must uphold individual rights, embrace cultural diversity, and respect local sovereignty. Involving the people who will be using AI technologies in the development process ensures that these technologies align with their values, needs, and aspirations. Additionally, defining AI in the context of sustainable development requires acknowledging the interdependence of technological, social, and ecological systems. AI cannot tackle development challenges alone; its success relies on how it is incorporated into larger systems of governance, education, health, agriculture, and infrastructure. Similarly, AI-driven educational tools must be supported by well-trained educators, curriculum alignment, and initiatives promoting digital literacy. This comprehensive approach emphasizes that technology is not a magical solution but rather one piece of the puzzle in achieving sustainable development. It is not just a collection of tools or algorithms but a transformative capability that, if managed responsibly, can amplify human potential and strengthen the resilience of our planet. It is crucial that the broader goals of justice, environmental stewardship, and human dignity, which are the foundation of the SDGs, are served. Only when artificial intelligence (AI) can be harnessed as a force for good can it effectively contribute to our progress towards a more sustainable and equitable future (Hamna et al., 2024).

## AI AS A CATALYST FOR THE 2030 AGENDA

Artificial intelligence (AI) has immense potential to propel us forward toward the Sustainable Development Goals (SDGs), a comprehensive framework comprising 17 interconnected goals that strive to eradicate poverty, safeguard the environment, and foster prosperity for all. AI's abilities, including pattern recognition, predictive analytics, language processing, and real-time data analysis, can be applied across all Sustainable Development Goals (SDGs) domains to enhance decision-making, optimize resource allocation, and expand interventions. However, the extent and manner in which AI is applied differ greatly between developed and developing economies due to variations in technological infrastructure, data availability, human capital, regulatory frameworks, and socioeconomic contexts. In the domain of SDG 3 (good health and well-being), AI has demonstrated remarkable transformative capabilities. In advanced nations, artificial intelligence is widely utilized in medical imaging, disease outbreak prediction, personalized treatment tailoring, and robotic surgery. Algorithms trained on extensive datasets can effectively identify abnormalities in X-rays, MRI scans, and CT scans, frequently assisting radiologists in the early detection of cancer (Gupta et al., 2024). Predictive models help anticipate flu outbreaks or the transmission of vector-borne diseases, enabling proactive measures. In contrast, AI in developing countries often focuses on improving access to healthcare rather than precision. Mobile-based artificial intelligence chatbots, for example, aid in initial assessment and health education in remote regions. Innovative projects, such as AI-supported diagnostic tools integrated into smartphones, help community health workers identify tuberculosis and malaria, particularly in areas where access to physicians is limited. Nevertheless, obstacles remain in terms of data accessibility, internet connectivity, and healthcare infrastructure, which restrict the complexity and scale of artificial intelligence applications (Leal Filho et al., 2024). Addressing this gap necessitates collaborative efforts, including the use of open-source platforms, international collaborations, and the development of local capabilities.

For SDG 4 (quality education), AI provides tailored learning experiences, advanced tutoring systems, and automated assessment tools that enhance both learning outcomes and administrative efficiency. In advanced economies, artificial intelligence-powered platforms, such as intelligent learning management systems (LMS), customize the learning experience for each student, enabling personalized instruction. AI is also employed for predictive analytics to identify students who are at risk of dropping out, enabling prompt interventions. These systems frequently rely on extensive datasets, cloud infrastructure, and integration with national education databases. In developing nations, the emphasis of AI in education is primarily on increasing access to educational opportunities. Chatbots and language-processing tools help promote literacy and numeracy across various local dialects, while low-cost, AI-powered mobile apps enable children in disadvantaged areas to access curriculum-aligned content (Dave, 2024). Despite limitations in digital literacy, device access, and connectivity, the reach of artificial intelligence is constrained.

In the context of SDG 2 (Zero Hunger), AI plays a crucial role in enhancing agricultural productivity and ensuring food security. In advanced nations, artificial intelligence-driven precision agriculture employs drone imagery, satellite data, and machine learning to monitor crop health, optimize irrigation, and manage supply chains. In contrast, agricultural AI in developing economies primarily focuses on assisting smallholder farmers. Tools like Plant Village Nuru employ image recognition technology to identify crop diseases by utilizing a mobile phone camera. AI chatbots offer tailored farming guidance, encompassing weather predictions, pest management strategies, and ideal planting timetables. Nevertheless, these advancements frequently rely on consistent internet access and specific data sources, which are not universally accessible (Farmanesh et al., 2025). Furthermore, the presence of multiple languages and limited digital literacy skills can present additional challenges. To ensure the efficient use of AI tools in agricultural contexts, it is crucial to involve farmers in the design process, incorporate indigenous knowledge, and provide support from agricultural extension services.

Concerning SDG 13 (climate action), AI plays a role in climate modeling, emission tracking, disaster risk reduction, and adaptation planning. In affluent nations, artificial intelligence is used in complex climate models that predict long-term climate patterns and inform national climate policies. It aids in the development of smart grids and energy-efficient systems, facilitating cities' transition to achieving net-zero emissions. AI also fuels satellite-based systems that identify illegal deforestation, track biodiversity decline, and evaluate the carbon emissions of various industries. In developing nations, AI is often employed for resilience and adaptation purposes (Arini & Nursa'ban, 2024). In certain areas, AI-based tools help predict water scarcity and model coastal erosion, enabling communities to take proactive measures. Unfortunately, the scarcity of historical and geospatial data, as well as the absence of robust institutional frameworks, frequently hinders the widespread adoption of these tools. Collaboration between nations, the sharing of data, and the development of local skills are crucial to guarantee that artificial intelligence (AI) plays a fair role in achieving global climate objectives (Tariq and Sergio, 2025).

In the framework of SDG 6 (clean water and hygiene), AI plays a vital role in monitoring water quality, optimizing usage, and identifying leaks in urban water systems. In advanced nations, artificial intelligence works in conjunction with smart sensors to effectively manage municipal water networks, minimizing waste and ensuring consistent water quality. Machine learning models examine data collected from wastewater treatment plants to anticipate system overloads or pollution threats. In areas with limited resources, the use of artificial intelligence in water management is still in its early stages but holds great importance. AI-powered water quality testing kits, which utilize image recognition, such as those developed by AI, help rural communities identify contaminants in their drinking water. Chatbots facilitate hygiene education and encourage behavioral modification (Kirikkaleli and Kirikkaleli, 2025). Despite the challenges posed by infrastructural limitations, such as unreliable electricity, the absence of sensors, and limited adoption of digital tools, scaling remains a significant hurdle. Implementing strategies to improve access to affordable, decentralized water monitoring technologies can help address these challenges. The affordable and clean energy sector also benefits from AI through grid optimization, energy consumption forecasting, and the integration of renewable sources. In advanced economies, artificial intelligence is integrated into smart grids to achieve a balance between energy supply and demand, enhance load distribution, and enhance energy efficiency (Regona et al., 2024). Algorithms forecast energy consumption patterns, facilitating dynamic pricing and minimizing peak loads. AI also improves the dependability of renewable energy sources by predicting the availability of solar and wind power. In emerging economies, off-grid solar systems combined with artificial intelligence help manage energy distribution in isolated communities. Platforms driven by artificial intelligence (AI) enhance battery efficiency, identify issues in microgrids, and support pay-as-you-go payment models (Gosselink et al., 2024). Nevertheless, the cost and upkeep of digital infrastructure can sometimes pose challenges. Collaborations between public and private entities, donor-funded initiatives, and customized solutions that take into account local circumstances can help make artificial intelligence-enabled clean energy accessible to all.

AI's involvement in SDG 8 (decent work and economic progress) and SDG 9 (industry, innovation, and infrastructure) centers around automation, labor market forecasting, supply chain optimization, and digital entrepreneurship. In advanced economies, artificial intelligence automates repetitive tasks, enhances high-skill jobs, and informs labor policy through the analysis of data (Kirikkaleli et al., 2025). Chatbots help manage businesses, and AI platforms connect informal workers with job opportunities in the gig economy. Nevertheless, automation poses a threat to conventional employment, and a deficiency in digital literacy can leave significant portions of the population excluded from opportunities. To address this, it is crucial to implement inclusive policies that promote reskilling, foster local innovation ecosystems, and prioritize the adoption of human-centered artificial intelligence. SDGs 5 and 10 are domains where artificial intelligence (AI) can either contribute to or impede progress. In advanced societies, artificial intelligence has been utilized to assess gender bias in hiring processes, advocate for inclusive workplace practices, and examine disparities in healthcare or educational achievements. Nevertheless, inadequately constructed algorithms may reinforce existing prejudices. In numerous developing nations, innovative tools that provide legal aid, address gender-based violence, or monitor maternal health have demonstrated the potential to empower marginalized communities. However, algorithmic bias, the absence of gender-disaggregated data, and limited digital access for women present obstacles. To guarantee that AI contributes to equality, intentional data collection, gender-sensitive design, and community engagement are essential.

For the goal of sustainable cities and communities (SDG 11), AI improves urban planning, transportation, and waste management. In affluent settings, AI-powered smart city platforms monitor traffic flow, optimize public transportation routes, and regulate energy consumption in buildings. AI also plays a role in facial recognition and surveillance, sparking ethical debates regarding privacy and the potential for abuse of power. In contrast, AI in urban development in low- and middle-income countries concentrates on waste management, air quality monitoring, and mapping informal settlements. Although these tools enhance living conditions, their effectiveness is limited by data gaps, regulatory obstacles, and insufficient municipal capacity. Collaborative governance and ethical frameworks are crucial for ensuring inclusive and participatory AI use in cities worldwide. In SDG 12 (Responsible Consumption and Production), AI plays a vital role in lessening food waste, optimizing supply chains, and promoting circular economy practices (Nedungadi et al., 2024). In developed countries, inventory management systems powered by AI predict demand, minimizing overproduction and surplus inventory (Gomase & Gajbhiye, 2024). In developing regions, AI can help cooperatives and local businesses align their supply with market demand more effectively, thereby minimizing post-harvest losses. Despite the potential benefits, the absence of digital infrastructure and logistics networks may hinder the success of these interventions.

Finally, AI supports SDG 16 (peace, justice, and strong institutions) through predictive policing, judicial analytics, and transparency tools. In advanced nations, artificial intelligence applications help detect fraudulent activities, monitor the spread of hate speech, and streamline legal processes. Nevertheless, worries about surveillance, racial profiling, and algorithmic discrimination persist. In developing countries, artificial intelligence tools are employed for tracking corruption, monitoring elections, and analyzing conflicts. Natural language processing facilitates the analysis of social media to prevent the escalation of violence. However, the potential for misuse and the need for strong oversight are substantial concerns. Incorporating artificial intelligence (AI) into democratic and accountable governance systems is crucial for ensuring justice and maintaining institutional integrity (Elias et al., 2024). These distinctions highlight the importance of inclusive innovation, fair resource allocation, and global collaboration. Addressing the global AI divide by sharing knowledge, establishing ethical standards, and making sustained investments is not only a technical necessity but also a moral imperative, crucial for achieving a sustainable and inclusive future.

However, the realization of AI's full potential is heavily reliant on several key factors, namely, the availability of data, the development of digital infrastructure, and the readiness of institutions. These three pillars serve as the bedrock for the successful development, implementation, and expansion of artificial intelligence technologies, enabling their contribution to sustainable development in various global settings (Mienye et al., 2024). Without them, even the most advanced artificial intelligence solutions risk being underutilized, misaligned, or ineffective in addressing the complex challenges associated with the Sustainable Development Goals (SDGs) agenda. Data availability is the most crucial factor in enabling artificial intelligence (AI), as it serves as the foundation for the algorithms that drive intelligent systems. It is crucial to ensure that the data used for training AI models is representative across various factors such as geography, income level, gender, age, and ethnicity to prevent the perpetuation of biases or inequalities. In the context of SDG 3 (good health and well-being), having access to comprehensive health records, disease surveillance data, and real-time clinical inputs is crucial for developing effective and fair diagnostic and predictive tools. Similarly, in SDG 4 (quality education), artificial intelligence-based learning platforms rely on student performance data, engagement metrics, and feedback loops to deliver customized educational content (Tariq, 2025).

Nevertheless, the worldwide dispersion of information is highly imbalanced. In numerous low-income and developing nations, the process of gathering data is disjointed, outdated, or entirely nonexistent in crucial areas such as public health, education, agriculture, and environmental monitoring. Even when data is available, it is frequently not digitized, lacks standardization, or is stored in isolated repositories across various institutions. Additionally, privacy regulations, data sovereignty concerns, and the lack of established governance frameworks can restrict the sharing and utilization of data for the advancement of AI. It poses a major obstacle to the implementation of AI for SDG applications, particularly in situations where demand is most significant (Lampropoulos et al., 2024). Overcoming this challenge necessitates strategic investments in national statistical systems, open data initiatives, and public-private data partnerships that prioritize ethical, inclusive, and secure data sharing. Digital infrastructure is the second crucial factor that determines whether artificial intelligence (AI) technologies can be implemented on a large scale. It encompasses physical infrastructure, such as broadband internet, mobile connectivity, data centers, and cloud services, as well as digital utilities like computing power, artificial intelligence development platforms, and cybersecurity systems (Leal Filho et al., 2024). Highly advanced artificial intelligence models, particularly those that require real-time data processing or substantial computational power, heavily rely on a robust digital infrastructure. In advanced nations, the widespread availability of fast internet, increasing device usage, and scalable cloud platforms enable the implementation of AI in complex fields such as precision farming, smart cities, and personalized healthcare (Al-Raeei, 2024). The foundational infrastructure not only enables the smooth operation of AI applications but also facilitates their ongoing enhancement through real-time data integration and feedback.

In contrast, digital infrastructure in many developing countries is lacking, especially in rural and underserved regions. The lack of consistent internet connectivity, frequent power outages, and the high cost of data usage pose significant challenges to the implementation and maintenance of AI systems (Shahvaroughi Farahani & Ghasemi, 2024). For instance, an AI-powered early warning system for floods or disease outbreaks may not be effective if the communities in danger cannot receive or respond to alerts due to inadequate network coverage. Additionally, the absence of cost-effective computing devices and localized digital content exacerbates the exclusion of populations that could potentially benefit from AI-driven services. Addressing this gap necessitates not only investments in infrastructure but also the implementation of policies that ensure universal access, affordability, and resilience (Raihan, 2024). Cutting-edge technologies, such as satellite-based internet, community data centers, and edge computing, can enable artificial intelligence capabilities to reach remote and underserved communities. Institutional readiness is the third and most complex enabler of AI-driven SDG progress. It encompasses the ability of governments, civil society, and the private sector to comprehend, control, execute, and expand AI solutions in a way that aligns with development objectives. It encompasses establishing the necessary legal and regulatory frameworks, promoting collaboration among different sectors, developing human resources, and ensuring ethical supervision (Ramanet al., 2024). In nations with strong institutional readiness, artificial intelligence (AI) is more likely to be incorporated into national development plans, guided by well-defined policies on data privacy, cybersecurity, intellectual property, and algorithmic accountability. These organizations can mobilize public funding for AI research, encourage responsible innovation, and establish monitoring systems to assess the impact of AI on achieving the Sustainable Development Goals.

Conversely, inadequate institutional capacity can lead to disjointed initiatives, improper utilization of AI technologies, or a lack of progress in policy-making (Okonkwo et al., 2024). Governments may lack the necessary technical expertise to assess artificial intelligence systems, while public institutions may face challenges in procuring, integrating, and overseeing these systems. In these situations, AI projects are frequently initiated by donors or external organizations without proper consideration of local requirements or capabilities (Madavarapu et al., 2024). The lack of robust institutions increases the likelihood that AI will exacerbate inequalities, violate rights, or erode trust. Building institutional readiness is not just about organizing workshops to enhance capacity; it also involves developing a comprehensive approach. It necessitates a sustained commitment to education, public administration reform, inter-agency collaboration, and mechanisms that allow citizens to actively participate in shaping technology governance.

Just as important is the development of local innovation ecosystems that enable countries to create context-specific artificial intelligence (AI) solutions rather than simply adopting existing technologies. It involves establishing collaborations between universities, startups, non-profit organizations, and government agencies to jointly develop artificial intelligence (AI) tools that tackle significant development issues. For instance, local developers are typically more knowledgeable about linguistic diversity, cultural subtleties, and contextual significance, all of which are crucial for the successful implementation of artificial intelligence in fields like education, agriculture, or healthcare. Additionally, inclusive institutional ecosystems can foster the ethical development of AI by involving stakeholders from marginalized communities, ensuring that AI systems align with their needs and values. The relationship between data availability, digital infrastructure, and institutional readiness is constantly evolving and mutually beneficial. For example, better infrastructure can enhance data collection capabilities. At the same time, stronger institutions can drive the strategic use of both data and infrastructure to benefit the public (Singh et al., 2024). Conversely, any gaps in any one area can significantly diminish the overall effectiveness of the others. For instance, even the most comprehensive data sets may not result in practical applications of artificial intelligence if there is no infrastructure in place to process them or institutions to utilize the insights they provide.

In summary, the advancement of AI in contributing to the SDGs is not solely dependent on technological innovation but on the foundational enablers that facilitate its implementation (Baig et al., 2024). The availability of data guarantees that artificial intelligence systems are trained using information that is relevant, representative, and up-to-date. Digital infrastructure serves as the platform through which artificial intelligence (AI) functions and delivers its benefits to individuals. Institutional readiness ensures that artificial intelligence (AI) is developed and implemented in a manner that aligns with national objectives, upholds ethical standards, and fosters inclusivity within society. Consequently, global initiatives aimed at utilizing artificial intelligence for sustainable development should focus on allocating resources, formulating policies, and fostering collaborations that bolster these essential pillars, especially in areas with the greatest developmental requirements. Only by taking action and embracing the potential of artificial intelligence can we create a more equitable, resilient, and environmentally friendly world (Tariq, 2025).

## AI IN ACTION: CASE STUDIES

Within the realm of 'AI for good,' numerous case studies demonstrate how AI-powered solutions are transforming healthcare diagnostics, enhancing agricultural productivity, and improving disaster preparedness and response. As an illustration, Google's DeepMind has partnered with the UK's National Health Service to develop artificial intelligence systems that can accurately diagnose eye diseases, matching the proficiency of top ophthalmologists (Kazlauskaitė et al., 2024). In sub-Saharan Africa, AI models are being employed to analyze chest X-rays for tuberculosis detection, alleviating the strain on limited radiologists. In the field of agriculture, IBM's Watson decision platform has been utilized in India to provide smallholder farmers with predictive information on weather patterns, soil quality, and pest infestations, leading to improved crop productivity and more environmentally friendly farming methods. Simultaneously, organizations such as Planet Labs and the United Nations World Food Programme employ artificial intelligence-driven satellite image analysis to assess vegetation health and food insecurity in crisis areas, facilitating more prompt and precise humanitarian interventions (Tariq and Sergio, 2025).

In governance, artificial intelligence (AI) is playing a role in improving transparency, streamlining public service delivery, and facilitating the intelligent planning of urban areas. Estonia, renowned for its advanced digital government systems, has integrated AI to automate and optimize processes such as business registration, tax filings, and social benefits distribution, resulting in reduced administrative tasks and faster service delivery. An example of AI in action is Brazil's Operation Serenata de Amor, a civil society initiative that employs AI to analyze public expense claims made by elected officials, identifying any suspicious transactions and advocating for government accountability. In innovative city projects, Singapore utilizes artificial intelligence (AI) for traffic management, energy optimization, and urban development planning. Its advanced transportation system utilizes real-time artificial intelligence data analytics to alleviate traffic congestion, optimize bus routes, and enhance commuting efficiency. These governance-focused applications showcase how artificial intelligence (AI) can enhance citizen trust in institutions while also improving operational efficiency.

Community-driven, context-specific innovations in the Global South demonstrate how localized AI applications can result in significant development achievements. For example, in Uganda, a collaboration between Makerere University and local farmers has led to the development of AI-powered mobile apps that can identify crop diseases by analyzing images, enabling farmers to promptly address the issues without requiring expert assistance. In India, Project Vaani, a joint initiative between Google and the Indian Institute of Science, utilizes voice-based artificial intelligence systems to bridge the digital divide for non-literate individuals by providing information in local languages and dialects (Hanna et al., 2024). In Kenya, mobile platforms that utilize artificial intelligence (AI) are employed to identify counterfeit medications by examining product barcodes, effectively tackling public health and safety concerns. These community-based initiatives demonstrate that AI can be inclusive and accessible when it is tailored to meet the specific needs, cultural contexts, and existing infrastructure of the local community (Kulkov et al., 2024).

## RISKS, ETHICS, AND GOVERNANCE CHALLENGES

As artificial intelligence (AI) systems become more prevalent in decision-making processes that impact millions of lives, their use in sustainable development should be approached with caution, fairness, and openness. Additionally, there is an immediate need for comprehensive global governance frameworks that integrate artificial intelligence (AI) technologies with human rights standards and Sustainable Development Goals (SDGs) principles to ensure their ethical and equitable implementation across various global contexts. Algorithmic bias occurs when artificial intelligence systems replicate or exacerbate existing inequalities present in the data used to train them. Because AI models learn from historical or observational data, they can unintentionally amplify and reinforce the discriminatory structures that exist in society. For instance, in the field of predictive policing or criminal justice, artificial intelligence systems trained on biased law enforcement data may unfairly target marginalized communities. Similarly, in healthcare, diagnostic models may not perform well for specific demographic groups if their training data does not adequately include individuals from those populations.

The danger of algorithmic bias is not confined to overtly discriminatory results. It can also manifest through more subtle forms of exclusion. For example, language processing models that have been primarily trained on English-language content may struggle to accurately process and understand languages spoken by indigenous or less-resourced communities, which can have significant implications for access to education, public services, or legal information. In these situations, the harm is not due to deliberate discrimination but rather the unintentional creation of systems that primarily serve the dominant or most represented groups within the population (Yadav et al., 2024). It emphasizes the importance of intentionally incorporating a wide range of datasets and involving various stakeholders in the design process, particularly those who are most at risk.

The problem of digital exclusion exacerbates the risks associated with the deployment of artificial intelligence. This "digital divide" is particularly evident in low-income, rural, or marginalized communities that already encounter systemic obstacles in accessing fundamental services. When AI-powered platforms become the primary or only means of accessing essential services, individuals who lack digital access may face increased exclusion. Instead of reducing inequality, the use of AI has the potential to exacerbate it unless specific measures are implemented to guarantee equal access and capacity-building opportunities for all. Besides physical and infrastructural obstacles, digital exclusion can also occur when individuals lack the necessary knowledge or control over their digital experiences. Numerous artificial intelligence systems can be confusing or unclear, making it challenging for users to comprehend the decision-making process or to question outcomes that seem unfair or inaccurate. It diminishes personal freedom and undermines trust in artificial intelligence systems, particularly when individuals are affected by automated decisions in domains such as welfare distribution, credit scoring, job recruitment, or immigration processing. These challenges highlight the pressing need for AI systems that are not only technically interpretable but also socially understandable.

Explainability is not just a technical aspect, it is a fundamental democratic requirement. When AI impacts access to rights and resources, those who are affected have a moral and legal right to know how and why decisions are made. It is particularly significant in public sector deployments, where government legitimacy and social trust are vital for efficient service delivery. Transparency should encompass not only individual explanations but also a comprehensive understanding of how artificial intelligence systems are developed, who is involved in their creation, where the data originates, and the ethical measures implemented to ensure responsible use. Inclusive AI, in this context, entails involving a wide range of stakeholders, such as women, minority groups, individuals with disabilities, and residents of developing regions, in the creation, evaluation, and management of AI systems. Participatory governance guarantees that AI solutions are culturally appropriate, socially acceptable, and responsive to the needs of the people they are designed to assist. In this manner, inclusion is not just a goal but a continuous process integrated into every stage of artificial intelligence (AI) development and implementation.

To tackle these interconnected risks and aspirations, global frameworks for AI governance are crucial. Although multiple nations and international organizations have provided recommendations or plans for artificial intelligence (AI), a unified and legally binding global framework that integrates AI development with human rights and the Sustainable Development Goals (SDGs) is still in the process of being established. It should encourage the establishment of common guidelines for algorithmic transparency, data privacy, and human oversight while also allowing for local adjustments and contextualization. The United Nations, through organizations such as UNESCO and the ITU, has begun establishing the necessary framework for effective governance. UNESCO's endorsement of the ethical considerations of artificial intelligence, as endorsed by member states in 2021, is one of the most comprehensive international frameworks designed to shape AI policy, focusing on human rights, environmental sustainability, and global equity. It highlights principles such as human-centeredness, fairness, accountability, and inclusiveness that align perfectly with the SDG framework. The suggestion emphasizes the need for evaluations that involve all relevant parties, enhance skills in resource-limited areas, and establish procedures for addressing any negative consequences. These provisions are crucial for guaranteeing that AI contributes positively to global development rather than hindering it.

In addition to uncoordinated initiatives, regional organizations and coalitions involving various stakeholders are actively contributing to the development of AI governance. Similarly, the Global Partnership on AI (GPai) encourages collaboration on AI standards, research, and ethics on an international scale, while initiatives like AI for Good offer platforms for working together on AI applications that contribute to sustainable development. For these frameworks to have a meaningful impact, they must be accompanied by enforceable commitments, effective enforcement mechanisms, and adequate resources that facilitate implementation in low- and middle-income countries. Ultimately, the incorporation of AI into the sustainable development landscape cannot be approached as a purely technical or economic endeavor. It should be rooted in a strong belief in the importance of human rights, social justice, and the health of our planet. It means recognizing the power asymmetries that currently shape AI development, where a few countries and corporations control the bulk of AI research, infrastructure, and deployment, and working actively to democratize both the benefits and governance of AI. It also means being cautious about the unintended consequences of artificial intelligence systems, such as surveillance, discrimination, environmental impacts, and job displacement.

## Digital Maturity and Ecosystem Readiness

The level of digital maturity plays a crucial role in the effective implementation and expansion of artificial intelligence (AI) interventions that contribute to achieving the Sustainable Development Goals (SDGs). It refers to an organization's or society's ability to effectively utilize digital technologies, incorporate them into their regular activities, mitigate potential risks, and ensure their alignment with long-term goals. As artificial intelligence solutions transition from small-scale experiments to widespread adoption in sectors such as healthcare, education, agriculture, and energy, the development of robust digital ecosystems becomes increasingly crucial. It determines not only the technological readiness but also the cultural, institutional, and infrastructural conditions necessary to support long-term innovation. Without a solid foundation in digital capabilities and a well-defined strategy, even the most promising AI tools may fail to deliver meaningful results or exacerbate existing inequalities (Leal Filho et al., 2024).

Digital maturity encompasses various aspects, such as the strength of infrastructure, the establishment of data governance frameworks, the development of digital skills, the integration across sectors, and the alignment of policies. Organizations and governments with high levels of digital maturity can effectively collect, analyze, and respond to data using artificial intelligence systems. For instance, in the healthcare sector (SDG 3), scalable artificial intelligence (AI) interventions, such as predictive diagnostics or health surveillance, depend on interoperable health records, secure data storage, and real-time data flows. Similarly, in education (SDG 4), adaptive learning platforms powered by AI require stable internet access, connected devices, and user literacy to operate on a large scale. As a result, digital maturity is not only a requirement but also a catalyst for the success of AI-driven development initiatives.

It allows for flexible scalability, which is crucial for transforming pilot projects into nationwide or multi-regional initiatives. Governments and non-profits can leverage cloud-based artificial intelligence platforms for various purposes, such as monitoring crop health using satellite imagery, efficiently managing disaster response logistics, or analyzing public sentiment in real-time. Cloud computing makes artificial intelligence tools more accessible and affordable, particularly for individuals and organizations with limited resources in developing economies. By linking physical devices and sensors to the internet, the IoT produces real-time, detailed data that is used to enhance AI models, resulting in more precise predictions and tailored interventions. In the field of agriculture (SDG 2), IoT devices can gather information on soil moisture, temperature, and crop health, which AI algorithms then utilize to enhance irrigation schedules and forecast pest infestations. In the field of energy systems (SDG 7), smart meters and grid sensors provide valuable data for artificial intelligence-driven energy demand forecasting and load balancing, resulting in enhanced efficiency and reduced waste. The combination of IoT and AI establishes a continuous learning process where AI utilizes sensor data to refine its responses and promote more innovative and sustainable resource management (Mienye et al., 2024).

Governance frameworks set guidelines for how data is collected, shared, protected, and utilized. They ensure that data, often referred to as the 'fuel' of artificial intelligence, is handled in an ethical, secure, and efficient manner. Without proper data governance structures in place, AI interventions are susceptible to infringing on privacy rights, exacerbating inequalities, or eroding public trust. Conversely, effective governance facilitates data interoperability across different sectors and jurisdictions, enabling comprehensive and integrated development solutions. For example, by connecting data on health, education, and social protection, governments can gain insights into vulnerable populations and develop targeted interventions that address multiple dimensions of need. Sound data governance enables cross-border collaborations and regional AI strategies that align with the Sustainable Development Goals (SDGs).

Creating sustainable digital ecosystems is the next step in guaranteeing that artificial intelligence-enabled interventions have a lasting impact on long-term development. A sustainable digital ecosystem encompasses not only technology and infrastructure but also institutions, policies, standards, and human resources. It highlights resilience, equity, and adaptability, traits that enable digital solutions to adjust and grow in the face of new challenges and opportunities. By investing in digital public infrastructure, including national identification systems, open data platforms, and cybersecurity measures, the groundwork is laid for the development of reliable and interconnected artificial intelligence applications. Simultaneously, collaborations between the public and private sectors can introduce innovation, attract investment, and achieve scale in AI projects while ensuring public interest and accountability.

Crucially, sustainable digital ecosystems also require investments in human skills and knowledge. It encompasses digital literacy, data science education, and specialized AI training, as well as fostering an inclusive digital culture that enables all segments of society, especially women, rural populations, and marginalized communities, to participate in and benefit from AI-driven development. A competent workforce and well-informed citizens are not only crucial for constructing and overseeing AI systems but also for fostering public participation in determining how AI is employed. The democratization of digital capabilities ensures that artificial intelligence tools are not limited to a privileged few but are instead accessible and adaptable to the general public. Policy and regulatory coherence are crucial for ensuring the long-term sustainability of digital ecosystems. Regulatory sandboxes can foster innovation while minimizing risks by enabling controlled experimentation with artificial intelligence applications. Legal frameworks must address concerns such as data ownership, algorithm accountability, intellectual property rights, and the transfer of data across borders. Collaboration among nations is crucial in this context, particularly for smaller or less affluent countries that may not have the resources to establish and enforce comprehensive AI regulations on their own.

Initiatives like 'Green AI' promote the reduction of carbon emissions associated with training large models, aligning with the goals of SDG 13 (Climate Action). Sustainable digital ecosystems should not only support the adoption of AI but also ensure that this adoption aligns with ecological sustainability and social responsibility.

## Policy and Strategic Recommendations

Achieving meaningful, sustainable development goals (SDGs) through artificial intelligence (AI) innovation necessitates a collaborative, multi-sectoral approach that harnesses the unique strengths of public, private, and academic stakeholders. Collaborations among the public, private, and academic sectors are crucial for advancing beyond isolated projects and small-scale experiments, aiming for comprehensive, scalable, and enduring AI solutions that directly contribute to achieving the Sustainable Development Goals. Governments establish regulatory frameworks, provide access to public data, and set development goals. Private companies contribute advanced technologies, financial support, and implementation expertise, while academia offers research, ethical analysis, and capacity-building initiatives.

By collaborating, these sectors can develop AI tools tailored to specific contexts, which can be easily scaled and adhere to ethical principles, particularly in crucial areas such as healthcare, education, agriculture, and climate adaptation (Nedungadi et al., 2024).

To foster collaborative endeavors, governments and international organizations must develop forward-thinking policies that promote responsible AI development with a focus on achieving sustainability goals. Policies should prioritize fairness in data distribution, transparency in algorithmic decision-making, and adherence to ethical design principles in artificial intelligence while encouraging innovations that align with the Sustainable Development Goals. Regulatory sandboxes, national AI strategies, and open data mandates can encourage experimentation while ensuring that necessary safeguards are in place. Furthermore, sustainability impact assessments, similar to environmental impact assessments, should be incorporated into the development pipelines of artificial intelligence (AI) to assess the long-term effects of algorithms on social inclusion, ecological well-being, and economic equity. Policies should also promote equal access to AI infrastructure and tools, guaranteeing that underserved areas and marginalized communities are not left behind in the digital transformation journey (Obaideen et al., 2024).

Equally important is investing in capacity-building and digital literacy to confirm that everyone can take part and benefit from the digital revolution in the long run. Simply having access to AI tools is not enough; communities need to have the knowledge, skills, and critical understanding to effectively engage with, influence, and benefit from AI technologies. Digital literacy programs should not only emphasize technical skills; they should also emphasize the importance of critical thinking and information literacy. However, they should also encompass ethical, civic, and contextual education regarding the societal implications of artificial intelligence. In developing economies and rural areas, where low digital readiness can lead to digital exclusion and exacerbate inequality, it is imperative. Programs specifically designed for young people, women, educators, and local leaders can make artificial intelligence knowledge accessible to all and foster innovation in local communities. Capacity-building efforts should encompass policymakers, civil society organizations, and journalists, empowering them to participate actively in AI governance and accountability initiatives.

In summary, closing the implementation gap for the AI-SDG necessitates a comprehensive approach that integrates innovation with inclusivity, oversight with collaboration, and scale with sustainability. Collaborations between public, private, and academic sectors can foster synergies and enable the practical application of artificial intelligence for sustainable development (Abdullah, 2024). It is crucial to establish responsible policy frameworks that steer technological advancements toward fair and transparent results. Simultaneously, developing human capacity guarantees that artificial intelligence adoption is inclusive rather than exploitative.

## CONCLUSION

Artificial intelligence has the possibility to significantly contribute to attaining the Sustainable Development Goals by promoting smarter decision-making, enhancing resource utilization, and providing real-time solutions to complex global issues. Its implementation in various sectors, including healthcare, education, agriculture, and climate action, has already shown substantial improvements in outcomes and scalability. To completely harness the potential of AI in sustainable development, it is essential to prioritize inclusivity, uphold ethical standards, and foster collaboration across diverse disciplines. To confirm the responsible use of artificial intelligence, frameworks must be established to mitigate risks such as bias, misuse of surveillance, and the exacerbation of existing social and economic inequalities. AI should enhance, rather than substitute, human expertise and community knowledge in sustainable development initiatives (Ziemba et al., 2024). As we approach the year 2030, adopting artificial intelligence (AI) as a means to promote positive change necessitates a commitment to fairness, transparency, and international collaboration. By implementing effective policies and fostering collaboration, artificial intelligence (AI) has the potential to serve as a driving force in creating a fairer, more inclusive, and environmentally sustainable world.

## REFERENCES


Abdullah, W. (2024). Artificial Intelligence for Achieving Sustainable Development Goals: Applications, Techniques and Progress. [Zagazig University]. *International Journal of Computers and Informatics*, *5*, 117–128.

Al-Raeei, M. (2024). Artificial intelligence for climate resilience: Advancing sustainable goals in SDGs 11 and 13 and its relationship to pandemics. *Discover Sustainability*, *5*(1), 513.

Arini, D., & Nursa'ban, M. (2024). Contribution of Artificial Intelligence (AI) in Education to Support the Achievement of Sustainable Development Goals (SDGs) 2030. *Jurnal Penelitian Pendidikan IPA, 10*(SpecialIssue), 39-45.

Baig, M. A. A., Huang, J., & Xu, J. (2024). AI for United Nations sustainable development goals: AI for UNSDGs.

Bocean, C. G. (2025). Sustainable Development in the Digital Age: Harnessing Emerging Digital Technologies to Catalyze Global SDG Achievement. *Applied Sciences (Basel, Switzerland)*, *15*(2), 816.

Dave, V. (2024). A systematic literature review of the effect/contribution of artificial intelligence technology towards achieving the sustainable development goals.

Elias, O., Esebre, S. D., Abijo, I., Timothy, A. M., Babayemi, T. D., Makinde, E. O., & Fatoki, I. E. (2024). Harnessing artificial intelligence to optimize financial technologies for achieving sustainable development goals. *World J. Adv. Res. Rev*, *23*, 616–625.

Farmanesh, P., Solati Dehkordi, N., Vehbi, A., & Chavali, K. (2025). Artificial Intelligence and Green Innovation in Small and Medium-Sized Enterprises and Competitive-Advantage Drive Toward Achieving Sustainable Development Goals. *Sustainability*, *17*(5), 2162.

Fazal, A., Ahmed, A., & Abbas, S. (2025). Importance of artificial intelligence in achieving sustainable development goals through financial inclusion. *Qualitative Research in Financial Markets*, *17*(2), 432–452.

Gomase, G., & Gajbhiye, C. (2024). The Contribution and Challenges of Artificial Intelligence (AI)-based techniques for achieving Sustainable Development Goals.

Gosselink, B. H., Brandt, K., Croak, M., DeSalvo, K., Gomes, B., Ibrahim, L., . . . Manyika, J. (2024). AI in action: Accelerating progress towards the Sustainable Development Goals. *arXiv preprint arXiv:2407.02711*.

Gupta, S., Gupta, S. B., & Gupta, M. (2024). Importance of artificial intelligence in achieving sdgs in India. *International Journal of Built Environment and Sustainability, 11*(2), 1–26.

Hanna, B., Xu, G., Wang, X., & Hossain, J. (2024, August). Leveraging Artificial Intelligence for Affordable and Clean Energy: Advancing UN Sustainable Development Goal 7. In *2024 11th International Conference on Behavioural and Social Computing (BESC)* (pp. 1-9). IEEE.

Kazlauskaitė, R., Ziemba, E. W., Ejdys, J., Mazurek, G., Stankevičienė, J., Duong, C. D., ... & Wach, K. (2024). Leveraging artificial intelligence to meet the sustainable development goals. *Journal of Economics and Management.*, 508-583.

Kirikkaleli, D., Aad, S., & Kirikkaleli, N. O. (2025). Sustainable development and investment in artificial intelligence in the USA. *Humanities & Social Sciences Communications, 12*(1), 1–7.

Kulkov, I., Kulkova, J., Rohrbeck, R., Menvielle, L., Kaartemo, V., & Makkonen, H. (2024). Artificial intelligence-driven sustainable development: Examining organizational, technical, and processing approaches to achieving global goals. *Sustainable Development, 32*(3), 2253–2267.

Lampropoulos, G., Garzón, J., Misra, S., & Siakas, K. (2024). The role of artificial intelligence of things in achieving sustainable development goals: State of the art. *Sensors (Basel), 24*(4), 1091. PMID: 38400249

Leal Filho, W., Mbah, M. F., Dinis, M. A. P., Trevisan, L. V., de Lange, D., Mishra, A., & Aina, Y. A. (2024). The role of artificial intelligence in the implementation of the UN Sustainable Development Goal 11: Fostering sustainable cities and communities. *Cities (London, England), 150*, 105021.

Leal Filho, W., Ribeiro, P. C. C., Mazutti, J., Lange Salvia, A., Bonato Marcolin, C., Lima Silva Borsatto, J. M., & Viera Trevisan, L. (2024). Using artificial intelligence to implement the UN sustainable development goals at higher education institutions. *International Journal of Sustainable Development and World Ecology, 31*(6), 726–745.

Madavarapu, J. B., Kasula, B. Y., Whig, P., & Kautish, S. (2024). AI-Powered Solutions Advancing UN Sustainable Development Goals: A Case Study in Tackling Humanity's Challenges. In *Digital Technologies to Implement the UN Sustainable Development Goals* (pp. 47–67). Springer Nature Switzerland.

Mienye, I. D., Sun, Y., & Ileberi, E. (2024). Artificial intelligence and sustainable development in Africa: A comprehensive review. *Machine Learning with Applications*, •••, 100591.

Nedungadi, P., Surendran, S., Tang, K. Y., & Raman, R. (2024). Big Data and AI Algorithms for Sustainable Development Goals: A Topic Modeling Analysis. *IEEE Access : Practical Innovations, Open Solutions*.

Obaideen, K., Albasha, L., Iqbal, U., & Mir, H. (2024). Wireless power transfer: Applications, challenges, barriers, and the role of AI in achieving sustainable development goals-A bibliometric analysis. *Energy Strategy Reviews*, *53*, 101376.

Okonkwo, E., Ndu-Anunobi, G. U., & Umeokafor, C. C. (2024). HARNESSING ARTIFICIAL INTELLIGENCE FOR SUSTAINABLE DEVELOPMENT: A PATHWAY TO ACHIEVING SUSTAINABLE DEVELOPMENT GOALS IN AFRICA USING NIGERIA AS A STUDY. *INTERNATIONAL JOURNAL OF PUBLIC ADMINISTRATION AND DEVELOPMENT STUDIES*, *1*(2), 37–58.

Raihan, A. (2024). Financial technology optimization using artificial intelligence (AI) to accomplish sustainable development goals (SDGs). In *Proceedings of the International Conference on on Digital Finance, Green Innovation, and Sustainable Development*.

Raman, R., Gunasekar, S., Kaliyaperumal, D., & Nedungadi, P. (2024). Navigating the Nexus of Artificial Intelligence and Renewable Energy for the Advancement of Sustainable Development Goals. *Sustainability*, *16*(21), 9144.

Regona, M., Yigitcanlar, T., Hon, C., & Teo, M. (2024). Artificial intelligence and sustainable development goals: Systematic literature review of the construction industry. *Sustainable Cities and Society*, •••, 105499.

erbu, R. S., & Mârza, B. . (2024). From Crisis to Opportunity: Embracing Sustainable Development Goals and Artificial Intelligence in the Transformative Innovations World. In *Ukraine's Journey to Recovery, Reform and Post-War Reconstruction: A Blueprint for Security, Resilience and Development* (pp. 49–61). Springer Nature Switzerland.

Shahvaroughi Farahani, M., & Ghasemi, G. (2024). How artificial intelligence plays a role in achieving sustainable development goals? [situations.]. *Sustainable Economies.*, *2*(3), 66.

Singh, A., Kanaujia, A., Singh, V. K., & Vinuesa, R. (2024). Artificial intelligence for Sustainable Development Goals: Bibliometric patterns and concept evolution trajectories. *Sustainable Development*, *32*(1), 724–754.

Tariq, M. U. (2025). *AI-Driven Learning and Engagement in Higher Education.* IGI Global., DOI: 10.4018/979-8-3693-4074-5

Tariq, M. U. (2025). Digital Accountability: Revolutionizing Public Sector Transparency and Service Delivery. In Santos Ferreira, A., & Lourenço dos Santos, C. (Eds.), *Enhancing Public Sector Accountability and Services Through Digital Innovation* (pp. 129–154). IGI Global Scientific Publishing., DOI: 10.4018/979-8-3693-9251-5.ch004

Tariq, M. U. (2025). Decolonizing Education Systems Through Action Research and Action Learning. In Mapotse, T., Tetteh, E., & Matsekoleng, T. (Eds.), *Enabling Indigenous Knowledge Systems in Action Research and Action Learning* (pp. 107–128). IGI Global Scientific Publishing., DOI: 10.4018/979-8-3693-3542-0.ch006

Tariq, M. U., & Sergio, R. (Eds.). (2025). *Cases on AI-Driven Solutions to Environmental Challenges.* IGI Global, 2025. https://doi.org/DOI: 10.4018/979-8-3693-7483-2

Tariq, M. U., & Sergio, R. (Eds.). (2025). *Convergence of AI, Education, and Business for Sustainability.* IGI Global., DOI: 10.4018/979-8-3373-1917-9

Yadav, P., Tudela, L. A. M., & Marco-Lajara, B. (2024). The role of AI in assessing and achieving the sustainable development goals (SDGs). In *Issues of Sustainability in AI and New-Age Thematic Investing* (pp. 1–17). IGI Global.

Ziemba, E. W., Duong, C. D., Ejdys, J., Gonzalez-Perez, M. A., Kazlauskaitė, R., Korzynski, P., & Wach, K. (2024). Leveraging artificial intelligence to meet the sustainable development goals. *Journal of Economics and Management*, *46*, 508–583.

## KEY TERMS AND DEFINITIONS:

**Ethical AI:** Responsible design prioritizing fairness and accountability.
**Digital Inclusion:** Confirming equitable access to digital technologies.
**Predictive Analytics:** Using data patterns to forecast outcomes.

# Chapter 4
# Accelerating Progress on Sustainable Development Goals Using AI

**S. Ida Evangeline**
https://orcid.org/0000-0003-2997-7897
*Government College of Engineering, Tirunelveli, India*

## ABSTRACT

*Artificial Intelligence (AI) is rapidly emerging as a transformative force in global development, offering new capabilities to accelerate progress across the United Nations Sustainable Development Goals (SDGs). This chapter explores the multi-dimensional role of AI within the broader context of digital maturity and ecosystem readiness. It begins by mapping core AI capabilities—such as machine learning, natural language processing, computer vision, and predictive analytics—to specific SDG targets, illustrating their relevance to sectors including health, education, agriculture, energy, and financial inclusion. It uses global case studies to show how AI contributes to better service delivery, risk prediction and targeted development programs. It further explores the negative sides of using AI, for example, algorithmic bias, privacy issues, the effects it has on the environment and the worsening of digital divide. These issues are discussed using the term digital maturity, highlighting how infrastructure, organizational strength and open governance matter. It presents ideas for responsible AI based on ethics, laws that protect rights, inclusive design and projects that help the public. It recommends that governments, development agencies and stakeholders in technology create AI strategies that are easy to understand, open to everyone, adaptable and follow what is important to their communities. It is argued by the chapter that, though AI by itself is not perfect, it can greatly assist in promoting sustainable development, as long as it is directed by equity, accountability and global cooperation.*

DOI: 10.4018/979-8-3373-7584-7.ch004

## 1. INTRODUCTION

In 2015, the United Nations General Assembly adopted the 2030 Agenda for Sustainable Development, establishing 17 Sustainable Development Goals (SDGs) as a universal call to action to end poverty, protect the planet, and ensure prosperity for all. The targets which are tied together and ambitious, act as a guide for development everywhere (Kulkov et al. 2024). While we get closer to 2030, it is clear that achieving several SDGs is slowing down or even reversing, mainly because of major global problems such as pandemics, unrest between countries, changes in the climate and rising economic and social inequalities. Because of this, we need to examine strategies and tools that can speed up progress toward sustainability.

Artificial Intelligence (AI) has emerged as one of the most consequential technological developments of the 21st century. Using machine learning, natural language processing, computer vision and robotics, AI systems can handle tasks that humans needed to do, often more quickly and on a larger scale. It impacts many areas, changing industries, altering workplaces and changing the way decisions are made. Many governments, development groups and researchers now see AI as important for achieving the SDGs, in addition to helping economies grow (Al-Raeei, 2025).

This chapter situates AI within the evolving landscape of digital transformation and digital maturity. Digital maturity refers to the readiness of institutions, societies, and ecosystems to adopt, govern, and derive value from digital technologies. It involves the hardware, software, laws, people and cultural habits that guide how digital tools are used and changed. In addition to raw power and large amounts of information, AI needs a digitally advanced setting to operate responsibly and do its best work. Also, the idea of digital ecosystems, made up of linked platforms, policies, institutions and users, highlights how digital transformation affects the whole system. AI systems will support a just and sustainable world only if these ecosystems are inclusive, interoperable, secure and in line with what is valued by society.

This chapter explores the dual role of AI: both as a catalyst for accelerating specific SDG targets and as a mirror reflecting the strengths and weaknesses of underlying digital ecosystems. It starts by showing how technologies, including predictive analytics and adaptive learning systems, currently support the SDGs such as those related to health, education and climate issues. Then, it gives specific examples of how AI is being applied in various fields to solve development issues.

Yet the deployment of AI is not without risks. Algorithmic discrimination, surveillance misuse, ecological costs, and deepening digital divides raise serious ethical and operational concerns. In places where digital skills are low, AI can bring more difficulties since the governance and technical systems may not be strong enough to make the most of AI or prevent harm. For this reason, this chapter looks closely at models for responsible AI governance, studying various policies, shared decision-making approaches and new ideas that support inclusive development.

Drawing on interdisciplinary research, global case studies, and policy analyses, this chapter provides a comprehensive and critical perspective on the role of AI in sustainable development. It points out that AI should be understood as a system that is shaped by society, culture and politics. By placing AI within the structure of digital maturity and the goals of the SDGs, this chapter shows how digital transformation can play a role in both achieving and supporting sustainability.

## 2. MAPPING AI CAPABILITIES TO SDGS

To appreciate the transformative potential of Artificial Intelligence (AI) for sustainable development, it is crucial to systematically examine how core AI capabilities align with the targets and indicators of the Sustainable Development Goals (SDGs). AI is better thought of as an environment with various techniques, structures and devices that can imitate, increase or handle parts of human thinking. AI-driven interventions across sectors rely mostly on machine learning, natural language processing (NLP), computer vision and predictive analytics (Regona et al. 2024).

Machine learning (ML) is a foundational technique in AI that enables systems to learn from data and improve performance over time without being explicitly programmed. ML models are especially good at pattern recognition and classification which is why they are useful in development contexts that rely on predictive modeling. ML is applied to predict when diseases will spread (SDG 3), forecast crop yields based on climate changes (SDG 2) and simulate how traffic moves to address crowding and pollution in cities (SDG 11 & 13). By combining different kinds of data such as satellite images, climate information and data from social media, ML helps organizations make flexible decisions as the environment changes (Singh et al. 2024).

Natural language processing (NLP) allows machines to interpret, generate, and translate human language. This capability is crucial for broadening access to information and enhancing inclusivity, especially in multilingual and low-literacy contexts. Thanks to NLP, AI chatbots can share maternal health advice (SDG 3), automated translation helps spread educational information correctly (SDG 4) and digital tools help people share their opinions on governance matters (SDG 16). It also helps analyze policy papers, making it easier to check if national strategies match the targets set by the SDGs. In addition, applying NLP in local languages can help overcome language problems and support communities who have been excluded because of language (Kamkar et al. 2024).

Computer vision, a subfield of AI focused on extracting information from visual data, is central to applications that rely on image and video analysis. Thanks to AI vision, drones in farming can watch over crops, identify pests and measure soil moisture, both ensuring food security and helping to use resources efficiently (SDG 2 & 12). Using AI on satellite data allows us to find out about illegal mining, deforestation or the spreading of cities (SDG 13 & 15). AI is used in health to interpret scans and skin images with great accuracy which helps diagnose patients in regions that do not have specialists (SDG 3). They show how using visual intelligence widens the scope of services and helps keep development areas secure (Garg et al. 2024).

Predictive analytics, often combining multiple AI techniques, enables forecasting and scenario planning based on complex, real-time data inputs. Many governments and development organizations now rely on predictive tools to handle their supply chains, get ready for potential humanitarian crises and model how changes in policies might affect the future. In the field of energy (SDG 7), AI helps predict changes in demand and improves how the power grid operates. Education (SDG 4) relies on predictive analytics to identify students who could drop out, so targeted steps can be taken to help them. With these capabilities, governments can become more efficient and start anticipating problems which is a big shift from simply reacting to them (Rashid et al. 2025).

Crucially, the mapping of AI capabilities to SDGs must account for social, cultural, and institutional context. The results an AI model gives can change a lot based on the input data, the technology available and the rules in a particular society. A precision agriculture model developed for North America may not work well in Sub-Saharan Africa unless it is changed to match the local conditions and ways of farming. Also, an AI that has been trained with data from Western populations might not make accurate diagnoses for people from ethnically diverse groups. For this reason, technical skills should be joined with understanding the context, local factors and involving the community.

This section lays the conceptual foundation for subsequent discussions by clarifying how AI's functional components can be directed toward specific SDG outcomes. After mapping, in the following section, we will focus on how AI is used in real situations in health, education, energy, agriculture and finance. The examples highlight both the potential and the difficulties in taking AI progress and making it useful for the environment.

## 3. SECTORAL APPLICATIONS OF AI IN SUSTAINABLE DEVELOPMENT

The breadth of the Sustainable Development Goals (SDGs) reflects the multidimensional nature of human development, encompassing health, education, poverty reduction, environmental sustainability, economic inclusion, and more. In every field, Artificial Intelligence (AI) is showing it can produce new ideas, manage complex tasks and offer services in a fairer and more efficient manner. This section explains how AI is used in healthcare, education, energy and climate, agriculture and financial inclusion, using practical cases to demonstrate how it can help achieve different SDGs (Manikandan et al. 2025).

### 3.1 Health and Well-Being (SDG 3)

In the health sector, AI is revolutionizing diagnostics, public health surveillance, personalized care, and resource optimization. Using machine learning, radiographic images are now examined to spot diseases such as tuberculosis, breast cancer and diabetic retinopathy earlier. In regions where there are not enough trained radiologists, these models become very helpful. An example is Google's AI used for screening diabetic retinopathy in rural clinics in India and Thailand which has helped prevent unnecessary blindness (Ahmad et al. 2025).

Beyond diagnostics, AI is being used to improve epidemic forecasting and response. During the COVID-19 crisis, BlueDot and HealthMap looked at global news, airline information and health records using natural language processing and data mining, to spot outbreaks early. Governments have also used predictive models to assign ICU beds, project the highest infection levels and plan lockdowns. AI chatbots and virtual health assistants have also been used to spread correct health information, limit the spread of false news and give medical advice to people who do not have easy access to healthcare providers (Fazal et al. 2025).

### 3.2 Quality Education (SDG 4)

AI-driven education technologies are reshaping the learning experience through personalized learning environments, real-time assessment, and accessibility enhancements. Such systems as Mindspark in India and ALEKS in the United States change the pace and level of educational content to meet each learner's abilities which helps underperforming students improve their learning. They rely on machine learning to monitor students and modify teaching methods, so learning is more personalized and effective (Cho & Ackom, 2025).

Natural language processing plays a pivotal role in breaking linguistic barriers and enhancing inclusivity. With NLP, Google Translate and Duolingo help users access knowledge in their native languages from all over the world. AI supports assistive devices for students with disabilities such as systems that let hearing-impaired students write with speech and provide summaries to learners with mental challenges. AI is now applied in higher education to automate tasks, study student learning and assist in maintaining student numbers by using early warning systems (Wang et al. 2025).

## 3.3 Clean Energy and Climate Action (SDGs 7 & 13)

AI has a growing role in enhancing energy efficiency, integrating renewable energy, and supporting climate adaptation and mitigation strategies. AI in smart energy grids predicts electricity demand, distributes power evenly and stores extra energy which helps to use more solar or wind energy. Denmark and Germany are examples of nations using AI to keep grids stable, reduce their carbon footprint and increase the share of renewable energy (Adewoyin et al. 2025).

In the climate sector, AI is helping to model environmental systems and monitor ecological change at unprecedented scale. By using both remote sensing data and AI, experts can find out about illegal deforestation, follow glacier shrinkage and estimate emissions from factories. AI has also been used to study the future results of climate policies, analyze the risks of climate change to cities and towns and help with preparing for floods and wildfires (Malkova, 2025).

## 3.4 Sustainable Agriculture and Food Security (SDG 2)

AI is transforming agriculture by making it more precise, efficient, and resilient. AI systems can use computer vision and sensor data to spot crop diseases, estimate the best time to harvest and improve how water is distributed to crops. With these apps, farmers can grow more crops, use less water and depend less on chemicals. As an example, PlantVillage Nuru enables farmers in East Africa to check and diagnose plant diseases instantly through their phones and is given recommendations for dealing with the issue (Kumaran et al. 2025).

AI is also enabling smarter food supply chains by predicting market demand, managing logistics, and reducing post-harvest losses. AI models are used in places where climate is uncertain to predict how weather will affect farming which supports farmers and helps plan for food security. When used alongside mobile devices and digital finance, AI helps smallholder farmers by giving them fast advice, access to markets and insurance coverage (Amuda, 2025).

### 3.5 Economic Growth and Financial Inclusion (SDGs 8 & 10)

AI applications in finance are opening new pathways for economic empowerment, especially for individuals excluded from traditional financial systems. AI is applied in Kenya, the Philippines and India to evaluate credit risk using mobile phone records, social network activity and utility bill payments. These models make it possible for microfinance institutions and fintech platforms to give credit and insurance to people who do not have a formal credit record which encourages entrepreneurship and fairness in the economy (Fazal et al. 2025).

AI also supports job matching platforms and workforce development programs. AI-powered tools such as Pymetrics are used to test a job seeker's mental and emotional traits, allowing them to be placed in jobs that suit their skills and likes. Governments and employment agencies are now using the same methods to find skills gaps and project labor trends. AI is also applied to notice fraud and ensure banks stick to regulations which makes the financial sector more transparent and reliable (Iorember et al. 2025).

These sectoral applications underscore AI's multifaceted potential to deliver targeted, scalable, and cost-effective solutions across a wide array of development challenges. Even so, getting these benefits across many places requires both technological progress and careful consideration of local situations, values and how capable institutions are. The following section looks at the wider opportunities AI opens up for development practice and policy.

## 4. OPPORTUNITIES AND VALUE ADDITION THROUGH AI

The appeal of Artificial Intelligence (AI) in the context of sustainable development lies not only in its technical sophistication, but also in its ability to enable new paradigms of problem-solving. AI brings about new ways to make public, private and nonprofit sectors more efficient, fair and accurate in their decisions. When AI is used in development projects, it can make interventions of better quality, speedier and on a larger scale than was possible before (Kumar, 2025).

One of the most compelling value propositions of AI is its capacity for real-time data processing and intelligent automation. In places where there is little money and few workers, AI makes it much easier to analyze data, find answers and take the right actions. Humanitarian logistics can use AI to quickly assess what is needed by analyzing satellite pictures and social media, find problems in the supply chain and ensure aid is spread efficiently. Using such tools makes operations more efficient and responsive which is very important in cases like disasters or epidemics (Ghosh et al. 2025).

Another major benefit lies in AI's ability to improve targeting and personalization of services. By using AI, education, health and financial services can be made to fit the unique requirements and characteristics of people or groups. Learning platforms tailor lesson content to fit where a student is and AI-based diagnostic systems suggest treatment options linked to past patient information. Thanks to these approaches, there is less waste, better results and a better experience for all, with a special focus on underserved populations who are usually given the same intervention (Alijoyo et al. 2025).

AI also facilitates predictive foresight and strategic planning, helping governments and development actors shift from reactive to anticipatory governance. By predicting food shortages, unrest or outbreaks, predictive analytics enables early actions that address the root causes and stop crises from happening. This is very important in areas that are highly vulnerable to climate change, as AI-based models can predict the outcomes of extreme weather, assist in preparing for disasters and guide future resilience plans (Carayannis et al. 2025).

A less visible but equally powerful dimension of AI's contribution is its ability to enhance system integration and coordination. Development that is sustainable involves bringing together experts from health, education, energy, infrastructure and governance. AI can connect these areas using the same data structures and platforms that can interact. A city could use integrated AI to find links between how students perform in school and their health, housing situation and means of transportation, helping develop policies that address the main causes rather than just the problems (Yue et al. 2025).

Furthermore, AI contributes to resource optimization and environmental sustainability, enabling smarter use of scarce resources such as energy, water, and arable land. AI is employed in cities to guide traffic and lower emissions by making traffic lights change and offering people real-time travel advice. In farming, AI studies soil sensors and satellite pictures to apply fertilizer and water in the best way which brings down both expenses and damage to the environment. In industries, AI saves energy by observing machines and forecasting when they will need maintenance (Ruoxing et al. 2025).

Critically, AI also presents a strategic opportunity for democratizing data and decentralizing innovation. The right environment for AI can allow grassroots organizations, small enterprises and local governments to use the tools. Thanks to low-code development and open-source AI, non-technical people can now develop local solutions that use data. AI, when used with participatory methods, can help communities keep their traditions, values and cultures, helping them stay in control of their own development (Dunleavy & Margetts, 2025).

However, the realization of these opportunities is not automatic. Several factors are important for them to work: digital infrastructure for all, strong data platforms, capable institutions and ethical guidelines. If these are not in place, AI could increase inequality, leave out marginalized people and reduce democracy. The next sections go into depth about these risks, starting with an examination of the ethical, operational and governance difficulties that come with using AI in development activities.

## 5. RISKS, CHALLENGES, AND ETHICAL CONSIDERATIONS

While the promises of Artificial Intelligence (AI) in sustainable development are substantial, so too are the risks and unintended consequences that accompany its adoption. The ability of AI to address issues and improve decisions can also lead to greater harms, the spread of bias and more inequalities if not managed properly. The section analyzes the main threats and dilemmas that AI presents to the Sustainable Development Goals (SDGs), underlining the value of forethought, inclusive planning and paying attention to local needs.

### 5.1 Algorithmic Bias and Discrimination

One of the most well-documented risks associated with AI is algorithmic bias, where outputs produced by machine learning models reflect—and often amplify—existing social inequalities embedded in the training data. AI systems may end up being discriminatory if their training data is lacking, uneven or biased from the past. For example, if predictive models in healthcare rely mostly on data from rich cities, they might not catch the diseases of people from other groups which leads to unfairness in care. Researchers have found that facial recognition technology tends to make more mistakes with people who have darker skin or a non-binary gender identity (Hanna et al. 2025).

The challenge of bias is particularly acute in the Global South, where data scarcity is common and international models are often transferred without localization. To limit bias, different and inclusive data should be used, all stakeholders should be considered in creating the AI and the systems should be regularly checked. In addition, algorithmic fairness relies on including it within human rights standards that ensure people can get help, be heard and know what is happening.

## 5.2 Data Privacy, Consent, and Surveillance

AI systems typically require vast amounts of data to function effectively, raising serious concerns about privacy, consent, and the potential for surveillance. Where people do not have much experience with digital tools or strong legal rights, data gathering can turn into taking advantage of them. In some digital health projects, personal health data is collected without clear permission, is sometimes not encrypted and may be shared without users being aware (Yan et al. 2025).

The expansion of AI-powered surveillance tools—such as facial recognition and predictive policing—has further complicated the ethical landscape. If these tools are used for security or service improvements, they can easily lead to more intrusive monitoring and reduce civil rights, mainly in authoritarian governments or countries with fragile democracy. For this reason, it is necessary to have rights-based data governance which covers enforceable privacy rules, clear ways to hold people accountable and processes for consent that match the culture and laws in each area (Sander, 2025).

## 5.3 Exacerbation of the Digital Divide

Despite its potential to expand access and inclusion, AI can inadvertently deepen the digital divide, entrenching disparities in access to technology, education, and opportunity. AI systems usually depend on good data, strong internet connections and trained staff which not everyone can afford or access. Many rural communities, informal workers or people with disabilities may not be able to use AI-enabled services because they are unavailable or not suitable for them (Hastuty et al. 2025).

This digital exclusion can be further exacerbated when development funding prioritizes high-tech solutions without investing in the foundational digital infrastructure and capacity-building needed for equitable use. If AI-assisted farming platforms are launched without first making sure smallholder farmers have smartphones and can use them, the platforms may not be well used and could create new reliance on middlemen. Making sure AI helps, rather than harms, inclusive growth calls for efforts to narrow gaps in access, including using local information, thinking about gender and providing training for local people (Jha & Singh, 2025).

## 5.4 Environmental and Resource Footprint

AI systems, particularly those involving large-scale machine learning models, have a non-trivial environmental impact. Building powerful models uses a huge amount of energy and water which often leads to higher greenhouse gas emissions and puts pressure on local resources. Experts predict that data centers supporting

AI workloads currently use about 1–2% of the world's electricity and are likely to use much more unless energy efficiency steps and integrating renewable energy can control their growth (Barbedo, 2025).

In contexts where AI is promoted as part of climate action (e.g., smart agriculture, energy optimization), this paradox becomes especially troubling. Unless proper studies are done, the environmental damage caused by AI might outweigh its benefits. Those working in development should build energy-saving algorithms, ethical data handling and carbon transparency into all aspects of their work and purchasing (Wang et al. 2025).

## 5.5 Accountability and Governance Gaps

A cross-cutting challenge in AI deployment is the lack of clear governance structures to ensure accountability when systems fail or cause harm. In various areas, the law has not kept up with new technology, so issues related to liability, transparency and oversight are still unresolved (Robles & Mallinson, 2025). It is not always clear whether the developer, the deploying agency or the data provider should take responsibility when an AI system gives a wrong health recommendation, denies someone financial services or supports discriminatory policing.

This lack of clarity undermines trust and can stall public sector adoption of AI. To solve this, policymakers and international bodies have to create governance rules that clarify who is responsible and how audits and redress can be carried out. The introduction of algorithmic impact assessments, ethics review boards and AI ombudspersons can add more oversight and responsibility within organizations (Batool et al. 2025).

In sum, the integration of AI into sustainable development carries significant ethical, operational, and systemic risks that must be proactively addressed. Such risks are often linked which causes them to reinforce each other and mostly influence the most vulnerable groups. Dealing with these risks is not just about technology—it is a matter of principle and ethics. In the next part, we look at how the maturity of digital systems, their rules and how open they are help decide if AI is used responsibly and fairly.

# 6. DIGITAL MATURITY AND ECOSYSTEM READINESS

## 6.1 Understanding Digital Maturity

Digital maturity encompasses more than access to hardware or internet infrastructure; it refers to a society's comprehensive readiness to adopt and adapt digital technologies in ways that are effective, ethical, and developmentally aligned. It includes basic digital infrastructure and also covers having skilled people, strong organizations and public trust in digital technology. A mature digital environment is one where technologies can be used and their effects can be understood, regulated and influenced (Fornasiero et al. 2025).

## 6.2 Infrastructure and Capacity Foundations

A core requirement of digital maturity is reliable infrastructure. If there is no reliable electricity, mobile service or data centers, it becomes hard or even useless to use AI systems. Most AI systems need access to real-time information and cloud resources which can only be provided if digital networks and processing power do not stop. If such a foundation is absent, AI applications could fail to be used, even if they can be technically built (Lin et al. 2025).

Beyond infrastructure, digital maturity also depends on human capital. Societies that do well with AI are those with a trained workforce able to introduce, oversee and maintain AI systems. This group should consist of data scientists and engineers as well as policymakers, regulators and members of civil society who know about the social effects of AI. People in the community are better equipped to use and trust AI-powered services because of digital literacy.

## 6.3 Institutional and Governance Readiness

Institutions play a pivotal role in shaping how AI is used and regulated. A mature digital institution can check if AI is useful, add it to their services and make sure it supports policy goals. Alternatively, countries with weak or split institutions may apply AI without fully realizing what it means or they may turn to outside groups without proper control. Having the right systems is important, but so is having proper laws, adjustable processes and the ability to handle change and new ideas (Mangundu, 2025).

Governance structures must also keep pace with technological change. In several countries, AI is growing more quickly than the laws that watch over it. It is important for governments to decide on standards, check if they are followed and keep citizens safe. It is necessary to create clear policies covering data privacy, transparency, ethics and algorithmic accountability so that the public trusts the company.

## 6.4 The Role of Ecosystem Interconnectivity

Digital ecosystems extend beyond single organizations or sectors. These processes depend on governments, private corporations, NGOs, researchers and users all using platforms, policies and commonly accepted norms. Ecosystem readiness shows how much these actors agree on goals and how well their systems can work with each other. When an ecosystem grows, it enables different sectors to join forces, share data and work together to make AI tools that are useful and helpful for society (Gong et al. 2025).

Interoperability is especially important in development contexts where holistic, multi-sectoral solutions are often needed. By combining education, health and social protection information, it becomes simpler to provide tailored and quick public services. But for this integration to be successful, it is necessary to have compatible technology, trust among institutions, clear laws for using data and a strong desire to make innovation accessible to all (Ordibazar et al. 2025).

## 6.5 Trust, Localization, and Inclusion

Trust is foundational to any digital ecosystem. If people and communities believe digital technologies are being used ethically and transparently, they are more willing to try and use AI-enabled services. Trust is built by being clear about data collection, making sure there are mechanisms for accountability and involving a range of voices in decision-making (Alzboon et al. 2025).

Equally important is the ability to localize AI tools. Many AI models are developed in high-income contexts with data that may not reflect the realities of the Global South or marginalized populations. For algorithms, interfaces and outputs to work well in any culture, they must be changed to fit the local culture, language, environment and institutions. Without being localized, AI could turn out to be useless or dangerous in areas such as health, education and social protection (Malhotra & Ramalingam, 2025).

## 6.6 Addressing Global and Local Disparities

Digital maturity is unevenly distributed across the globe and within national borders. Whereas a few countries are planning extensive national AI policies, others are having difficulties setting up basic digital infrastructure. In some advanced countries, the gap between cities and the countryside, unequal earnings and structural barriers can make it harder for everyone to use AI (Nong et al. 2025).

Bridging these disparities requires a developmental approach that prioritizes inclusive access, participatory design, and long-term capacity-building. Improving AI in sustainable development should be combined with increased investments in connectivity, digital skills, updates in institutions and involvement of the public. Only when this is done can AI help society instead of increasing inequality (Luu, 2025).

## 6.7 From Maturity to Meaningful Innovation

Ultimately, digital maturity and ecosystem readiness form the bedrock upon which AI can contribute meaningfully to sustainable development. When these foundations are absent, AI systems might reflect injustices that already exist, fail to be useful or cause undesired effects. If AI is supported by a responsible, ethical and open environment, it has the ability to boost innovation, improve governance and increase availability of public goods. This next part looks at ways to design and use AI to achieve the SDGs, relying on the ideas introduced earlier (Eliseo et al. 2025).

# 7. FRAMEWORKS FOR RESPONSIBLE AI IN SUSTAINABLE DEVELOPMENT

## 7.1 The Need for Structured Governance

As Artificial Intelligence (AI) becomes increasingly embedded in public services, development programs, and policy infrastructures, the need for structured, forward-looking governance frameworks becomes urgent. Though AI can play a role in tackling poverty, climate change and inequality, if it is not properly controlled, it can widen existing gaps, introduce more risks and damage the public's trust. This means that responsible AI governance is essential for matching technology with the ethical goals of the SDGs and cannot be seen as an extra step (Papagiannidis et al. 2025).

A framework for responsible AI must begin by acknowledging that AI systems operate within deeply social and political contexts. Besides using data and code, their work is influenced by how priorities are set, who will benefit and what is expected in the organization. For this reason, ethics, in terms of fairness, accountability, privacy, transparency and inclusivity, should be involved at every stage of AI, starting with its design and purchase and ending with its deployment and management (Li et al. 2025).

## 7.2 Ethical Principles and Rights-Based Foundations

At the heart of responsible AI governance lies the commitment to human rights and social justice. Principles from groups like UNESCO, the OECD and the European Commission are often the starting point for ethical AI frameworks. They state that AI needs to be fair, clear, explainable, secure and centered on people. Making sure that AI technologies improve the well-being of everyone, do not do any harm and are open to those who are poor, marginalized or not online is required in development (Sanchez et al. 2025).

Operationalizing these principles requires more than high-level declarations. Governments and organizations need actionable mechanisms for implementation. It requires setting up legal rules to secure data privacy, prevent discrimination and allow the public to observe and question actions. To ensure accountability, it is important to have bodies such as ethics councils, data protection authorities and algorithmic review boards with the authority, means and knowledge to work in this area (Law et al. 2025).

In contexts where formal institutions are weak, rights-based approaches to AI governance must also be community-driven. With participatory ethics, community technology assessments and civic oversight platforms, local people can have a say in choosing, adapting and examining AI tools. Because of these mechanisms, AI systems are both accountable and fit the needs of their context.

## 7.3 Capacity-Building for Governance and Innovation

One of the most significant barriers to responsible AI implementation in many parts of the world is the lack of technical, regulatory, and institutional capacity. It is important for those in charge to understand what AI offers and also its risks to effectively handle the decisions involved in deploying it. For capacity building to be effective, it should cover various aspects (Jha & Singh, 2025).

On one level, this means investing in education and training for AI developers, data scientists, and policy professionals. It is important to have courses that blend technical skills with the study of ethics, law and society to help develop a group of AI experts who are equally skilled in programming and human rights (Limón et al. 2025).

At the institutional level, development agencies and governments must support public-sector modernization. This means giving ministries digital tools, improving how agencies communicate and setting up ways for everyone to learn and adapt over time. Universities, think tanks and groups in civil society should also be supported because they can provide research relevant to the country, offer views different from the government's and join discussions on policies (Filgueiras, 2025).

Capacity-building should be particularly attentive to the Global South. Traditionally, only a few countries and institutions have worked on AI which has kept resources and influence from being equally distributed. Solving these imbalances calls for investing in local innovation, sharing knowledge across countries and using cooperation models that stress fairness and sharing between countries.

## 7.4 Public-Interest AI and the Role of Open Ecosystems

One of the core challenges in the current AI landscape is the dominance of proprietary platforms, commercial incentives, and closed systems. Such dynamics usually focus on making profits and limit who gets access to data, algorithms and infrastructure. For this reason, AI frameworks should support the creation of public benefit AI, designed to serve important developmental goals like better health care, stronger climate action or more equal education (Machado et al. 2025).

Open-source AI models, public data repositories, and shared infrastructure initiatives are essential for democratizing innovation. If these resources are managed well, ethical guidelines are followed and they can be adapted locally, they make it possible for smaller organizations, local governments and community groups to use AI. Models such as data trusts, AI built by groups and open innovation challenges help to spread public-interest AI and encourage many people to oversee it (Robles & Mallinson, 2025).

Importantly, public investment plays a key role in catalyzing such ecosystems. It is important for governments and development institutions to invest in AI that benefits society, encourage ethical AI by using it in procurement and help create long-lasting infrastructure for everyone to use.

## 7.5 Regulatory Innovation and Adaptive Oversight

Given the dynamic nature of AI technologies, static or overly prescriptive regulation may be ineffective or counterproductive. It is important for oversight to change and develop based on new kinds of use cases, risks and what society expects. This also means using special environments called regulatory sandboxes to test AI, as well as regularly updating regulations after consulting with the public and using evidence (Ajmal et al. 2025).

Transparency and explainability are also crucial regulatory priorities. When AI is used in the public sector, mainly for resource allocation, deciding eligibility or watching over citizens, it should be subject to disclosure so independent review can take place. Also, it is important to provide grievance mechanisms for people and groups who are hurt by AI decisions, making sure they can get timely, fair and accessible redress (Kothandapani, 2025).

Ultimately, governance systems must recognize the inherently experimental nature of AI in development contexts. Mistakes, failures of models and events that were not expected will happen. Responsible frameworks are identified by having strong feedback mechanisms which make it possible to learn, improve and be held accountable to the public.

## 7.6 Toward a Development-Centered AI Governance Paradigm

Bringing these elements together, the challenge is not simply to govern AI, but to do so in ways that are aligned with the deeper goals of sustainable development: equity, empowerment, environmental stewardship, and global solidarity. It means the focus should shift from using technology to govern, to using development goals to guide how AI is used, so that its success is based on helping people flourish.

Such a shift demands bold political leadership, inclusive policymaking, and a commitment to fairness across all phases of the AI lifecycle. It further suggests a new way to understand innovation—as something that comes from a group effort and is based on the everyday lives of various communities rather than being the work of a few top experts (Shafik, 2025).

The next section builds on this foundation by showcasing concrete examples of responsible AI in action, drawing on global case studies that illustrate both the promise and complexity of translating these frameworks into practice.

# 8. CASE STUDIES AND BEST PRACTICES

While the theoretical potential of Artificial Intelligence (AI) to accelerate progress on the Sustainable Development Goals (SDGs) is well articulated, it is through real-world implementation that the possibilities and limitations of AI are most clearly illuminated. They allow us to see how AI technologies are applied in the real world, what helps them succeed, what problems still exist and how to integrate ethics and development into their use. It introduces several cases from different regions and sectors to highlight the responsible use of AI to solve difficult development problems.

## 8.1 AI for Public Health Surveillance in Ghana: Advancing SDG 3

In Ghana, a collaboration between IBM Research Africa and the Ghana Health Service led to the development of a predictive AI model designed to improve malaria surveillance and response. Using data from weather, health care centers and satellites, the system could predict malaria outbreaks at the district level with great accuracy (Boatemaa et al. 2024).

This initiative demonstrates the power of AI to enhance anticipatory governance in health. Significantly, it points out that using AI as part of existing public health structures is more effective than presenting it as a separate advancement. Since Ghana's health system was well-integrated and shared data, the model was able to give useful insights that fit the country's priorities. Just as important was having health workers and epidemiologists take part in both designing and analyzing the technology, so it would meet the community's needs and be trusted (Mensah, 2023).

## 8.2 Adaptive Learning Platforms in India: Personalizing Education for Equity (SDG 4)

India faces deep educational disparities, particularly across socio-economic and linguistic lines. Mindspark, an AI-based adaptive learning system, was used in many urban and peri-urban schools to help deal with this situation. Using the information from their performance, Mindspark adjusts the subjects and their level of difficulty for every student in real time (Ghosh, 2024).

Students who used Mindspark were found by the Abdul Latif Jameel Poverty Action Lab (J-PAL) to achieve greater learning gains than those taught in the usual way and the biggest improvement was seen in students who struggled more in their studies. This case shows that AI can help achieve equity in education by offering students instruction that fits their needs (Sethi & Singh, 2024).

Besides its algorithm, Mindspark also needed support from teachers, parental involvement and integration with what was being taught in classrooms. In addition, running in various languages and matching regional teaching standards proves that localization matters in designing AI.

## 8.3 AI and Precision Agriculture in Kenya: Empowering Smallholder Farmers (SDG 2)

In Kenya, the *PlantVillage Nuru* mobile application offers a practical example of how AI can enhance agricultural productivity and resilience among smallholder farmers. Together with the United Nations FAO, Penn State University created Nuru to detect plant diseases in cassava, maize and potato using computer vision and a smartphone camera (Raimi et al. 2021).

Farmers receive instant diagnostic feedback and tailored advice on treatment options, delivered in local languages. Nuru also aggregates field-level data to inform regional agricultural planning and research. The service has been introduced in several East African countries, helping tens of thousands of farmers (Aroba & Rudolph, 2024).

The case stands out because it uses low-cost tools and involves communities in extension. Educating people on digital technology and joining forces with agricultural cooperatives have been key to adoption. Furthermore, since Nuru is open-access, other researchers and groups can use and modify it which encourages growth and innovation across the entire community.

## 8.4 Smart Grid Optimization in Denmark: Integrating AI with Climate Goals (SDGs 7 and 13)

Denmark's leadership in renewable energy integration is supported by sophisticated AI systems that manage its national smart grid. They help predict how much electricity will be needed and produced, ensure a good balance of power and find any unusual issues in the energy grid. By doing this, a greater amount of wind and solar electricity can be added to the grid without affecting its reliability (Kolhe, 2025).

In Denmark, AI is integrated into a strong digital system that covers data management, meter readings and jointly created policies. Because the energy system is open and people can take part in decision-making, trust has helped people choose and remain committed to decarbonization (Arévalo & Jurado, 2024).

It shows how AI can help businesses become more efficient and also protect the environment. It proves that having technical skills is not enough; strong institutions and long-term planning are also needed to make a difference.

## 8.5 Fintech and AI for Financial Inclusion in the Philippines: Expanding Access to Credit (SDGs 8 and 10)

In the Philippines, some fintech companies, for example Tala and LenddoEFL, apply AI to judge a person's creditworthiness using their mobile habits, texting habits and online activities. These models give those with no formal credit history such as informal workers and rural people, a way in to the formal financial system.

Using mobile apps, users can get microloans instantly and this helps them create a credit profile for future use. Rapid decisions can be made with AI which also cuts down on transaction costs. Still, the moral aspects of credit scoring based on behavioral data have encouraged discussions with regulators and people in society (Danladi et al. 2023).

The case points out the possibilities and the risks that come with AI-based financial inclusion. On one side, it helps democratize financial services; on the other, it leads to concerns about giving permission, privacy and how algorithms work. The central bank in the Philippines has joined in these developments by introducing sandboxes and guidelines for ethics to look after consumers.

## 8.6 Cross-Cutting Lessons and Reflections

These case studies collectively illuminate key themes relevant to the responsible deployment of AI in sustainable development. They highlight the need to fit AI tools to what matters locally such as people's needs, strengths and beliefs. They also explain that working with many stakeholders promotes trust, legitimacy and sustainability. To be successful, AI in health, education, agriculture or finance should be designed with users, checked regularly and included in larger systems within institutions (Uglev, 2023).

Third, these examples prove that how developed an ecosystem is dictates how effective AI is. When digital infrastructure, governance and capacity are working together, AI allows for faster innovation and concrete achievements. If these conditions are missing, the best technology can still fail or cause damage.

Case studies prove that designers should consider ethics and inclusion first, not wait until the end. If AI systems are built to value equity, openness and user power, they are more likely to succeed in making positive and lasting changes.

In the next section, practical steps and recommendations are given to guide policymakers, technologists and development practitioners in using AI responsibly and effectively as the years progress.

# 9. FUTURE OUTLOOK AND POLICY RECOMMENDATIONS

## 9.1 Charting the Road Ahead for AI and the SDGs

As the global community approaches the 2030 deadline for achieving the Sustainable Development Goals (SDGs), the urgency to identify and scale transformative solutions has never been greater. AI, even though it is not fully developed, has already started to affect the way development is done and has increased the impact of interventions. At the same time, using this potential calls for a planned and future-thinking approach, where new technologies are carefully managed with ethical rules, fairness and sustainability (Samanvitha et al. 2025).

Looking ahead, the role of AI in development will be shaped by a complex interplay of technological advancements, governance architectures, investment flows, and societal attitudes toward risk and innovation. The new developments in generative AI, autonomous systems and federated learning create new chances, but they also introduce fresh risks such as people losing their jobs, more misinformation and the selling of private and environmental data. So, people working on AI development should design policies that see AI as an interactive part of human and environmental life and not only as a technological resource (Meitei et al. 2025).

## 9.2 Integrating AI into National Development and Digital Strategies

For AI to become a meaningful instrument of sustainable development, it must be integrated into national policy frameworks that link digital transformation directly to SDG targets. A number of countries are making national AI strategies, but not all of these plans are clear about linking AI to development or ethics. Governments are advised to design integrated plans that use AI within both digital and economic strategies, to make sure all ministries are working together (Alqahtani & Wafula, 2025).

These strategies should prioritize inclusive access, ethical governance, and the use of AI in public service delivery. This may entail using AI for social services, climate change response and educating everyone and including ethical thinking and risk evaluation in all purchasing and policy checks. The main aim is for AI to become open and useful for all people, instead of being controlled by a few (Ogunseye et al. 2025).

## 9.3 Strengthening Global and Regional Governance Architectures

AI's cross-border nature demands governance mechanisms that transcend national boundaries. A global effort is necessary to align ethics, share good practices and avoid regulatory differences. The United Nations, the African Union and regional development banks are important for encouraging dialogue, supporting new ideas and upholding rules that accept various cultural and political values (Wang et al. 2025).

Emerging initiatives—such as UNESCO's Recommendation on the Ethics of Artificial Intelligence—offer valuable starting points. They must be turned into real actions with strong agreements, step-by-step plans and extra support designed for countries in the Global South. Working together on AI governance and development in the sectors of agriculture, disaster response and health provides a strong model for countries to collaborate instead of depending on one another (Dunleavy & Margetts, 2025).

## 9.4 Investing in Public-Interest Innovation and Infrastructure

To ensure that AI serves developmental priorities, greater investment is needed in public-interest technologies. Organizations, agencies and governments should finance AI models, data repositories and research centers that serve missions rather than commercial interests. With these investments, countries can depend less on large global technology companies and build their own innovation systems that are focused on social and environmental issues (Richter et al. 2025).

At the same time, infrastructure must be built with equity and sustainability in mind. Steps like boosting Internet access in rural areas, making data centers greener with renewable energy and allowing public and non-profit groups to make use of cloud and AI services are part of this. Well-designed AI will rely on inclusive, interoperable and environmentally safe infrastructure (Sayari, 2025).

## 9.5 Building Institutional and Societal Capacity

AI governance and deployment require not only rules and infrastructure, but also people with the knowledge, skills, and ethical grounding to design and oversee AI responsibly. Training and support should be offered to those who build AI, work with data and those who oversee government and public organizations. It is important for training to include both technical content and knowledge of human rights, systems approaches and participatory methods (Trujillo-Cabezas, 2025).

It is also important to involve the public so that trust is built, ethical questions are discussed and the government is held responsible by its citizens. Civic forums, citizen assemblies and inclusive consultation can guide the choices made in AI to represent public values and the experiences of people. AI literacy should be included in school curricula to help kids get ready for a future with intelligent systems.

## 9.6 Promoting Agile, Adaptive, and Evidence-Based Policy

AI technologies are evolving rapidly, and governance mechanisms must be designed with sufficient flexibility to keep pace. Policymakers should use flexible rules that make it possible to try, get quick feedback and make changes as needed. Regulatory sandboxes are used, as well as scenario planning and horizon scanning, so that emerging risks can be anticipated and handled.

Evidence-based policymaking is equally important. Impact evaluation systems should be used by governments and partners to assess AI tools on their technical, social, ethical and environmental effects. Ensuring that AI systems are beneficial to the public and keep up with new development needs can be done through independent audits, long-term studies and research involving all parties (Lakshminarasimham, 2025).

## 9.7 Embracing AI as a Catalyst, Not a Panacea

Perhaps the most important policy insight is that AI, while powerful, is not a substitute for inclusive governance, strong institutions, or human solidarity. It can boost existing strengths and speed up service delivery, but it may also worsen inequality and cause additional problems if used without thought. Rather than relying on only technical solutions, those working on policy and development should ensure AI is used in ways that value equity, accountability and sustainability (Parinsi et al. 2025).

Basically, the future of AI and sustainable development is shaped by the decisions societies make in areas such as politics, ethics and collaboration, not only by technological progress. If AI is used wisely and involves all parties, it can play a key role in making development fairer, stronger and more focused on people.

The final section offers a concluding synthesis, reflecting on the central themes of this chapter and reaffirming the need for AI to be shaped not just by what is possible, but by what is just, inclusive, and aligned with the global pursuit of sustainable development.

## 10. CONCLUSION

Artificial Intelligence (AI) stands at the frontier of technological innovation with the potential to reshape how the world addresses the grand challenges encapsulated in the Sustainable Development Goals (SDGs). This chapter has shown that AI can make development interventions more effective, accessible and responsive such as by forecasting disease outbreaks, saving energy, individualizing education and boosting crop yields. These abilities can result in both minor improvements and major progress in several parts of sustainable development.

Still, AI can have both positive and negative effects and this is not always certain. Its usefulness depends on how mature and open the digital networks where it functions are. Ignoring issues such as algorithmic bias, data privacy, digital divides and environmental sustainability might make AI contribute to existing issues or introduce new risks. So, AI should be understood as a system where technology interacts with power, policy and human actions, rather than just as a technical tool.

In order to make use of AI for the SDGs, countries and organizations must put in place strong digital infrastructure, knowledgeable people and ethical and relevant governance. With responsible AI, teamwork in governance and open innovation, this technology can help bring about ethical, inclusive and sustainable growth.

The right use of AI is not only about getting better development results—it is also about reinventing the way we pursue progress today. Using AI technology that follows equity, accountability and collective strength can assist societies in achieving the SDGs and in ways that are fairer, more durable and ready for the future.

## REFERENCES


Adewoyin, M. A., Adediwin, O., & Audu, A. J. (2025). Artificial intelligence and sustainable energy development: A review of applications, challenges, and future directions. *International Journal of Multidisciplinary Research and Growth Evaluation*, *6*(2), 196–203.

Ahmad, U., Aman, A., Khan, A. A., & Ali, S. E. A. (2025). Optimizing crowdfunding for mineral resources of Dutch economy: The role of fintech in achieving sustainable development goals through artificial intelligence. *Resources Policy*, *100*, 105413.

Ajmal, C. S., Yerram, S., Abishek, V., Nizam, V. M., Aglave, G., Patnam, J. D., & Srivastava, S. (2025). Innovative Approaches in Regulatory Affairs: Leveraging Artificial Intelligence and Machine Learning for Efficient Compliance and Decision-Making. *The AAPS Journal*, *27*(1), 22. PMID: 39776314

Al-Raeei, M. (2025). The smart future for sustainable development: Artificial intelligence solutions for sustainable urbanization. *Sustainable Development*, *33*(1), 508–517.

Alijoyo, F. A., Aziz, T. S. A., Omer, N., Yusuf, N., Kumar, M. D., Ramesh, A. V. N., & El-Ebiary, Y. A. B. (2025). Personalized marketing: Leveraging AI for culturally aware segmentation and targeting. *Alexandria Engineering Journal*, *119*, 8–21.

Alqahtani, N., & Wafula, Z. (2025). Artificial intelligence Integration: Pedagogical strategies and policies at leading universities. *Innovative Higher Education*, *50*(2), 665–684.

Alzboon, M. S., Al-Shorman, H. M., Alka'awneh, S. M. N., Saatchi, S. G., Alqaraleh, M. K. S., Samara, E. I. M., & Haija, A. A. A. (2025). The Role of Perceived Trust in Embracing Artificial Intelligence Technologies: Insights from SMEs. In *Intelligence-Driven Circular Economy: Regeneration Towards Sustainability and Social Responsibility—Volume 2* (pp. 1–15). Springer Nature Switzerland.

Amuda, Y. J. (2025). Artificial intelligence for food production among smallholder farmers: Towards achieving sustainable development goals (SDGs) in Nigeria. *Journal of Ecohumanism*, *4*(1), 175–185.

Arévalo, P., & Jurado, F. (2024). Impact of artificial intelligence on the planning and operation of distributed energy systems in smart grids. *Energies*, *17*(17), 4501.

Aroba, O. J., & Rudolph, M. (2024). Systematic literature review on the application of precision agriculture using artificial intelligence by small-scale farmers in Africa and its societal impact. *Journal of Infrastructure. Policy and Development, 8*(13), 8872.

Barbedo, J. G. A. (2025). A review of artificial intelligence techniques for wheat crop monitoring and management. *Agronomy (Basel), 15*(5), 1157.

Batool, A., Zowghi, D., & Bano, M. (2025). AI governance: A systematic literature review. *AI and Ethics*, •••, 1–15.

Boatemaa, R., Asare, S. O., Akabadin, S. C., Agyabeng, V., & Addy, A. (2024). The role of AI in Enhancing Disease Surveillance and Outbreak Response in Developing Countries. *Ghana Journal of Nursing and Midwifery, 1*(4), 16–29.

Carayannis, E. G., Dumitrescu, R., Falkowski, T., Papamichail, G., & Zota, N. R. (2025). Enhancing SME Resilience through Artificial Intelligence and Strategic Foresight: A Framework for Sustainable Competitiveness. *Technology in Society*, •••, 102835.

Cho, H., & Ackom, E. (2025). Artificial Intelligence (AI)-driven approach to climate action and sustainable development. *Nature Communications, 16*(1), 1228. PMID: 39890783

Danladi, S., Prasad, M. S. V., Modibbo, U. M., Ahmadi, S. A., & Ghasemi, P. (2023). Attaining sustainable development goals through financial inclusion: Exploring collaborative approaches to Fintech adoption in developing economies. *Sustainability, 15*(17), 13039.

Dunleavy, P., & Margetts, H. (2025). Data science, artificial intelligence and the third wave of digital era governance. *Public Policy and Administration, 40*(2), 185–214.

Eliseo, M. A., Junior, L. C., & Silveira, I. F. (2025). A Comprehensive and Structured Maturity Model for Measuring AI Adoption Levels in Industry 4.0. *CLEI Electronic Journal, 28*(1), 3–1.

Fazal, A., Ahmed, A., & Abbas, S. (2025). Importance of artificial intelligence in achieving sustainable development goals through financial inclusion. *Qualitative Research in Financial Markets, 17*(2), 432–452.

Filgueiras, F. (2025). Artificial intelligence and governance challenges in Latin America–the game between decolonization and dependence. In *Handbook on Governance and Data Science* (pp. 198–221). Edward Elgar Publishing.

Fornasiero, R., Kiebler, L., Falsafi, M., & Sardesai, S. (2025). Proposing a maturity model for assessing artificial intelligence and big data in the process industry. *International Journal of Production Research, 63*(4), 1235–1255.

Garg, T., Kumar, U., Yadav, H., & Jain, A. (2024, April). Fostering Sustainable Growth via the Fusion of Artificial Intelligence and Computer Vision. In *International Conference on Sustainable Development through Machine Learning, AI and IoT* (pp. 102-109). Cham: Springer Nature Switzerland.

Ghosh, S., Sarkar, S. K., & Roy, P. (2025). Application of Automation and Artificial Intelligence (AI) in Green Transportation System. In *Driving Green Transportation System Through Artificial Intelligence and Automation: Approaches, Technologies and Applications* (pp. 21–42). Springer Nature Switzerland.

Ghosh, S. S. (2024). Transforming the Indian Education Landscape: The Impact of Personalized Learning and Adaptive Technologies in Continuing Education. In *Embracing Technological Advancements for Lifelong Learning* (pp. 278-299). IGI Global.

Gong, Y., Ma, F., Wang, H., Tzachor, A., Sun, W., Zhu, J., & Schandl, H. (2025). The evolution of research at the intersection of industrial ecology and artificial intelligence. *Journal of Industrial Ecology, 29*(2), 440–457.

Hanna, M. G., Pantanowitz, L., Jackson, B., Palmer, O., Visweswaran, S., Pantanowitz, J., & Rashidi, H. H. (2025). Ethical and bias considerations in artificial intelligence/machine learning. *Modern Pathology, 38*(3), 100686. PMID: 39694331

Hastuty, A., Maswati, M., Saharuddin, M., Sukri, A. M., & Halik, A. (2025). Artificial intelligence: A review of the philosophy of Islamic educational science. *Journal of Research in Instructional, 5*(1), 90–102.

Iorember, P. T., Hounkanrin, D. O., Diyoke, K., & Tang, C. F. (2025). Tracing financial inclusion pathway to sustainable development: The criticality of population growth and energy intensity using a machine learning approach. *African Journal of Economic and Management Studies.*

Jha, A., & Singh, S. R. (2025). Bridging the Divide: Capacity Building for AI Adoption in Developing Countries. In *AI Strategies for Social Entrepreneurship and Sustainable Economic Development* (pp. 133-150). IGI Global Scientific Publishing.

Kamkar, M., Leonard, K. C., Ferrer, I., Loo, S. C. J., Biddinger, E. J., Brady, D., & Serrano, J. F. (2024). Artificial Intelligence (AI) for sustainable resource management and chemical processes. *ACS Sustainable Resource Management, 1*(2), 178–180.

Kolhe, M. L. (2025). Advancing Sustainable Electrical Energy Technologies: A Multifaceted Approach Towards SDG Achievement. *Processes (Basel, Switzerland), 13*(1), 210.

Kothandapani, H. P. (2025). AI-Driven Regulatory Compliance: Transforming Financial Oversight through Large Language Models and Automation. *Emerging Science Research*, 12-24.

Kulkov, I., Kulkova, J., Rohrbeck, R., Menvielle, L., Kaartemo, V., & Makkonen, H. (2024). Artificial intelligence-driven sustainable development: Examining organizational, technical, and processing approaches to achieving global goals. *Sustainable Development, 32*(3), 2253–2267.

Kumar, S. (2025). A review on new marketing management theory 6.0: A new paradigm in consumer engagement. [Kuwait chapter]. *Arabian Journal of Business and Management Review, 14*(1), 1–5.

Kumaran, M. S., Keerthika, V., Reddy, P. S., & Rajendra, A. (2025). Rural Ecosystem Monitoring in Food Security Analysis Based on Sustainable Agriculture: Artificial Intelligence Application. *Remote Sensing in Earth Systems Sciences, 8*(1), 56–64.

Lakshminarasimham, K. C. (2025). Technology Leadership for Program Success: Integrating AI and Agile Methods for Modern Enterprises. In *Integrating Blue-Green Infrastructure Into Urban Development* (pp. 489-506). IGI Global Scientific Publishing.

Law, R., Ye, H., & Lei, S. S. I. (2025). Ethical artificial intelligence (AI): Principles and practices. *International Journal of Contemporary Hospitality Management, 37*(1), 279–295.

Li, Y., Fan, Y., & Nie, L. (2025). Making governance agile: Exploring the role of artificial intelligence in China's local governance. *Public Policy and Administration, 40*(2), 276–301.

Limón, M. E. R., Osuna, J. H. O., Hernández, G. T., & Rico, F. N. M. (2025). AI in public administration-transformative opportunities for climate resilience and sustainable development. *Revista de Ciencias Tecnológicas, 8*(2), 1–21.

Lin, Y., Yousaf, Z., Grigorescu, A., & Popovici, N. (2025). Harnessing digital foundations and artificial intelligence synergies: Unraveling the role of digital platforms, artificial intelligence, and strategic adaptability in organizational innovativeness. *Journal of Innovation & Knowledge, 10*(2), 100670.

Luu, H. S. (2025). Laboratory Data as a Potential Source of Bias in Healthcare Artificial intelligence and machine learning models. *Annals of Laboratory Medicine*, *45*(1), 12–21. PMID: 39444135

Machado, H., Silva, S., & Neiva, L. (2025). Publics' views on ethical challenges of artificial intelligence: A scoping review. *AI and Ethics*, *5*(1), 139–167.

Malhotra, G., & Ramalingam, M. (2025). Perceived anthropomorphism and purchase intention using artificial intelligence technology: Examining the moderated effect of trust. *Journal of Enterprise Information Management*, *38*(2), 401–423.

Malkova, Y. (2025). Artificial intelligence and sustainable power. In *The Sustainable Power Grid* (pp. 43–58). Elsevier.

Mangundu, J. (2025). Navigating Artificial Intelligence Governance: Insights from South African Higher Education IT Decision-Makers. *The African Journal of Information Systems*, *17*(1), 1.

Manikandan, S., Kaviya, R. S., Shreeharan, D. H., Subbaiya, R., Vickram, S., Karmegam, N., & Govarthanan, M. (2025). Artificial intelligence-driven sustainability: Enhancing carbon capture for sustainable development goals–A review. *Sustainable Development*, *33*(2), 2004–2029.

Meitei, A. J., Rai, P., & Rajkishan, S. S. (2025). Application of AI/ML techniques in achieving SDGs: A bibliometric study. *Environment, Development and Sustainability*, *27*(1), 281–317.

Mensah, G. B. (2023). AI-Augmented Public Health Administration in sub-Saharan Africa: Addressing Challenges in Ghana's Cyberlaws Regimes for Smooth and Effective Use. *International Journal of Legal Science and Innovation*, *5*(6), 26–54.

Nong, P., Adler-Milstein, J., Apathy, N. C., Holmgren, A. J., & Everson, J. (2025). Current Use And Evaluation Of Artificial Intelligence And Predictive Models In US Hospitals: Article examines uses and evaluation of artificial intelligence and predictive models in US hospitals. *Health Affairs*, *44*(1), 90–98. PMID: 39761454

Ogunseye, O. O., Ajayi, O. T., Fabusoro, A., Abba, A. O., & Adepoju, B. (2025). Leveraging Artificial Intelligence for Advancing Key Sectors of National Growth and Development. *Asian Journal of Current Research*, *10*(1), 45–55.

Ordibazar, A. H., Hussain, O. K., Chakrabortty, R. K., Irannezhad, E., & Saberi, M. (2025). Artificial intelligence applications for supply chain risk management considering interconnectivity, external events exposures and transparency: a systematic literature review. *Modern Supply Chain Research and Applications*, (ahead-of-print).

Papagiannidis, E., Mikalef, P., & Conboy, K. (2025). Responsible artificial intelligence governance: A review and research framework. *The Journal of Strategic Information Systems*, *34*(2), 101885.

Parinsi, W. K., Musa, A. D. L., & Musa, K. S. P. (2025). The Role of AI in Driving Sustainable HRM: A Phenomenological Study on the Use of People Analytics for Corporate Carbon Footprint Reduction. [JUMPER]. *Journal Management & Economics Review*, *2*(6), 191–196.

Raimi, L., Panait, M., & Sule, R. (2021). Leveraging precision agriculture for sustainable food security in sub-Saharan Africa: A theoretical discourse. *Shifting Patterns of Agricultural Trade: The Protectionism Outbreak and Food Security*, 491-509.

Rashid, A., Baloch, N., Rasheed, R., & Ngah, A. H. (2025). Big data analytics-artificial intelligence and sustainable performance through green supply chain practices in manufacturing firms of a developing country. *Journal of Science and Technology Policy Management*, *16*(1), 42–67.

Regona, M., Yigitcanlar, T., Hon, C., & Teo, M. (2024). Artificial intelligence and sustainable development goals: Systematic literature review of the construction industry. *Sustainable Cities and Society*, •••, 105499.

Richter, V., Katzenbach, C., & Zeng, J. (2025). Negotiating AI (s) futures: Competing imaginaries of AI by stakeholders in the US, China, and Germany. *Journal of Science Communication*, *24*(2), A08.

Robles, P., & Mallinson, D. J. (2025). Artificial intelligence technology, public trust, and effective governance. *The Review of Policy Research*, *42*(1), 11–28.

Ruoxing, C., Jianning, W., Basem, A., Hussein, R. A., Salahshour, S., & Baghaei, S. (2025). Examining the application of strategic management and artificial intelligence, with a focus on artificial neural network modeling to enhance human resource optimization with advertising and brand campaigns. *Engineering Applications of Artificial Intelligence*, *143*, 110029.

Samanvitha, C., Dharmendra, H., Nethravathi, N., & Velmurugan, P. R. (2025). Artificial Intelligence for Sustainable Futures: Navigating Social and Environmental Responsibility. In *Advancements in Intelligent Process Automation* (pp. 129-154). IGI Global.

Sanchez, T. W., Brenman, M., & Ye, X. (2025). The ethical concerns of artificial intelligence in urban planning. *Journal of the American Planning Association*, *91*(2), 294–307.

Sander, B. (2025). Confronting risks at the intersection of climate change and artificial intelligence: The promise and perils of rights-based approaches. *Netherlands Quarterly of Human Rights*, •••, 09240519251336962.

Sayari, K. T. (2025). Infrastructure and Investment Needs for AI Implementation in Education. In *Teachers' Roles and Perspectives on AI Integration in Schools* (pp. 141–162). IGI Global Scientific Publishing.

Sethi, S., & Singh, M. (2024). *Blended Learning and AI in Higher Education: Adapt, Evolve, Thrive*. Cambridge Scholars Publishing.

Shafik, W. (2025). The Darkside of Artificial Intelligence and the Metaverse in Scientific Research and Publishing: Navigating the Academic Standards in the Digital Era. In *Navigating AI and the Metaverse in Scientific Research* (pp. 275–304). IGI Global Scientific Publishing.

Singh, A., Kanaujia, A., Singh, V. K., & Vinuesa, R. (2024). Artificial intelligence for Sustainable Development Goals: Bibliometric patterns and concept evolution trajectories. *Sustainable Development*, *32*(1), 724–754.

Trujillo-Cabezas, R. (2025). Exploring the link between foresight and artificial intelligence methods to strengthen collective future-building in contexts of social instability. *foresight, 27*(2), 267-305.

Uglev, V. (2023, September). Case Study of Organization of Decision-Making and Feedback Synthesis in Intelligent Tutoring Systems with a Cross-Cutting Approach. In *Novel & Intelligent Digital Systems Conferences* (pp. 114–124). Springer Nature Switzerland.

Wang, Q., Sun, T., & Li, R. (2025). Does artificial intelligence promote green innovation? An assessment based on direct, indirect, spillover, and heterogeneity effects. *Energy & Environment*, *36*(2), 1005–1037.

Wang, Q., Zhang, F., & Li, R. (2025). Artificial intelligence and sustainable development during urbanization: Perspectives on AI R&D innovation, AI infrastructure, and AI market advantage. *Sustainable Development*, *33*(1), 1136–1156.

Wang, Z., Gao, Y., Zhou, Y., & Xue, L. (2025). Digital governance and AI: Boosting OFDI's impact on regional innovation performance. *Science & Public Policy*, •••, scae087.

Yan, B., Li, K., Xu, M., Dong, Y., Zhang, Y., Ren, Z., & Cheng, X. (2025). On protecting the data privacy of Large Language Models (LLMs) and LLM agents: A literature review. *High-Confidence Computing*, •••, 100300.

Yue, H., Wei, Y., Yuan, H., & Li, H. (2025). Revitalizing urban industrial heritage: Enhancing public trust in government through smart city development and open big data analysis using artificial neural network (ANN) modeling. *Cities (London, England)*, *156*, 105538.

Zhou, B., & Guan, S. (2025). Ethical and Psychological Challenges in Human-AI Romantic Relationships: An Interdisciplinary Critical Study. *Innovative Applications of AI*, *2*(1), 39–45.

# Chapter 5
# Artificial Intelligence for Sustainable Development: A Systematic Review of Literature

**Kritika Gupta**
https://orcid.org/0000-0001-6496-9337
*Chandigarh University, India*

## ABSTRACT

*Purpose: This study presents a systematic literature review on the application of artificial intelligence (AI) in sustainable development and environmental sciences to identify existing research gaps and encourage future studies. Design/methodology/approach: A total of 32 peer-reviewed articles published between 2008 and 2024 were analyzed, all sourced from the Scopus database, using a structured coding framework. Findings: The review highlights a significant lack of research on AI's role in sustainable development in underrepresented regions, particularly in Africa and South America. It also emphasizes the need for more robust methodologies, including larger sample sizes and quantitative approaches, to enhance the reliability and generalizability of findings. Research limitations: The study is limited to articles indexed in Scopus, which, despite being a single source, is one of the most comprehensive and reputable academic databases. The selected time frame (2008–2024) ensures the inclusion of relevant, high-quality research while minimizing bias.*

## 1. INTRODUCTION

The rapid evolution of Artificial Intelligence (AI) technologies has transformed the capability of modern societies to address complex global problems. From healthcare diagnostics to precision agriculture to energy management to climate modeling,

DOI: 10.4018/979-8-3373-7584-7.ch005

AI has fundamentally transformed the capabilities of sectors. Simultaneously, the global community is trying to progress on the UN Sustainable Development Goals (SDGs)—a 2015 initiative consisting of 17 interconnected Goals, established with the aim of eradicating poverty, protecting the planet, and ensuring prosperity for all by 2030 (UN, 2015). The world is facing growing environmental degradation, economic inequality, and social inequalities, as well as the incorporation of AI into the concepts of sustainable development with a unique set of opportunities, and important challenges. In this situation, it is important to conduct a systematic review of the literature and timely to understand how AI might be leveraged to support the SDGs.

Artificial Intelligence, refers basically, to computer systems that can perform a number of tasks which typically require human intelligence such as learning, reasoning, problem solving, and perception (Russell &Norvig, 2020). AI includes a number of subfields including machine learning (ML), deep learning natural language processing (NLP), computer vision robotics. If implemented carefully, AI technologies could support decision making, reduce resource use, foster innovation and advancement, with sustainable practices (Vinuesa et al., 2020). AI technologies will be increasingly infused into our daily lives and will ultimately be instrumental in tackling the ongoing puzzles of sustainable development – particularly, when faced with challenges that benefit from the amalgamation and analyses of big and complex data, to support real-time informed decision making. AI will be able to make significant contributions to all three pillars of sustainable development which includes, environmental, economic, and social dimensions. From an environmental perspective, AI could support modelling climate patterns more accurately, monitor deforestation with satellite images, and enhance the energy systems' efficiency in smart grids (Rolnick et al., 2022). The economic dimension can support more vigilant use of industrial processes for more sustainable practices, the application and assessment of circular economies, and the increased transparency of supply chains. From a social perspective, it can assist with access to high-quality health and education, provide equitable forms of governance, and promote evidence-based decision making (Zhang et al., 2023). These examples, used alongside SDGs, imply AI has the potential to be a powerful force for transformational change.

Yet, there are many serious issues that accompany the excitement for AI's ability to facilitate sustainable development. Some issues include the risks to data privacy, biased algorithmic processes, a lack of transparency, and unequal access to AI could exacerbate existing social and economic inequalities (Bender et al., 2021; Strubell et al., 2019). In addition, the environmental impacts of feeding and running very large AI models cannot be ignored, since the training takes up a significant amount of energy and storage when data storage is vastly increased. A 2023 report from Reuters (2023) observed that indirect emissions from major tech companies had risen by over 150% in less than three years, mainly due to the expansion of AI infrastructures. Moreover, the geopolitical balances of power affect the pace and prospects of AI innovations. As a select few nation states and tech corporations monopolise research, development, and policy, these processes can create new "technological dependencies," making low-income countries purely consumers of AI tools and generally unable to develop solutions that work for their context. Such imbalances undermine agency and the sovereignty to engage in, and contribute to a participatory form of global inclusive Sustainable development (UNESCO, 2021). Therefore, cross-border collaboration and inclusive governance frameworks across all technology types and structures, and democratized access to all technology choices including AI tools for inclusive countries, are critical to ensuring equitable sharing of technological advancement benefits.

There is a growing awareness across academia, industry and policy that we need to be more responsible about governing AI development. There are several scholars, including Floridi et al. (2018), and Vinuesa et al. (2020), that have raised the need for frameworks that incorporate ethical legal and societal considerations in the development of AI systems. This includes considerations of fairness, transparency, accountability and environmental responsibility. Further, the academic community recognise that sustainable development has an inherent interdisciplinary and cross-sectoral nature. It will require collaboration between computer scientists, environmental scientists, development economists and ethicists to build AI applications that are not only functional but ethical and equitable. There are a range of studies that have examined AI applications in Sustainable development from various sectors, including; agriculture (Kamilaris & Prenafeta-Boldú, 2018), energy systems (Nguyen et al., 2020), health care (Esteva et al., 2017) and urban development (Batty, 2018). For instance, AI diagnostic tools have led to improved disease detection and to personalized treatment (SDG 3), "smart" renewable energy systems with advanced predictive analytics have improved the integration of renewable energy into the energy transition systems (SDG 7), and "smart" city technologies have improved traffic and waste management (SDG 11). All of these examples contribute in a direct way to SDG 13, climate action, which can benefit from AI-enabled climate modelling and AA-enabled early warning systems. Nevertheless, different dimensions of SDGs are still underrepresented in the literature. For example, those dimensions under SDG 5 (Gender Equality), SDG 10 (Reduced Inequalities) and SDG 16 (Peace, Justice and Strong Institutions) have been substantially less researched by AI researchers/practitioners (Vinuesa et al., 2020). This means that it would be prudent to establish a broader and more inclusive research agenda for academics and practitioners alike to promote AI innovation for all dimensions of sustainable development. It should also be noted the ironic role of AI in Sustainable development. On one hand, AI is a powerful tool for environmental conservation and support to resource efficiency.

On the other hand, AI can also negatively contribute to environmental outcomes. Large AI systems have high computational demands which creates greater energy consumption, which often comes from 'dirty' (non-renewable) energy sources, Strubell et al (2019) discussed the carbon footprint of training sophisticated Natural Language Processing (NLP) models, as well as discussing research focusing on developing more energy-efficient AI technologies, both in terms of architectures and infrastructure for AI models. In environmental contexts, AI technologies have also been used for biodiversity monitoring, pollution and contamination tracking, and disaster response and preparedness. For example, Rolnick et al (2022) illustrated that the satellite and sensor data supporting AI technologies may use machine learning algorithms to detect deforestation, track and assess air and water quality and model extreme weather events. In keeping with this, Hodge et al. (2020) stated that AI could potentially expedite the transition to low-carbon economies through the optimization of renewable energy distribution and consumption. As well, Gupta and Singh (2024) described, AI-enabled smart grids and predictive maintenance systems were increasing energy efficiency and fostering responsible energy consumption. Yet, even with these potential benefits, ethical dilemmas and logistically complicated barriers remain in various implementations of AI in environmental sciences, such as data availability and data quality, algorithmic transparency, as well as interdisciplinary gulf between technologists and environmental practitioners that prevent the realization of the full potential of AI in Sustainable development. Also, algorithmically driven decisions made in environmental settings of heightened consequence - like in disaster response, or when distributing resources - present issues of accountability, inclusivity, and risk.

In order to address these concerns, AI research must be situated within frameworks to understand sustainability that prioritize long-term ecological balance, social justice and participatory, equitable development. Responsible AI practices should include transparent reporting of energy consumption, the conscious reduction of algorithm bias, community engagement in technology implementation, and digital literacy efforts to educate historically underserved communities. Through a synthesis of a rich cadre of interdisciplinary literature, this study provides an overview of the way in which AI is being used in the support of sustainable development, where gaps exist and how we can shape together the future of AI and sustainable development through deliberate research, policy, and practice. Through this exercise the study aims to deepen understanding of the duality of AI—both as an enabler and as barrier—of a sustainable and equitable future for all. This study reviews current examples, barriers, and potentials for AI within Sustainable development in an effort to assess how AI can be used as a mechanism to help resolve environmental challenges and to restore long-term ecological balance drawing upon knowledge from multiple fields.

## 2. THEORETICAL FRAMEWORK

A thorough examination of the articles downloaded from the Scopus-indexed database was undertaken so that keywords and major theme areas could be established in the literature. The present review identified four main areas of emphasis: the role of artificial intelligence (AI) in sustainable development, the extent of AI in environmental protection and conservation, the application of Sustainable development practices in the corporate sector using AI, and the effects of AI on environmental awareness. As such, these themes provide a systematic understanding of how AI can help promote Sustainable development and environmental sciences.

### 2.1 Artificial Intelligence and Its Role in Sustainable Development

Recent scholarship has increasingly emphasized the transformative potential of artificial intelligence (AI) as a catalyst for inclusive development and shared prosperity, particularly within the Global South. Mutambara (2025) highlights AI's capacity to drive economic growth while addressing pressing social challenges in developing regions. His comprehensive work outlines how AI technologies can support sectors such as agriculture, healthcare, and education by improving efficiency and accessibility, thereby fostering inclusive development. Mutambara argues that harnessing AI responsibly can help bridge existing development gaps and promote equitable economic participation, contributing significantly to sustainable development goals (SDGs).

Complementing this perspective, Dhar and Mallick (2025) critically explore the philosophical and socio-cultural dimensions of AI through the lens of posthumanism in the Global South. They argue for a rethinking of AI's role beyond purely technological paradigms, stressing the importance of context-specific interpretations that incorporate indigenous knowledge systems and local realities. This approach foregrounds equity and inclusivity, urging researchers and practitioners to consider diverse epistemologies and socio-political factors when deploying AI solutions. Their work underscores the need to challenge dominant narratives and power structures embedded within AI development, which often marginalize vulnerable populations.

Together, these studies reinforce the view that AI's potential in the Global South must be understood through an interdisciplinary and inclusive framework. They highlight the dual challenge of leveraging AI for development while addressing ethical, social, and cultural complexities unique to these regions. This evolving discourse invites further empirical investigation into how AI can be adapted to support sustainable and equitable outcomes across diverse socio-economic landscapes.

Recognized as a game-changer for sustainable development, artificial intelligence (AI) offers new and data informed ways to tackle complex environmental, social and economic problems. Technology in general is often viewed as a means to increased efficiency but AI also affords an opportunity to transition to more sustainable systems based on better decision-making, predictive analytics and automation. Technological determinism and systems theory are two major theoretical perspectives that lay the conceptual foundation for how AI fits into sustainable development. Deeming technology as a causal force that drives society's structures, behaviors and environmental outcomes, technological determinism suggests that technological change is not only a catalyst for change, but a driver of systemic change. New technological abilities can shape how societies interact with their environment and how resources are managed (Brynjolfsson & McAfee, 2014). AI technologies will provide concrete meaning to sustainable development by:

- Improving resource use, maximizing use of natural resources and minimizing waste;
- Improving energy efficiency through smart grid technology, smart building systems and energy demand forecasting;
- Supporting green innovation, such as AI-enabled precision farming, climate modeling, and pollution tracking;
- Facilitating data integration and real-time monitoring that informs policy decisions for sustainability.

These capacities are aligned with achieving several of the Sustainable Development Goals (SDGs) set by the United Nations, namely, SDG 7 (Affordable and Clean Energy), SDG 11 (Sustainable Cities and Communities), SDG 12 (Responsible Consumption and Production), and SDG 13 (Climate Action) (Vinuesa et al., 2020). AI can be regarded as a powerful stimulant to enhance and accelerate our progress towards sustainability targets in the ways that human systems interact with the planet. Alongside this idea, systems theory conceptualizes the complexity and interdependence of ecological, social and economic systems, and promotes the idea that sustainable development challenges cannot be solved in isolation, but must be considered in a broader, integrative way that considers systems feedback loops, interdependencies and emergent behaviours (Meadows, 2008). This means that the introduction of AI into sustainability practices may require consideration of the systemic implications, rather than just the technical efficiencies attributed to these new AI capabilities.

Systems theory can inform the ethical and strategic use of AI through:

- Cross-sectoral integration, supporting assurance of solutions that do not produce unintended consequences in other sectors (e.g., energy solutions harming water, or inequities);
- Stakeholder engagement and ownership, acknowledging all diverse actors (government, community, business, and NGO) are part of interconnected systems in environmental sustainability transitions;
- Adaptive and resilient system building, where AI systems are designed to respond to changing environmental and social conditions within resilient systems;
- Transparent decision-making, where trade-offs between economic growth, environmental sustainability, and social well-being are openly assessed.

We now have more sophisticated insight into AI for sustainable development by integrating these two theoretical lenses: Technological determinism explains how AI can serve as a leverage point for transformative change, while systems theory serves as a framework for fostering change properly, ethically, and sustainably over the long term. Together they articulate key ideas about embedding AI in a wider socio-ecological context, which supports innovation that is not just good enough, but also just and ecological.

## 2.2 Scope of Artificial Intelligence in Environmental Protection and Conservation

The integration of Artificial Intelligence (AI) can be meaningfully examined as it relates to environmental protection and conservation through the theoretical frameworks of ecological modernization theory and data-driven decision-making. These frameworks help paint a picture of how AI technologies could alter environmental management processes and facilitate improved sustainability outcomes. Ecological modernization theory asserts that technological innovation is a significant promoter of changes within industrial systems and social practices that affect the natural environment towards more environmentally sustainable practices (Mol & Spaargaren, 2000). It does not mean that technological development is bad for the environment; instead, this area of modernity highlights the potential for technological development to drive ecological modernization. AI identifies and establishes a new potential to decouple economic growth from environmental degradation through cleaner-, more efficient-, and adaptable systems to drive forward this idea of ecological modernization and transition. Furthermore, AI supports ecological modernization, primarily through supporting:

- Quality for resources to divert methane emissions in order to use predictive algorithms to figure out waste reduction;
- Efficiency for pollution, geography analysis for emissions in region by building a predictive model for application to different scenarios and mitigation potential;
- Protection for wildlife and biodiversity, automation of species ID using image recognition, acoustic monitoring and tracking;
- Custody for habitat, GIS satellite images need classification, land-use description, AI use for developing models are able to identify/locate deforestation and encroachment limits over time in real-time.

For instance, AI-enabled systems can analyze pictures from camera traps that are used for endangered species identification, poaching recognition, and population dynamics, increasing conservation efficacy while decreasing the need for human oversight (Rolnick et al., 2022). These needs are consistent with the core principals of ecological modernization, which emphasizes the role of technology as a part of sustainable environmental governance. In addition to this logic, the understanding of data-based decision-making is also involved in how it is important to act or take action on large collections of environmental data. Environmental systems are complex, unpredictable, and rapidly changing, and to understand how these types of systems change or adapt we need up-to-date and high-quality information in order to recognize trends and make appropriate responses. Additionally, AI technologies, especially machine learning, remote sensing, and big data, can enable us to process and make sense of the vast amounts of data that are produced by many different sources including:

- Satellite imagery, which is used to track land-use change, forest cover, and urban growth;
- Sensor networks that provide real-time measurements of air and water quality, soil moisture, or greenhouse gas emissions;
- Climate models that project sea-level rise or other changes in weather patterns or ecosystem dynamics.

These AI-augmented tools will assist researchers, conservators, and decision-makers in detecting environmental stressors more quickly, predicting shifts in ecosystems, and assessing impacts of interventions. For instance, machine learning models can assimilate climate data and estimate chances of drought; as a result, governments can react faster in deciding how to allocate resources for response and where to initiate emergency efforts. Similarly, remote sensing techniques empowered with AI (i.e. remote cameras) can survey and detect coral bleaching events, or track glacial retreat, at an efficiency equal to or exceeding traditional survey methods. The greatest value in data-driven decisions is converting raw data into actionable insights. In addition, AI supports evidence-based environmental governance by employing real-time and predictive analysis. This supports more rapid, exact, and proactive forms of response to environmental challenges. In doing so, conservation is made more effective, but resilience is increased, due to a more identified direction in actions taken to spatial shifts associated with climate change, biodiversity decline, and resource depletion..While ecological modernization theory places more emphasis on society's structural transformation through technology, data-driven decision making relies on AI's way of working with information and facilitating decisions. When combined, these frameworks indicate how AI will shape the future of the monitoring, management and protection of the natural world, as well as providing scalable and sustainable responses to our most serious environmental issues.

## 2.3 Implementing Sustainable development Practices in the Corporate World with Artificial Intelligence

The role of Artificial Intelligence (AI) in corporate sustainable development goals can be conceptualised through two relevant theoretical perspectives: stakeholder theory and the resource-based view (RBV) of the firm. These frameworks complement one another as they explain how and why firms might exploit AI to achieve sustainability goals and improve competitive advantage. Stakeholder theory can be understood as advancing the proposition of Freeman (1984), that organizations have an ethical obligation to take into account the interests and well-being of all stakeholders—not just shareholders—when developing and executing business strategies. Stakeholders include the organisation's investors, employees, customers, suppliers, regulators, and the community at large. From a sustainable development perspective, stakeholder theory highlights an organization's ethical obligation to pursue both environmental and social objectives in addition to financial ones. In other words, AI provides corporations the means to achieve sustainability goals in an open and balanced way, with reliance on data and evidence.

Using AI-powered solutions, businesses can:

- Decrease carbon emissions with smart energy management systems, as well as emissions forecasting tools.
- Enhance their supply chains through better route optimization, resource use reduction, and ensuring ethical sourcing with real-time monitoring.
- Simplify reporting and compliance, automating the tracking of sustainability measure with AI, and creating more detail in ESG (environmental, social, and governance) disclosures.

These apps do not just support regulatory compliance and limit operational risks; they also nurture trust and alignment with stakeholder expectations. AI's ability to automate complicated tasks and analyze large amounts of data allows companies to make better-informed decisions that address sustainability aims and stakeholder interests. As a second perspective, the firm's resource-based view (RBV) (Barney, 1991) is a strategy viewpoint, which states that competitive advantage comes from a firm's capability to develop and deploy resources in ways that are valuable, rare, inimitable, and non-substitutable. In this viewpoint, AI is defined as a strategic resource that enables to capacity to innovate, operational excellence, and responsiveness, which are needed even more in sustainable business practices. AI can provide value to sustainability-driven innovation:

- Predictive analytics enable companies to determine energy usage, mitigate potential equipment failure, and minimize material loss;
- Automation of production processes improves efficiencies while lowering negative environmental impacts;
- Machine learning models also facilitate more informed, real-time dynamic decision making to respond to sustainability challenges for firms.

Organizations that leverage AI in their sustainable development strategies can improve both their environmental and social performance while distinctly separating them from competitors. This is particularly relevant as consumers, investors, and regulators are increasingly focused on the environmental aspect of responsible businesses and climate-conscious business models. By utilizing AI to design sustainable products, reduce the natural resources that organizations consume, and innovate sustainable services, companies can lead the growing green economy. In tandem, stakeholder theory and the resource-based view (RBV), offer a holistic perspective on the fabric of organizational strategy in terms of adopting AI and corporate sustainability strategy. While stakeholder theory focuses on the external ethical responsibility and stakeholder alignment; the RBV incorporates internal organizational capabilities to drive sustained competitive advantage. Together, these frameworks illustrate how AI enables organizations to satisfy changing stakeholder requirements and contribute to competitive success in the long term; by embedding sustainability throughout the organization and its value creation process.

## 2.4 Artificial Intelligence and Its Impact on Environmental Awareness

The influence of Artificial Intelligence (AI) on environmental awareness and understanding can be illustrated through communication theory (theory of communication) and behavioral economics. One framework that fits with communication theory is Roger's (2013) Diffusion of Innovations framework, which outlines how a new idea or technology spreads throughout a social system. AI-enabled tools, such as mobile applications, smart devices, and interactive data visualization platforms, help spread environmental knowledge. In the case of information about environmental impacts, AI allows for clear translation of sophisticated environmental data to the public. This can expand understanding and engagement with a larger segments of the public, and build environmental literacy. For example, an AI-enabled platform may monitor air quality or water pollution, track rates of deforestation, predict climate-related events, and highlight users' insights into sustainable consumption behaviors. It was previously mentioned that such platforms make scientific information more public-facing and shape public perceptions by tracking real-time, local environmental impacts and presenting the data intuitively and effectively (Rolnick et al., 2022). Greenwashing poses a significant challenge to sustainable development by undermining transparency and consumer trust. Recent studies show that misleading environmental claims negatively affect consumer attitudes and reduce genuine green purchasing (Gupta & Singh, 2024a, 2024b, 2024c). Additionally, greenwashed word of mouth can distort consumer behavior, hindering progress toward responsible consumption goals (Singh, Gupta, & Kapur, 2022). Addressing greenwashing is therefore crucial for advancing authentic sustainability practices.

Used effectively, this technology could promote the diffusion of environmentally responsible and willing to change behaviors and help develop a shared conception of ecological conditions. From a behavioral economics perspective, the best example of how AI can play a role in environmental sustainability may be in how it informs practical decision making, and fosters behavior change. Using Thaler and Sunstein (2009) as a basis for our understanding, we can think of AI technologies as "choice architects" that can employ personalized feedback, small nudges, and behavioral cues to steer humans towards more environmentally friendly actions. For example, AI-enabled systems can:

- Generate alerts in real-time if energy or water usage is excessive;
- Suggest green products depending on the user's consumption patterns; and
- Track and reward sustainable actions such as recycling or using public transport.

Such characteristics draw on behavioral economics principles - such as defaults, framing, and reinforcement - so that sustainable choices are easier, more attractive, and more similar to the values and habits of users. For individuals and organizations, these tools can ultimately change consumption patterns, minimize waste, stimulate efficiency incentives, and provide pathways for more environmentally responsible behaviours over time. By drawing on both communication theory and behavioral economics, we see that AI raises awareness about environmental issues and encourages real behavioural change. AI technology promotes two processes: informing stakeholders and shaping behaviour, and enables stakeholders to be more active in sustainability as an individual and a community. So, AI is a powerful enabler of environmental stewardship, and enables more informed, deliberate, and sustainable interactions with nature.

The earlier studies reviewed about the role of Artificial Intelligence (AI) in Sustainable Development and Environmental Sciences used systematic review methods, which help to identify gaps in research and develop a broader picture of the field (Gupta & Singh, 2024). This study has a systematic approach, starting with searching relevant research articles published between 2008 and 2024 from the Scopus-indexed database using the keywords “sustainable development” and “artificial intelligence”. After adding exclusion and inclusion criteria for article selection according to this study protocol (see table 2), 32 articles were chosen for full analysis. A data classification sheet was developed to facilitate a systematic assessment of the key characteristics of the studies that we coded logically, so the literature could be synthesized and categorized. Ultimately, this coding can structure the extant knowledge and lead to a meaningful articulation of evidence needs to close the significant literature gaps for further research on AI, sustainable development and environmental sciences.

*Figure 1. The Procedure Followed in Selecting the Research Article for the Study.*

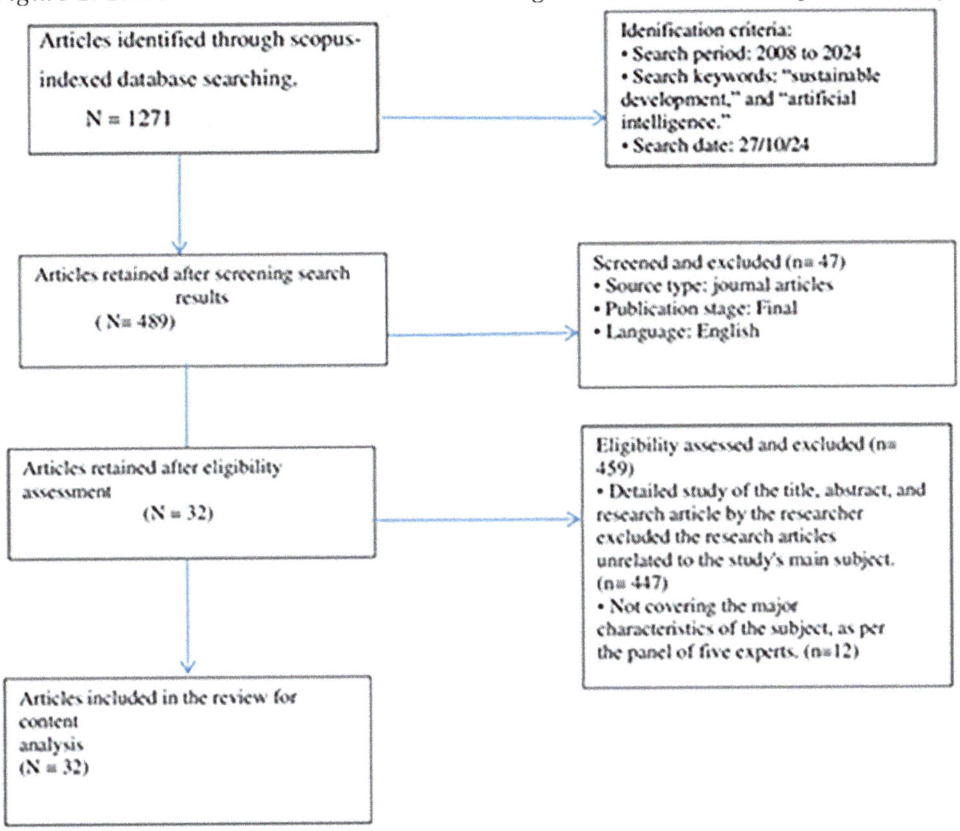


The selection of the research articles is represented in Figure 1. Initially, 1,271 articles were sourced from the Scopus-indexed database using the keywords "AI in Sustainable Development" and "AI in Environmental Sciences." Upon screening relevance, 32 articles were directly related to Sustainable Development practices, environment conservation and relevant to the application of AI in environmental sustainability. In other buttons, 447 articles were excluded from the study as they were irrelevant to the core focus of the topic of research. This selection process ensured that the final analysis focused on studies that would be suitable, relevant, and significant in a focused manner in terms of AI's contribution to sustainable development and environmental development.

*Table 1. Categories for Classification and Coding in this Research Chapter*

| CATEGORY | MEANING | CODES FOR ALTERNATIVES |
|---|---|---|
| 1 | CONTEXT | T. Studies done in Developed Countries<br>U. Studies done in Developing Countries<br>V. Non-Applicable |
| 2 | GEOGRAPHIC REGION | T. Europe<br>U. Asia<br>V. North America<br>W. South America<br>X. Africa<br>Y. Australia<br>Z. Others |
| 3 | TIME PERIOD | T. Till 2015<br>U. 2016-2017<br>V. 2018-2019<br>W. 2020-2021<br>X. 2022-2023<br>Y. 2023 – Till date |
| 4 | MAIN SUBJECT | T. Sustainable development<br>U. Artificial Intelligence<br>V. Environmental Sciences<br>W. Others |
| 5. | METHOD | T. Qualitative<br>U. Quantitative<br>V. Case Study<br>W. Others |
| 6 | SAMPLE SIZE | T. Less than 250 or 250<br>U. 251-500<br>V. 501-750<br>W. More than 751<br>X. Non- Applicable |
| 7 | TOPICS | T. Sustainable Development<br>U. Sustainability and Environmental Impact<br>V. Use and Impact of AI in Environmental Sciences<br>W. Sustainable practices<br>X. Sustainability Reporting<br>Y. Role of AI in Corporate Sustainability<br>Z. Others |

Following a close examination of the collection of articles selected for the review, a classification scheme was generated based on the main characteristics located in the literature. A classification scheme is included in table 1. The classification encompasses seven categories with logical codes - T, U, V, W, X, etc. Each article can be coded with multiple codes with a particular category if it had relevant aspects.

The first classification distinguishes the context of each study, and it is coded T for developed countries; U for developing countries; and V for other contexts. Understanding this context is important since it clarifies what geographical part of the world most studies have occurred in and where more studies could be conducted. The “others” or “not applicable” applies to studies that do not examine either developed, or developing countries.

The second classification refers to geographic location of the research and allocated the following codes: T for Europe, U for Asia, V for North America, W for South America, X for Africa, Y for Australia and Z for anywhere else that did not fall into any of these categories.

The third classification indicates the years of the study period, roughly from 2008 -2024. T through Z are to represent years in the period of time(seconds) the known range/year of research articles.

The fourth classification identifies the major topics under the research articles. T is the code for Sustainable Development, U for Artificial Intelligence, and V for Environmental Sciences.

The fifth classification covers the research methods used, with codes T for qualitative studies, U for quantitative studies, V for case studies, and W for other research methods. This classification specifies what research methods are evident within the studies focusing on AI in Sustainable Development and Environmental Sciences.

The sixth classification covers the sample size in each study, T, U, V, W, and X cover each sample size as indicators of sample size. The sample size is vitally important to the validity of research in that a smaller sample can limit reliability and variability with larger samples being richer and more reliable but also more intricate and needs more resources to manage.

The seventh classification specifies the primary subjects into more targeted subtopics with codes T-Z. Detailed classifications are a useful way to show us the 'areas of focus' within the larger main subject areas. This also allows you to recognize what research areas have been well researched and have ample sources and data. It also allows you to identify research subtopics that do not sufficiently develop any sources, data, or research.

## 3. RESEARCH METHODOLOGY

*Table 2. Classification and Categorization of each research article for the study*

| Context | Geographical Region | Time Period | Main Subject | Method | Sample Size | Topic |
|---|---|---|---|---|---|---|
| ‘T’<br>‘T’<br>‘T’ | ‘V’<br>‘Y’<br>‘U’ | ‘T’’<br>‘T’<br>‘Y’ | ‘T’<br>‘V’<br>‘T’ | ‘V’<br>‘U’<br>‘U’ | ‘X’<br>‘X’<br>‘X’ | ‘U’<br>‘V’<br>‘W’ |
| ‘T’ | ‘V’ | ‘W’ | ‘T’ | ‘U’ | ‘X’ | ‘W’ |
| ‘U’ | ‘W’ | ‘Y’ | ‘T’ | ‘T’ | ‘X’ | ‘W’ |
| T’ | ‘U’ | ‘Y’ | ‘T’, ‘V’ | ‘T’ | ‘T’ | ‘U’ |
| ‘T’ | ‘U’ | ‘Y’ | ‘U’, ‘V’ | ‘U’ | ‘X’ | ‘V’ |
| ‘T’ | ‘V’ | ‘X’ | ‘V’ | ‘U’ | ‘X’ | ‘U’ |
| ‘T’ | ‘U’ | ‘Y’ | ‘T’ | ‘W’ | ‘X’ | ‘T’ |
| ‘V’ | ‘Z’ | ‘Y’ | ‘T’ | ‘W’ | ‘X’ | ‘T’ |
| ‘U’ | ‘U’ | ‘Y’ | ‘T’ | ‘W’ | ‘W’ | ‘X’ |
| ‘T’ | ‘V’ | ‘X’ | ‘V’ | ‘T’ | ‘X’ | ‘V’ |
| ‘T’ | ‘V’ | ‘Y’ | ‘V’ | ‘W’ | ‘V’ | ‘V’ |
| ‘U’ | ‘U’ | ‘Y’ | ‘V’ | ‘T’ | ‘X’ | ‘V’ |
| ‘U’ | ‘U’’ | ‘X’ | ‘T’, ‘U’ | ‘T’ | ‘X’ | ‘Y’ |
| ‘T’ | ‘T’ | ‘Y’ | ‘V’ | ‘W’ | ‘X’ | ‘U’ |
| ‘T’ | ‘T’ | ‘Y’ | ‘V’ | ‘U’ | ‘X’ | ‘V’ |
| ‘U’<br>‘T’ | ‘X’ | ‘Y’ | ‘V’ | ‘U’ | ‘X’ | ‘V’ |
| | ‘U’ | ‘Y’ | ‘V’ | ‘W’ | ‘X’ | ‘U’ |
| ‘T’ | ‘T’ | ‘Y’ | ‘U’ | ‘W’ | ‘X’ | ‘Y’ |
| ‘T’ | ‘T’ | ‘W’ | ‘U’ | ‘W’ | ‘X’ | ‘V’ |
| ‘T’ | ‘T’ | ‘Y’ | ‘U’ | ‘W’ | ‘W’ | ‘V’ |
| ‘U’ | ‘U’ | ‘W’ | ‘U’ | ‘W’ | ‘X’ | ‘V’ |
| ‘T’ | ‘T’ | ‘W’ | ‘V’ | ‘U’ | ‘X’ | ‘U’ |
| ‘T’ | ‘U’ | ‘Y’ | ‘V’ | ‘W’ | ‘X’ | ‘U’ |
| ‘T’ | ‘U’ | ‘X’ | ‘V’ | ‘W’ | ‘X’ | ‘V’ |
| ‘T’ | ‘U’ | ‘Y’ | ‘T’ | ‘W’ | ‘W’ | ‘W’ |
| ‘T’ | ‘U’ | ‘V’ | ‘T’ | ‘U’ | ‘X’ | ‘T’ |
| ‘T’ | ‘U’ | ‘Y’ | ‘U’ | ‘W’ | ‘X’ | ‘U’,’Y’ |
| ‘U’ | ‘W’ | ’Y’ | ‘V’ | ‘W’ | ‘T’ | ‘U’ |
| ‘U’ | ‘U’ | ‘Y’ | ‘V’ | ‘T’ | ‘X’ | ‘V’ |
| ‘U’ | ‘W’ | ‘X’ | ‘T’ | ‘T’ | ‘X’ | ‘T’ |
| | | | | | | |

Source: Authors’ compilation.

This type of extended classification will allow for better examination of research themes and gaps by extending the main subject classification to detailed subtopic classification. These classifications and coding as shown in (table 2), combined as an organized framework for collecting and organizing the literature, will provide a way to comprehensively analyze the research that has been conducted to date, and help guide papers for future research.

## 4. RESULTS AND DISCUSSION

*Figure 2. The Context of Studies Analyzed. Source: Authors' compilation. Categories: T-studies done in developed countries*

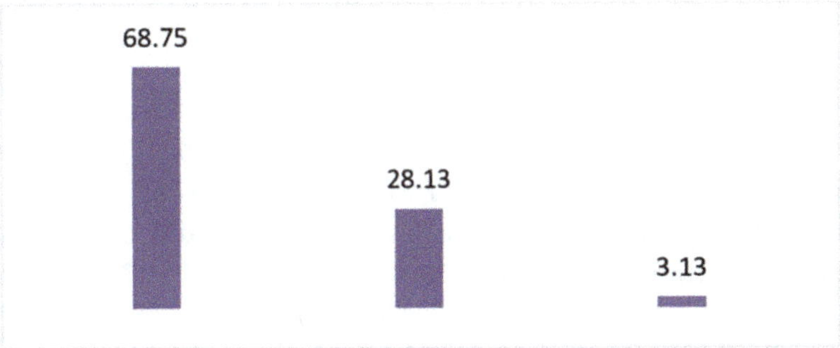


**Figure 2 shows the first categorization of studies by geographical context. For the studies to be categorized, we used the following codes - T for studies from developed countries, Q for studies from developing countries and R for studies from other or undefined contexts. After examining the 32 studies included in this review, we found an overwhelming majority of studies from T developed countries, with 68.75% of studies in developed countries (T), compared to 28.13% of studies in developing countries (Q) and only 3.13% of studies in 'other contexts' (R). This analysis indicates that there is a large geographical imbalance in the literature pertaining to climate change adaptation in the built environment, with the preponderance of studies appearing in developed countries and very few in developing countries identifying a significant knowledge gap for future studies.**

*Figure 3. The Geographic Region in the Studies Analyzed. Source: Authors' compilation. Categories: T-Europe, U-Asia, V-NorthAmerica, W-SouthAmerica, X-Africa, Y-Australia, and Z-others.*

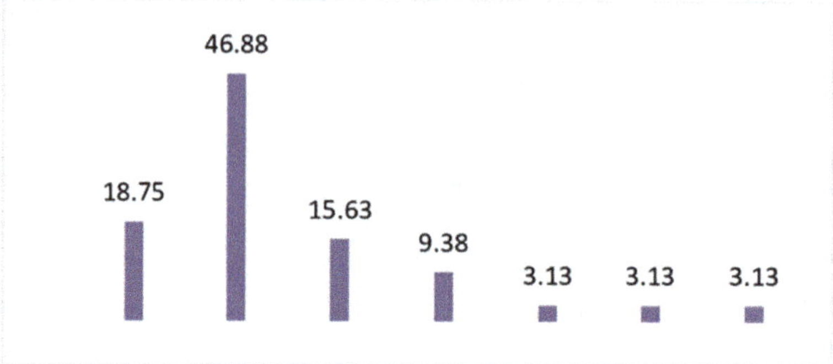


**Figure 3 shows a second classification describing the locations of the studies. The studies were coded as follows: T for Europe, U for Asia, V for North America, W for South America, X for Africa, Y for Australia, and Z for other regions not included in the categories above. The distribution of the 32 research articles in Fig. 5 indicates that the most studies (46.88%) were conducted in Asia (the highest geographical response). Europe had the second highest representation (18.75%), and North America had the third (15.63%). The proportion of studies completed in South America (9.38%), Africa (3.13%), and Australia (3.13%) was significantly lower. Additionally, 3.13% of the studies were conducted in other geographical locations not stated above. These results imply that there is a regional cluster of research in Asia and that there are comparatively fewer studies from the other continents, indicating that less researched regions of the world may be areas for future research.**

*Figure 4.* **Source: Authors' Compilation. Categories: T-till 2015, U-2016-2017, V-2018-2019, W-2020-2021, X-2022-2023, and Y-2023 till date.**

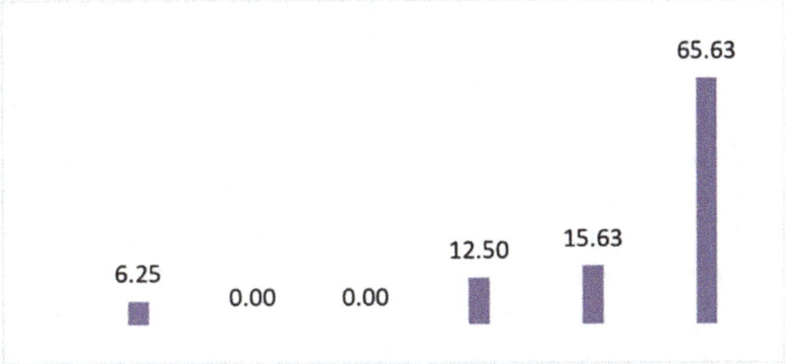


**The third classification is illustrated in Figure 4 which sites the studies based on their duration. The studies, which reflect older times periods were rated from T, which is like up to 2015, U for 2016-2017, V for 2018-2019, W for 2020-2021, X for 2022-2023, and Y for 2023 to date. The findings are presented on Fig. 6. The findings indicate that the vast majority of studies (65.63%) are undertaken during 2023 to date, which shows how topical this research field is becoming. Other studies are categorized by (15.63%) 2022-2023, (12.50%) 2020-2021; 2021-221—6.25%. The finding indicates that there has been a demonstrated existing scholarly interest in research on the topic in recent years as not only a limited number of studies existed prior, but an increase happened in subsequent years.**

*Figure 5.* **Source: Authors' compilation. Categories: T-Sustainable development, U-Artificial Intelligence, and V-Environmental Science**

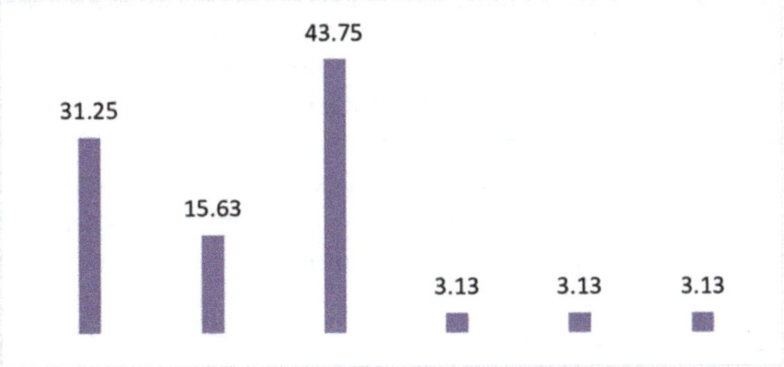

Figure 5 displays the fourth classification by identifying research articles based on their prevailing substantive topics. The codes assigned include T for Sustainable Development, U for Artificial Intelligence, and V for Environmental Sciences. In context of the data illustrated in Fig. 7, the greatest percentage of studies are under the category of Environmental Sciences (43.75%), making it the most researched topic, followed by Sustainable Development studies (31.25%), and studies on Artificial Intelligence (15.63%). Some articles in the research dealt with intersections of these topics, including Sustainable Development practices placed within Environmental Sciences (3.13%), AI usage in Sustainable Development practices (3.13%), and AI usage in Environmental Sciences (3.13%). The large percentage in Environmental Sciences indicates some meaning there is something significant taking place, however the percentages also suggest underlying emerging topics of research on AI and sustainability practices.

*Figure 6. Source: Authors' Compilation. Categories: T-qualitative, U-quantitative, V-case study, and W-others.*

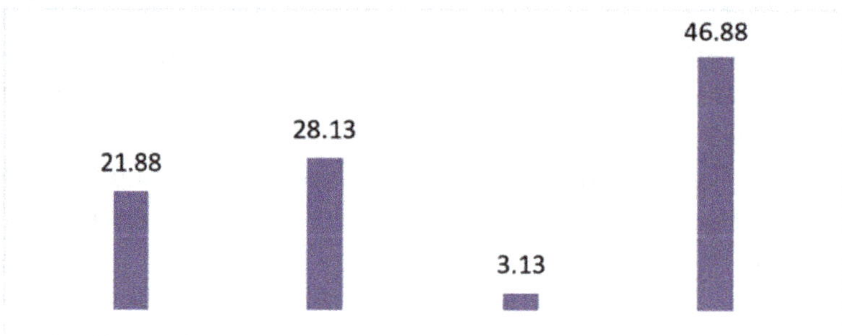


Figure 6 illustrates the fifth classification of attributes of the magnitude, as a classification, of the research methodologies chosen by the authors of the studies we reviewed. The employed methodological lettering system is as follows: T for Qualitative means, U for Quantitative means, V for Case studies, W for Other means. As depicted visually in Fig. 8, the questionnaires we used to classify the reviewed studies in terms of methodologies show very clear differences among the research designs used. Only 3.13% of studies, used 'case study' approaches suggesting the 'case study' approach is rarely used in the current research. In the dividing of qualitative and quantitative research, there is a greater proportion of authors reuse quantitative means (28.13%) rather than qualitative, (21.88%) studies. However, the majority of authors, plus the detailed methodology, used other methodologies like literature reviews, conceptual analyses, or mixed method. Overall, authors do not tend to restrict to traditional use of empirical research designs, which was good to see. This indicates there is opportunity for more methodology diversity in the form of case studies which may help to inform practice in the area.

*Figure 7.* Source: Authors' compilation. Categories: T-less than 250 or 250, U-251-500, V-501-750, W-more than 750, and X- non-applicable.

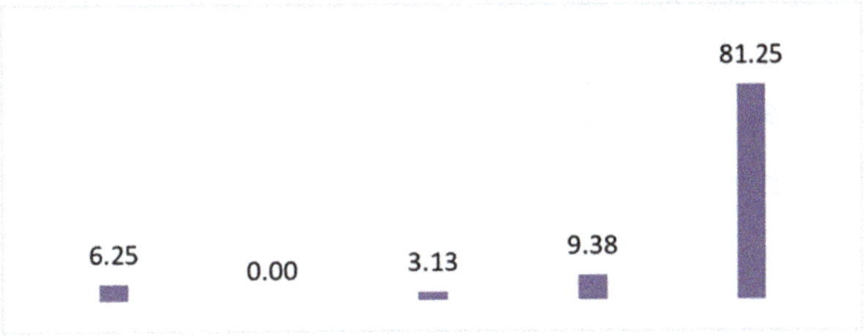


Figure 7 shows the sixth categorization, in which papers are classified best on their sample size. The coding structure is shown: T for sample sizes with 250 or fewer; U for sample sizes of 251-500; V for sample sizes of 501-750; W for sample sizes of more than 751; and X for non-applicable cases (theoretical studies; review papers; etc . without defined samples). Among the papers with a defined sample size, a majority were preferable to large sample sizes, with 9.38% of studies using more than 751 participants or data points. There were just slightly smaller sample sizes than 250, at 6.25% followed closely by 501-750 samples, at 3.13%. The results indicate some level of preference for the larger sample sizes where possible, however much research remains that uses smaller samples or does not identify sample size, highlighting differences in scale and approach.

*Figure 8. Source: Authors' compilations. Categories: T-sustainable development, U-sustainable development and environmental impact, V- use and impat of AI in environmental sciences, W- sustainable practices, X- online retail policies, Y- sustainable development reporting, and Z-others.*

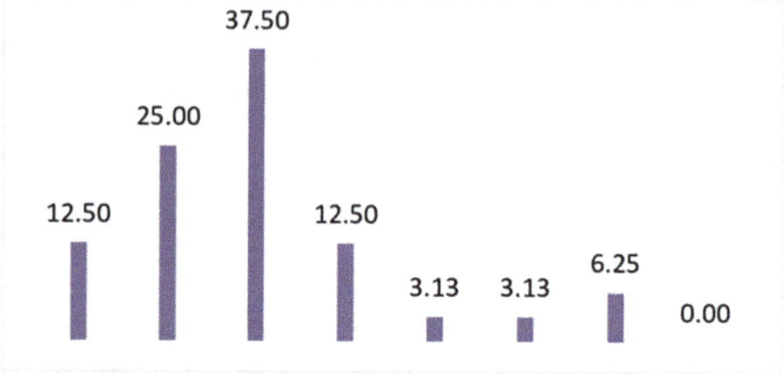


In Figure 8, the seventh classification shows the reviewed studies and their respective topics. The codes are: T - Sustainable Development, U - Sustainable Development and Environmental Impact, V - Use and Impact of AI in Environmental Sciences, W - Sustainable Practices, X - Sustainable Development Reporting, Y - AI and Corporate Sustainable Development, Z - Miscellaneous Topics. As shown in Fig. 10, the majority of the literature was on Use and Impact of AI in Environmental Sciences (37.50% of all studies), which was followed by literature on Sustainable Development and Environmental Impact (25%).

There were also a moderate number of studies on Sustainable Development (12.50%) and Sustainable Practices (12.50%). However, there are quite a few theme gaps. Specifically, 3.13% of studies addressed Sustainable Development Reporting, and an equal proportion (3.13%) discussed the Role of AI in Corporate Sustainable Development and Environmental Protection. Furthermore, very few studies investigated the effects of AI in Corporate Sustainable Development Practices.

These findings imply a concentration of research in environmental and AI applications; however, there are considerable gaps in corporate focussed sustainability themes and Sustainable Development Reporting practices. This means there are important new avenues for future research.

## 5. CONCLUSION

This systematic review analyzed peer-reviewed articles from 2008 to 2024, and all articles were obtained from Scopus indexed database. The search used the keywords "Artificial Intelligence in Sustainable Development and Environmental Sciences" in a focused effort to examine emerging technologies particularly artificial intelligence and its relationship with sustainability related disciplines. After a comprehensive screening and selection process, thirty-two peer-reviewed research articles were discovered and reviewed. The review found a significant pattern in that most of the research in terms of volume and scope, was found primarily in the developed world. This suggests an imbalance in the distribution of academia and resources in an effort to fully study AI in sustainable development and environmental sciences; thus, suggesting there is a disparity in both awareness and implementation capabilities, geographically. The selected articles were systematically analyzed using a coding framework that contained eight thematic classifications and allowed each selected article to be coded by focus, research approach used, application area and article outcomes. From the coding framework patterns were identified in the literature and gaps were identified in each of the eight thematic categories.

As outlined above, there are four primary gaps in the literature, and they represent areas where both academicians and practitioners can push for both action and contribution; there is also room for further research and development opportunities for AI for the environment and sustainable development. The first gap is the lack of studies on developing nations; while developed countries are pursuing opportunities for employing AI across environmental monitoring, climate modeling, management of natural and other resources, and sustainability assessments, these areas of application are largely unexplored in the context of developing economies. This imbalance is concerning given that many developing countries endure serious environmental issues such as deforestation, disposal of waste, air, and water pollution, and the effects of climate change. Additionally, the ways in which AI can assist countries in resource optimization, policy development, and disaster preparedness is mostly untested in these regions. Future studies need to consider closing this gap, which may involve undertaking case studies that are located, conducting analyses that are region-specific and conducting assessments of AI within local contexts, particularly around sustainable development in the Global South. Another significant gap is the lack of diversity in approaches to research; many studies are based on qualitative methods or conceptual discussions without any empirical research/validation. Although these contributions are important, they often do not possess the infusion of rigor and repeatability that would allow for conclusions useful for action. There is an urgent need for future studies to employ a diversity of methods including:

- Quantitative analysis with large-scale datasets
- Experimental designs that test effectiveness of AI tools in situ
- Comparative case studies across regions and sectors
- Longitudinal degree studies of the long-term effects of AI on AI trajectories

Researchers can strengthen the credibility, depth, and generalizability of their data, providing a more robust evidence base for others. Many of the studies you have read in the literature are limited by small sample size and lack of strong empirical evidence. These problems reduce the statistical power and generalizability of their conclusions and hinder the development of best practices that can be used on a larger scale between jurisdictions or sectors.

Future research should:

- Utilize large and diverse datasets, potentially by partnering with government agencies, environmental non-profits or open-data sites.
- Use cutting-edge AI techniques, e.g. machine learning, big data analysis, for identifying hidden patterns and relationships in environmental phenomena.
- Develop standardized evaluation metrics to enable comparisons between studies.

Developing the empirical basis for research in this area will help to create more robust evidence-based policies and AI driven tools for sustainability.

The final gap is due to the limited study of AI in corporate sustainable development and environmental protection. Some studies investigate AI in the public sector or even in scientific contexts, but too few studies look at how businesses are adopting AI into their sustainability reporting, environmental impact mitigation, supply chain management, or corporate social responsibility (CSR). There is significant attention being paid to Environmental, Social, and Governance (ESG) criteria as well as sustainability-driven models of corporate behaviour, thus, it is vital to research how AI can:

- Enhance corporate sustainability strategies
- Support real-time environmental monitoring and reporting
- Improve resource efficiency and reduce carbon footprints
- Facilitate compliance with international environmental standards

Investigating this synergy could have the capacity to fill technology, business, and sustainability gaps to provide better, larger scale environmental options for the private sector.

## Future Directions

The results of this study indicate that there is much work to do to fill four research gaps, which need to be addressed in order to advance the body of knowledge about AI for sustainable development and the environmental sciences. By placing attention on less researched areas, making advancements in method, increasing empirical evidence, and examining corporate sustainability initiatives, future studies can build upon and add to current bodies of knowledge. Furthermore, filling the gaps not only strengthens academic knowledge but also secures more responsible, just, and inventive uses of AI, addressing some of the most serious environmental issues of our time. It will also contribute to the global trend toward sustainable development and environmental care, which is seen as part of inclusive economic growth, through international accords such as the United Nations Sustainable Development Goals (SDGs).

## REFERENCES


Barney, J. (1991). Firm resources and sustained competitive advantage. *Journal of Management, 17*(1), 99–120.

Batty, M. (2018). *Inventing future cities*. MIT Press.

Bender, E. M., Gebru, T., McMillan-Major, A., & Shmitchell, S. (2021). On the dangers of stochastic parrots: Can language models be too big? *Proceedings of the 2021 ACM Conference on Fairness, Accountability, and Transparency*, 610–623. https://doi.org/DOI: 10.1145/3442188.3445922

Brynjolfsson, E., & McAfee, A. (2014). The second machine age: Work, progress, and prosperity in a time of brilliant technologies. WW Norton & company.

Dhar, N., & Mallick, B. (2025). *Re-thinking posthumanism across the global south: An introduction*. https://doi.org/DOI: 10.3726/b22159

Esteva, A., Kuprel, B., Novoa, R. A., Ko, J., Swetter, S. M., Blau, H. M., & Thrun, S. (2017). Dermatologist-level classification of skin cancer with deep neural networks. *Nature, 542*(7639), 115–118. DOI: 10.1038/nature21056 PMID: 28117445

Floridi, L., Cowls, J., Beltrametti, M., Chatila, R., Chazerand, P., Dignum, V., & Vayena, E. (2018). AI4People—an ethical framework for a good AI society: Opportunities, risks, principles, and recommendations. *Minds and Machines, 28*, 689–707. PMID: 30930541

Freeman, R. E. (1984). *Strategic management: A stakeholder approach*. Pitman.

Gupta, K., & Singh, N. (2024a). A systematic review of literature on greenwashing. Sustainability Development through Green Economics, 114, 75–90. https://doi.org/DOI: 10.1108/S1569-375920240000114005

Gupta, K., & Singh, N. (2024b). Greenwashing perception and attitude–intention relationship towards green product purchase: A mediating model. *Environment, Development and Sustainability*, •••, 1–24. DOI: 10.1007/s10668-024-05486-5

Gupta, K., & Singh, N. (2024c). Visualization of global research trends and future research directions of greenwashing by using bibliometric analysis. *Environment, Development and Sustainability*, •••, 1–21. DOI: 10.1007/s10668-024-04548-y

Gupta, S., & Singh, A. (2024). Importance of Artificial Intelligence in Achieving SDGs in India. *International Journal of Built Environment and Sustainability, 11*(2), 1–26. DOI: 10.11113/ijbes.v11.n2.1193

Hodge, B.-M. A., Palchak, D., Ela, E., & Milligan, M. (2020). Wind and solar integration in the US power system: Operational practices, challenges, and opportunities. Current Sustainable/Renewable. *Energy Reports*, *7*, 1–10. DOI: 10.1007/s40518-020-00146-6

Kamilaris, A., & Prenafeta-Boldú, F. X. (2018). Deep learning in agriculture: A survey. *Computers and Electronics in Agriculture*, *147*, 70–90. DOI: 10.1016/j.compag.2018.02.016

Meadows, D. H. (2008). *Thinking in systems: A primer*. Chelsea Green Publishing.

Mol, A. P., & Spaargaren, G. (2000). Ecological modernisation theory in debate:A review. *Environmental Politics*, *9*(1), 17–49.

Mutambara, A. G. O. (2025). *Artificial intelligence: A driver of inclusive development and shared prosperity for the global south*. https://doi.org/DOI: 10.1201/9781003511014

Nguyen, H. T., Nguyen, T. V., & Tran, T. D. (2020). Artificial intelligence in renewable energy systems. *Energy Reports*, *6*, 265–273. DOI: 10.1016/j.egyr.2020.11.156

Reuters. (2023). *Tech companies' indirect emissions rise 150% amid AI infrastructure growth*. https://www.reuters.com/sustainability/climate-energy/tech-giants-indirect-emissions-rose-150-three-years-ai-expands-un-agency-says-2025-06-05/

Rolnick, D., Donti, P. L., Kaack, L. H., Kochanski, K., Lacoste, A., Sankaran, K., & Bengio, Y. (2022). Tackling climate change with machine learning. *ACM Computing Surveys*, *55*(2), 1–96.

Russell, S. J., & Norvig, P. (2020). *Artificial intelligence: A modern approach* (4th ed.). Pearson.

Singh, N., Gupta, K., & Kapur, B. (2022). Greenwashed word of mouth (GWWOM): A vibrant influence on customer green behaviour. *Journal of Global Responsibility*, *13*(4), 472–487. DOI: 10.1108/JGR-11-2021-0094

Strubell, E., Ganesh, A., & McCallum, A. (2019). Energy and policy considerations for deep learning in NLP. *Proceedings of the 57th Annual Meeting of the Association for Computational Linguistics*, 3645–3650. https://doi.org/DOI: 10.18653/v1/P19-1355

Thaler, R. H., & Sunstein, C. R. (2009). *Nudge: Improving decisions about health, wealth, and happiness*. Penguin.

UNESCO. (2021). Recommendation on the ethics of artificial intelligence. United Nations Educational, Scientific and Cultural Organization. https://unesdoc.unesco.org/ark:/48223/pf0000381137

United Nations. (2015). Transforming our world: The 2030 Agenda for Sustainable Development. https://sdgs.un.org/2030agenda

Vinuesa, R., Azizpour, H., Leite, I., Balaam, M., Dignum, V., Domisch, S., & Nerini, F. F. (2020). The role of artificial intelligence in achieving the Sustainable Development Goals. *Nature Communications*, *11*(1), 233. PMID: 31932590

Zhang, J., Fan, R., & Shen, F. (2023, December). Introducing Automatic Verification Strategy in Online Study of Computational Science. In *2023 International Conference on Computational Science and Computational Intelligence (CSCI)* (pp. 1708-1713). IEEE.

# Chapter 6
# Exploration of Green Innovation Technology Adoption to Accelerate Sustainable Development in the Manufacturing Industry

**Suriya Ponnambalam**
https://orcid.org/0000-0002-8775-0474
*Bharath Institute of Higher Education and Research, India*

**M. K. Ilampoornan**
https://orcid.org/0000-0002-6233-8141
*Bharath Institute of Higher Education and Research, India*

## ABSTRACT

*This chapter discusses importance of integrating green innovation technology within the manufacturing industry to foster development. It emphasizes that such technologies can reduce environmental impacts, enhance resource efficiency, and contribute to regulatory compliance. Key themes include the drivers for adopting green innovations, such as competitive advantage, consumer demand for sustainable practices, and the need for cooperate social responsibility. This chapter argues that businesses that embrace these innovations can achieve sustainability goals while also achieve economic benefits, improved brand reputation, and long-term sustainability goals but also achieve economic benefits, improved brand reputation,*

DOI: 10.4018/979-8-3373-7584-7.ch006

*and long-term viability. By presenting case studies and practical examples, the chapter illustrates successful implementation of green technology in manufacturing processes, highlighting the potential for both environmental and economic gains.*

## 1. INTRODUCTION

The manufacturing industry plays a pivotal role in economic development, but its operations often come at the cost of environmental degradation. With increasing global pressure to mitigate climate change and resource depletion, there is a pressing need for industries to adopt sustainable practices. One promising pathway to achieving this balance is through the adoption of Green Innovation Technology (GIT)—innovations that promote both environmental sustainability and operational efficiency.

*Research Problem:* Despite the growing awareness of sustainability challenges, the adoption of green innovation in the manufacturing sector remains inconsistent and slow in many regions. Manufacturers face a range of barriers, including technological limitations, regulatory uncertainties, and economic constraints, which hinder the widespread implementation of GIT.

*Objective and Scope:* This chapter aims to explore the key drivers, influencing factors, and strategic frameworks that facilitate the adoption of green innovation technologies in the manufacturing sector. Specifically, it seeks to:

- Examine the regulatory, technical, and economic enablers of GIT.
- Analyze the role of innovation models and acceptance frameworks (such as TAM, EA-TAM, and UTAUT) in shaping green technology adoption.
- Identify strategies that accelerate sustainable development through innovation-led practices.
- The chapter adopts a literature-based conceptual exploration, drawing on empirical studies and theoretical models from both developed and emerging economies.

The chapter begins with a critical literature survey that synthesizes key themes in GIT research. It then examines factors influencing adoption, characteristics of effective green innovation strategies, and the relevance of various technology acceptance models. Later sections address corporate environmental responsibility, policy implications, and the mediating role of green behavior and innovation in sustainable development. The chapter concludes with recommendations and future research directions.

The adoption of green innovation technology (GIT) has occurred as a grave strategy designed for the manufacturing production to achieve sustainable development (SD). This exploration delves into the key drivers, strategies, and mechanisms that facilitate the adoption of GIT, drawing insights from various studies to deliver a thorough analysis of its function in accelerating SD. (Shahzad et al., 2022) develops a GIA model based on UTAUT, identifying constructs like performance expectancy and facilitating conditions that predict green behavioral intention, crucial for adopting green technologies in manufacturing to enhance sustainable development. (Mukhtar et al., 2024) reveals that comprehensive green technology adoption plays a crucial role in enhancing the sustainability performance of Malaysian manufacturing companies, with innovation capabilities positively moderating this relationship, thereby facilitating accelerated sustainable development within the industry.(Nzomo et al., 2023) highlights that green innovation strategies, including green products and processes, are essential for act sustainability inManufacturing firms certified under ISO 14001. However, a flexible regulatory framework is crucial to enhance the adoption of these innovations for sustainable development.(Fratta et al., 2024) discusses a Green Innovation Practice (GIP) for introducing low-emission inorganic binders in ferrous foundries, addressing pollution from organic binders. This approach aims to facilitatethe integration of green technology solutions, promoting sustainable development in the manufacturing division.(Yang, B. 2024) highlights that adopting a green technology innovation (GTI) strategy significantly enhances sustainable development in manufacturing, improving financial performance by about 20% and reducing environmental costs by approximately 21%, thus promoting operational productivity and environmental responsibility.

## 2. LITERATURE SURVEY

(Gupta, A. 2024) emphasizes that investing in green technology offers environmental benefits, cost savings, and regulatory compliance, thereby accelerating sustainable development in manufacturing. It highlights that such investments, combined with rework processes, enhance profitability and reduce carbon emissions significantly.(Omar et al.,2024) highlights that green manufacturing practices (GMGP) positively influence corporate sustainable performance (CSPR) through green innovation (GIN), suggesting that adopting GIN is crucial for manufacturing SMEs to enhance sustainability and achieve development goals successfully.(Mukhtar et al., 2023) emphasizes that green technology revolution is crucial for enhancing the sustainability outcomes of the Malaysian solar PV manufacturing sector, for which a conceptual framework is proposed to explore this relationship and suggesting that such innovations can accelerate sustainable development in manufacturing.According to Cheng et al. (2023), green process innovation and enhanced green productivity play a pivotal role in promoting sustainability within the cement and plastic industries of Pakistan and India, underlining the importance of environmental consciousness in facilitating sustainable development via technology adoption.

(Khakwani et al.,2024) highlights that green product innovation, digital transformation combined with eco-friendly manufacturing methods markedly contributes to improved organizational performance and sustainability in the manufacturing industry, emphasizing the importance of adopting environmentally-friendly technologies for sustainable development.According to Wang M. (2024), digital innovation is essential for implementing environmentally friendly production technologies, improving manufacturing efficiency, and minimizing both energy use and waste, and enhancing product and service innovation, ultimately accelerating sustainable development in the manufacturing industry amidst environmental challenges and resource shortages.(Shaban et al., 2024) highlights that green dynamic capabilities significantly influence Sustainable development in manufacturing companies is driven by green innovation, while environmental regulations influence and support the implementation of green innovation technologies to address sustainability challenges effectively.

(Lutfi et al., 2023) highlights that green innovation technologies are essential for manufacturing companies to improve their environmental outcomes and attain sustainable development goals.It identifies factors influencing adoption, including perceived benefits, top management support, and various pressures, emphasizing their role in promoting green practices.(Siyal et al., 2023) highlights thatTechnological compatibility, combined with institutional forces and the shift toward green transformation, drives green innovation adoption in manufacturing. This alignment enhances sustainability efforts, promoting ecological practices and carbon neutrality, ultimately accelerating sustainable development within the industry.Li et al. (2023) examine the impact of green innovation strategies—such as green process and product innovations—on sustainable performance in manufacturing, highlighting how green product innovation mediates this relationship and how employees' environmentally friendly behavior acts as a moderating factor. (Popoola et al., 2024) highlights that demand-pull factors, regulations, and organizational innovation significantly influence eco-innovation adoption in Nigeria's manufacturing sector, suggesting that awareness campaigns and partnerships can accelerate sustainable development through enhanced adoption of green technologies.(Ashraf et al., 2024) highlights thatGreen business strategies as well as capabilities play a vital role in strengthening green innovation within manufacturing firms, contributing to sustainable development. Value co-creation and absorptive ability are crucial for generating innovation and improving business performance in an environmentally conscious society.

Zhang et al. (2024) emphasize that the utilization of smart product platforms strongly promotes green technological innovation in the automotive manufacturing sector, with corporate innovation investment fully mediating this relationship, thus facilitating sustainable development and aligning with global environmental goals like NetZero.(Singh., 2024) highlights that institutional pressures drive green innovations, which significantly enhance green supply chain practices.This connection, influenced by the capability to leverage big data analytics, further accelerates sustainable development within the manufacturing industry, emphasizing the integrated nature of sustainability practices.(Javed et al., 2024) highlights that green innovation (GI) is influenced by Both internal and external green supply chain practices (GSCP), along with green training (GT), work together to strengthen competitive advantage and support sustainable development in the manufacturing industry through pro-environmental behavior.(Hariadi et al. (2023) stress that green initiatives—especially top management commitment and product stewardship—play a crucial role in advancing green product-service innovation, which in turn accelerates Sustainable Product-Service System Performance, thereby contributing to sustainable development in the manufacturing industry.

(Bhatia et al., 2022) explores how stakeholder and competitive pressures drive the adoption of Industry 4.0 technologies, which, through green process innovation, enhance environmental commitment and ultimately contribute to sustainable development in the manufacturing industry.(Tu et al. 2024) underscore the importance of green innovation in improving both the environmental as well as economic performance of manufacturing firms in China.With environmental regulations and green human resource management significantly influencing the implementation of green innovation contributes significantly to advancing sustainable development within the industry. (Borah et al.,2025) highlights thatthe ability to develop green technologies positively influences the strength of the relationship between green operational practices and green product innovation, suggesting that adopting green innovation technologies is crucial for manufacturing practices to improve sustainability and competitiveness in a changing business environment.(Sun et al., 2023) highlights that relational governance within innovation platforms positively impacts green innovation in manufacturing SMEs, indicating the importance of promoting collaborative innovation and effectively managing risk perceptions,can accelerate the adoption of green technologies, thereby contributing to sustainable development in the manufacturing industry.(Zhang et al., 2022) emphasizes that green technology innovation is crucial for sustainable development in China's manufacturing sector, with command-based environmental regulation most effectively promoting innovation capabilities, particularly in green product innovation, thereby addressing ecological challenges and enhancing economic growth.

(Richnák et al., 2022) highlightsGreen manufacturing and green logistics are closely connected to Industry 4.0 technologies, highlighting their collective impact on sustainable industrial practices, indicating that adopting sustainable technologies and innovations can accelerate sustainable development in the manufacturing industry, supporting with the Sustainable Development Goals (SDGs).(Ha et al., 2022) highlights that technological factors like relative advantage, compatibility, and simplicity significantly influence green innovation adoption in Vietnam's manufacturing sector, essential for enhancing competitiveness and achieving sustainable development while addressing environmental challenges.(Agarwal et al., 2020) discusses a Multi-Criteria Decision-Making (MCDM) approach to evaluate and adopt green manufacturing technologies, emphasizing their role in enhancing sustainability as well as innovation within the manufacturing industry, ultimately contributing to accelerated sustainable development.Kaur emphasizes that green innovation in SMEs enhances environmental sustainability by improving production efficiency, reducing waste, and fostering investment returns. It highlights the need for adopting green technologies to support sustainable development in the manufacturing sector in emerging economies.(Baquero 2024) highlights that integrating green learning orientation and effective resource orchestration enhances green innovation in manufacturing. By fostering a green culture and managing knowledge effectively, firms can accelerate sustainable development through improved green product and process innovations.

(Rashid et al., 2015) emphasizes that technological innovation, particularly in product and process eco-innovation, is crucial for manufacturing industries to achieve sustainability, driven by regulatory push, market pull, and firm strategies, fostering green practices and enhancing environmental performance.(Li et al.,2023) highlights that green manufacture and technology ominously enhance waste saving and energy use, which are essential for sustainability in manufacturing. It emphasizes prioritizing these factors to drive sustainable practices across all production industries.(Thi Ngoc Thuyen et al., 2024) identifies motivations for green innovation in Vietnamese manufacturing, highlighting technology, enterprise characteristics, and market pressures as key factors. It proposes a framework for understanding green practices, which can accelerate sustainable development in the manufacturing industry.(Alyahya et al., 2022) highlights that external pressures, such as governance, customer, and competitive pressures, significantly drive sustainable growthperforms, which in turn enhance green innovation in Saudi Arabian manufacturing, facilitating the adoption of environmentally friendly knowledges and performs for sustainable development.(Zhu et al., 2023) highlights that the adoption of green technologies and the cultivation of green dynamic capabilities play a key role in boosting green product innovation, which in turn fosters green competitive advantage, thereby accelerating sustainable growth in the developed industry. Prioritizing these practices is essential for improved green performance.

(Xu et al., 2022) highlights that green technology invention significantly arbitrates the relationship betweenThe relationship between CSR initiatives and a company's financial success and ecological performance, suggesting its crucial role in enhancing sustainable development within the manufacturing industry. (Ismail 2023) highlights that green dynamic capabilities facilitate the adoption of green technological revolutions, which significantly mediate the relationship between these capabilities as well as brand sustainability, thereby contributing to sustainable development in the manufacturing industry in Tanzania.(Wei et al., 2024) highlights that intelligent manufacturing enhances corporate environmental performance by fostering green technology innovation, thereby supporting sustainable development in the manufacturing industry. This transformation is particularly significant in non-state-owned, capital market-focused, and large-scale enterprises. (Li et al., 2022) highlights that green technology innovation in China's equipment manufacturing industry promotes global value chain upgrading by reducing pollution costs, optimizing export trade, and fostering green product and process origination, thus contributing to sustainable development in the manufacturing sector.(Li et al., 2023) highlights that digitalization of business models significantly enhances green technology innovation in manufacturing enterprises, with knowledge-sharing and knowledge-integration capabilities mediating this relationship, thus facilitating sustainable development through improved green innovation practices.(Huang et al., n.d.)reveals that China's Free Trade Zones significantly enhance green technology innovation in manufacturing, particularly in non-state-owned and less pollution-intensive firms, by alleviating financial constraints and improving human resources, thus accelerating sustainable development in the industry.(Li et al., 2022)discusses the construction of a green revolution system in manufacturing, emphasizing the role of big data and artificial intelligence in overcoming challenges and enhancing intelligent development, production, operation, and service, thereby supporting sustainable development goals in the industry

(Rusmayadi et al., 2023) indicates that green technology investment and renewable technology implementation significantly enhance energy efficiency and decrease carbon emissions in industrial firms, thereby accelerating sustainable development. These resultshighlight the importance of integrating green innovations for developed environmental and operational outcomes.(Alinda et al., 2024) highlights eco product innovation as a key driver of sustainability practices in Uganda's manufacturing sector, emphasizing the need for effective deployment of strategic resources aligned with comprehensive green innovation strategies to enhance eco-friendly practices and accelerate sustainable development.(Nawab 2024) highlights that green technology adoption (GTA) positively influences green competitive advantage (GCA) and sustainable development (SD) in manufacturing companies, emphasizing the importance of dynamic capabilities and organizational commitment in enhancing these outcomes for sustainable practices.(Wang et al.,2022) highlights thatInnovations in green technology play a crucial role in advancing and upgrading the manufacturing value chain, particularly under optimal formal and informal institutional environments, thereby facilitating sustainable development in the manufacturing industry through enhanced efficiency and competitiveness.(Xu et al., 2025) highlights that green Industrial Internet of Things (GIIoT) adoption, supported by dynamic capabilities and circular economy practices, significantly enhances environmental performance in manufacturing firms, thereby accelerating sustainable development through improved technological, operational, and cultural compatibilities.(Ogiemwonyi et al.,2024) highlights that green innovation (GI) pointedly enhances a manufacturing firm's conservational ethic and sustainable performance, suggesting that adopting GI is crucial for accelerating SD in the manufacturing industry, mainly in the context of Jordanian manufacturers.

(Malik et al., 2025) highlights that Green Organizational Innovations (GOI) mediate the relationship between Green Organizational Learning (GOL) and Organizational Performance (OP), emphasizing that adopting green innovations accelerates sustainable development in the manufacturing sector by enhancing performance through sustainability-oriented learning.(Huang 2024) highlights that institutional pressures stimulate green innovation adoption in Taiwan's electrical and electronics industry, with top management teams' responses mediating this relationship, ultimately enhancing firm performance and contributing to sustainable growth in the manufacturing sector.(Enbaia et al., 2024) highlights that green development and product improvements mediate the relationship between environmental ethics and sustainable performance, suggesting that adopting green innovation technologies can significantly enhance sustainability enterprises in the manufacturing industry, particularly when supported by a strong organizational green culture.(Hossain et al., 2024) highlights that the adoption of green smart technologies (GSTA) positively impacts green innovation performance (GIP) in Malaysian manufacturing companies, thereby enhancing sustainability and supporting the government's commitment to environmental goals and economic growth activities.(Jakhar et al., 2020) highlights that exploratory innovative capabilities in manufacturing firms can trigger sustainable behaviors, suggesting that adopting green innovation technologies may enhance responses to stakeholder pressures, ultimately accelerating sustainable development in the industry, mainly in the situation of Indian manufacturing firms.

## 2.1 Green Manufacturing Practices and Outcomes

Numerous studies highlight the role of green manufacturing practices in improving environmental and organizational performance. For instance, Gupta (2024) emphasizes the financial and ecological benefits of investing in green technologies and rework processes. Mukhtar et al. (2024) identify the moderating role of innovation capabilities in improving sustainability among Malaysian manufacturers. Similarly, Omar et al. (2024) and Cheng et al. (2023) show that adopting green process innovations enhances performance in SMEs and energy-intensive sectors like cement and plastics in South Asia.

These practices often include waste reduction, renewable energy integration, and process optimization, aligning with broader sustainability goals. In Africa, Popoola et al. (2024) highlight demand-pull factors and innovation awareness as key drivers of eco-innovation in Nigerian manufacturing firms.

## 2.2 Technology-Driven Innovation and Digital Transformation

The emergence of digital tools and Industry 4.0 technologies is recognized as a catalyst for green innovation. Wang (2024) and Khakwani et al. (2024) underscore the synergy between digital transformation and green product innovation in enhancing firm performance. Zhang et al. (2024) show how smart product platforms promote GIT adoption in automotive manufacturing. Green dynamic capabilities and green smart technologies (e.g., AI, IoT, blockchain) also play a key role in building competitive advantage and sustainability, as shown by Ashraf et al. (2024) and Hossain et al. (2024). These findings suggest that digital innovation serves as both an enabler and outcome of green manufacturing strategies.

## 2.3 Institutional and Regulatory Influences

Government regulation and institutional pressures significantly shape green innovation practices. Shahzad et al. (2022) and Nzomo et al. (2023) find that performance expectancy and flexible regulatory frameworks are crucial for motivating GIT adoption. Tu et al. (2024) link environmental regulations with green human resource management in Chinese firms. From a policy perspective, Fratta et al. (2024) and Zhang et al. (2022) emphasize that stricter environmental laws—such as carbon pricing and ISO certifications—encourage green process innovation and sustainable compliance. Alyahya et al. (2022) and Huang (2024) highlight that institutional pressures are especially influential in regions with emerging regulatory systems.

## 2.4 Firm-Level Drivers and Green Innovation Capabilities

Adoption of GIT is also influenced by internal factors, including leadership commitment, R&D capabilities, and employee engagement. Lutfi et al. (2023) and Siyal et al. (2023) identify top management support and technology compatibility as crucial for adoption in SMEs. Borah et al. (2025) and Baquero (2024) show that organizational capabilities—such as absorptive capacity, dynamic capability, and green learning orientation—mediate the relationship between innovation and sustainability outcomes. Moreover, Javed et al. (2024) and Ismail (2023) explore how green training and employee behavior foster pro-environmental practices, further enhancing innovation and firm competitiveness.

## 2.5 Summary and Research Gaps

The literature reveals a growing consensus that green innovation is essential for sustainable manufacturing, supported by digital technologies, institutional frameworks, and firm-level competencies. However, several gaps remain: Most studies are fragmented, focusing on isolated drivers without integrating models like TAM, UTAUT, or EA-TAM in manufacturing contexts. There is limited exploration of how green innovation mediates or moderates sustainability performance. Empirical work on comparative regional dynamics—especially in the Global South—is underdeveloped. These gaps justify the chapter's focus on synthesizing green innovation adoption drivers through theoretical lenses and conceptual frameworks. The following sections examine these frameworks in greater depth and relate them to green technology adoption strategies.

# 3.FACTORS INFLUENCING GREEN INNOVATION TECHNOLOGY ADOPTION

Green innovation technology adoption is influenced by multiple factors, including regulatory frameworks, organizational capabilities, and market dynamics. These factors determine how industries and businesses integrate environmentally sustainable technologies into their operations. The key factors can be categorized into three main areas:

## 3.1 Regulatory Pressures and Institutional Drivers

Government regulations and institutional policies are among the most critical drivers of GIT adoption. For instance, Tu et al. (2024) demonstrate how China's stringent environmental regulations, coupled with Green Human Resource Management (GHRM), have significantly increased green innovation in manufacturing enterprises. Similarly, Zhang et al. (2022) find that China's command-based regulation has effectively promoted green product innovation, particularly through ISO 14001 certification enforcement. In India, Borah et al. (2025) note that regulatory frameworks encouraging low-carbon production have led firms to integrate green operational practices with product innovation. These policy-level influences align with the "facilitating conditions" factor in UTAUT and support the EA-TAM argument that regulatory environments determine energy and technology investment behavior. Corporate Social Responsibility (CSR) is an integral institutional driver. In Malaysia, Mukhtar et al. (2024) highlight that CSR-oriented firms are more proactive in adopting green technologies due to reputational and stakeholder pressure. This is also reflected in the EA-TAM model, where CSR behavior fosters green investment and innovation alignment. Government policies, regulations, and institutional frameworks play a critical role in encouraging businesses and industries to adopt green innovation technologies. These pressures come from various sources:

- *Environmental Laws and Regulations:* Governments set strict emission control policies, waste management laws, and environmental protection acts to promote sustainability. Carbon taxation and cap-and-trade systems encourage industries to reduce their carbon footprint by investing in green technologies. Regulations like fuel efficiency standards, energy usage limits, and product sustainability certifications push firms toward eco-friendly innovation.
- *International Agreements and Sustainability Goals:*Global Global policy frameworks like the Paris Agreement and the UN Sustainable Development Goals (SDGs)require nations and businesses to focus on sustainable practices. Compliance with these agreements often leads to stricter national policies and industry-wide sustainability mandates.
- *Institutional Support and Incentives:*Numerous governments offer supports, tax credits, and grants to companies adopting green technologies. Research institutions, universities, and industry organizations help by providing technical guidance, research collaborations, and pilot programs for green innovations.
- *Corporate Social Responsibility (CSR) and Ethical Considerations:* Companies that embrace sustainability can improve their brand copy and attract eco-conscious financiers, customers, and partners. Adopting green technologies helps organizations meet their corporate social responsibility goals, reducing their negative environmental impact.

## 3.2 Technology Compatibility and Organizational Capabilities

The success of green technology adoption also depends on internal capabilities such as system compatibility, leadership support, and R&D strength. According to Khakwani et al. (2024), digital transformation and green manufacturing practices significantly boost firm performance when supported by innovation infrastructure. In the context of technology compatibility, Siyal et al. (2023) show that firms in Pakistan and Vietnam experience faster GIT adoption when new technologies align with existing workflows and production systems. This ties closely to the "effort expectancy" and "compatibility expectancy" elements in UTAUT and TAM. Organizational culture and leadership also play a pivotal role. Lutfi et al. (2023) find that SMEs in Jordan are more likely to adopt green innovations when top management demonstrates sustainability commitment and provides technical training—an example of how internal "facilitating conditions" influence adoption outcomes.

- *Compatibility with Existing Systems:* If green technologies seamlessly integrate with a company's current infrastructure, processes, and supply chains, adoption is more likely. Retrofitting older systems for green technology may require additional investment, which can slow down adoption. Organizations must assess technical feasibility, scalability, and operational impact before implementing new technologies.
- *Research and Development (R&D) Capabilities:*Companies with strong R&D departments are more likely to innovate and adopt energy-efficient materials, smart grids, and renewable energy solutions. Collaboration with universities and research institutions helps businesses access cutting-edge sustainable technologies.
- *Workforce Skills and Expertise:*Adoption success depends on whether employees have the technical knowledge and training to work with green technologies.Companies need to invest in upskilling programs, certifications, and knowledge-sharing platforms to enhance technological competence.
- *Leadership Commitment and Organizational Culture:*Strong commitment from top management ensures that sustainability goals align with business strategies.A corporate culture that values innovation, environmental responsibility, and long-term sustainability promotes green technology adoption.

## 3.3 Economic Incentives and Market Demand

The financial viability of green innovations—through cost savings, government subsidies, or consumer preferences—is another major driver. Gupta (2024) shows that rework and green investment significantly reduce carbon emissions and operational costs in Indian manufacturing firms. In China, Li et al. (2023) emphasize how green product innovation leads to improved export competitiveness, reflecting the economic motivation behind GIT. Market trends further reinforce economic drivers. For example, Ashraf et al. (2024) find that firms aligning with green consumer preferences and value co-creation enjoy enhanced business performance. These findings correlate with the "performance expectancy" construct in TAM and UTAUT. Green financing also plays a critical role. As noted by Rusmayadi et al. (2023), Indonesian firms that secure funding for renewable technologies see higher energy efficiency and lower emissions—aligning with EA-TAM's emphasis on energy-resource investment.

- *Cost Savings and Efficiency Gains:* Green innovations like energy-efficient manufacturing, smart grids, and water recycling systems reduce operational costs in the long run. Investment in solar energy, wind power, and electric vehicles helps businesses cut fuel and electricity expenses.
- *Consumer Preferences and Competitive Advantage:*Consumers increasingly prefer eco-friendly, biodegradable, and energy-efficient products.Companies that adopt green technologies can market themselves as sustainable brands, gaining a competitive edge over traditional businesses.
- *Financial Support and Investment Opportunities:*Many organizations secure green bonds, sustainability-linked loans, and government grants to fund eco-friendly projects.Private investors and venture capitalists are increasingly funding clean technology startups and green innovation firms.
- *Supply Chain and Industry Trends:*Businesses may face pressure from supply chain partners to adopt environmentally friendly practices.Large corporations often require their suppliers to meet sustainability standards, reducing waste and carbon emissions across the value chain.

## 4. CHARACTERISTICS OF GREEN INNOVATION TECHNOLOGY STRATEGY

Green Innovation Strategy integrates environmental sustainability with technological advancement by embedding eco-friendly practices into core business operations. It emphasizes compliance with environmental regulations, adoption of smart technologies, and alignment with business goals for efficiency and competitiveness. The strategy supports circular economy principles, stakeholder engagement, and market responsiveness. These characteristics complement earlier frameworks like TAM, UTAUT, and EA-TAM by linking innovation with regulatory, technical, and behavioral drivers of green technology adoption. A Green Innovation Technology

Strategy focuses on integrating environmentally sustainable solutions into business models, operations, and production processes. It aims to minimize eco-friendly impact while maximizing financial and public benefits. The key characteristics of such a strategy include:

i) Sustainability-Focused Innovation

- Emphasizes the improvement and application of eco-friendly technologies that decrease environmental harm.
- Encourages energy efficiency, waste reduction, and resource conservation in industrial processes.
- Supports the use of renewable energy sources such as solar, wind, and biofuels.

ii) Regulatory Compliance and Environmental Responsibility

- Aligns with government regulations, international agreements, and industry standards related to sustainability.
- Confirmspassivity with conservation laws, carbon reduction policies, and green certifications (e.g., ISO 14001).
- Helps businesses meet Corporate Social Responsibility (CSR) goals by adopting eco-conscious practices.

iii) Integration with Business Strategy

- Embeds green technology within the core business strategy rather than treating it as an add-on.
- Encourages sustainable supply chain organization, dropping the carbon footprint of production and logistics.
- Aligns with long-term profitability goals by improving resource efficiency and reducing costs.

iv) Circular Economy and Waste Minimization

- Promotes closed-loop production cycles, where waste materials are reused or recycled.
- Supports the design of products for reparability, durability and recyclability.
- Encourages productions to accept zero-waste manufacturing and responsible disposal methods.

v) Technology-Driven Innovation

- Leverages innovative technologies such asIoT, AI, and blockchain for smart energy management and efficiency.
- Encourages green product design, sustainable materials, and biodegradable packaging.
- Supports the use of smart grids, electric vehicles, and automation to optimize energy consumption.

vi) Market-Driven and Consumer-Oriented Approach

- Responds to the increasing demand for eco-friendly products and facilities.
- Builds brand reputation and competitive advantage by offering sustainable alternatives.
- Targets environmentally conscious consumers, investors, and stakeholders.

vii) Collaboration and Stakeholder Engagement

- Encourages partnerships with governments, research institutions, and NGOs to foster innovation.
- Engages employees, customers, and suppliers in sustainability initiatives.
- Promotes knowledge sharing, training, and education on green technology adoption.

viii) Long-Term Economic and Environmental Benefits

- Balances profitability with environmental impact, ensuring sustainable business growth.
- Reduces operational costs through energy efficiency and resource optimization.
- Contributes to climate change mitigation, biodiversity conservation, and pollution control.

## 5. TECHNOLOGY ACCEPTANCE MODEL (TAM)

The Energy-Augmented Technology Acceptance Model (EA-TAM) section has been significantly expanded to better articulate the conceptual link between energy demand, renewable energy investment, and sustainable technology adoption in manufacturing industries. A visual model illustrating the EA-TAM framework and its core variables has also been included to support clarity and facilitate understanding of its practical application. According to (Anser et al. 2020), the Technology Acceptance Model (TAM) explains how individuals accept and use specific information technologies and systems. The model highlights two key components: perceived usefulness and perceived ease of use, which indicates the importance, and subjective capacities of individuals to utilize computer-based applications in a way that maximizes the utility of his or her work and allows them to execute efficiently. The perceived ease of use refers to how an individual feels comfortable and capable of using computer-based programs with minimal effort. It was evident that both factors were influenced by a number of external circumstances that could temporarily halt the use of the actual system.

The Technology Acceptance Model (TAM) has evolved into two extended versions, TAM-2 and TAM-3, by incorporating various external factors influencing perceived usefulness and perceived ease of use (Anser et al., 2020). Perceived usefulness is measured through four components: the individual's social standing gained through technology use, relevance of the technology to job requirements, improvement in work quality, and satisfaction with task outcomes. Perceived ease of use includes six elements: computer proficiency, availability of external support systems, fear or anxiety associated with using technology, computer playfulness, perceived enjoyment, and overall ease of interaction. Both TAM-2 and TAM-3 operate under the utility maximization principle to enhance end-user system performance.

In a similar vein, Anser et al. (2020) developed an adapted TAM model specifically for travelers, integrating mobile technology into the broader category of information technology and systems to assess tourist acceptance based on perceived usefulness and ease of use. This adaptation highlights mobile technology as an essential tool for acquiring travel-related information, such as destination research, navigation assistance, hotel locations, flight reservations, and other travel services. The model incorporates both prior technological experience and leisure travel experience to better understand the actual use of mobile technology in tourism contexts, particularly in pleasure-seeking activities.

## 5.1 Energy–AugmentedTechnology Acceptance Model (EA-TAM)

The EA-TAM model illustrates that technology inherently demands energy to function effectively and support business processes. Consequently, energy demand remains a critical factor in driving economic activity and achieving the green development agenda. The model emphasizes that technology-related emissions, primarily released during the manufacturing phase, underscore the persistent need for green energy solutions to support sustainable development. To mitigate these emissions, the integration of renewable energy sources is essential in facilitating technology-driven growth. In light of these concerns, the study introduces the EA-

TAM model from both micro and macro perspectives, highlighting its relevance in aligning technological advancement with environmental sustainability.

- *From a firm's perspective, the energy-augmented Technology Acceptance Model (EA-TAM)* highlights the strategic role of renewable energy in guiding green investment decisions. These investments are seen as essential for enhancing logistics performance, export potential, technological progress, efficient resource utilization, competitiveness, and overall firm profitability. Moreover, the rising demand for green energy supports product innovation, which depends heavily on sustained R&D efforts aimed at cultivating a green mindset and a behavioral inclination toward adopting environmentally friendly systems. The EA-TAM model, from the firm's viewpoint, thus provides a practical framework for formulating green policies that lead to measurable environmental and economic benefits.
- From an industry standpoint, the EA-TAM model emphasizes the critical role of green factors in promoting green product usage. Key elements such as green supplier selection are instrumental in shaping green purchasing intentions. Additionally, practices like industrial green engineering, green procurement, green consumerism, green product recovery, and green innovation significantly enhance the perceived ease of adopting and using green products. However, the pathway to green innovation is often hindered by challenges such as regulatory constraints and elevated carbon pricing, which may negatively influence attitudes and preferences toward green product adoption. Despite these barriers, fostering strong green preferences can expand the range of eco-friendly product choices, ultimately encouraging broader adoption of green products across industries.

## 6. UNIFIED THEORY OF ACCEPTANCE OF USE OF TECHNOLOGY (UTAUT)

(Anser et al., 2020) expanded the unified theory of acceptance of the usage of technology (UTAUT) to the services sector, where technology is directly used to make hotel bookings/reservations online via company websites. Thus, the internet is a viable information technology aspect that connects computer systems all over the world and provides information such as hotel reservations, travel information, weather forecasts, and so on. Table 1 highlighting the key features, constructs, and applications of TAM, EA-TAM, and UTAUT with a specific focus on Green Innovation Technology (GIT) adoption in manufacturing.

*Table 1. Comparison of TAM, EA-TAM, and UTAUT in the Context of GIT Adoption*

| Model | Core Constructs | Unique Features | Application to GIT in Manufacturing |
|---|---|---|---|
| TAM (Technology Acceptance Model) | - Perceived Usefulness (PU)<br>- Perceived Ease of Use (PEOU)<br>- Behavioral Intention (BI) | Focuses on individual acceptance of technology based on utility and ease | Helps assess how workers or managers perceive the usefulness and ease of green technologies (e.g., smart meters, eco-manufacturing software) |
| EA-TAM (Energy-Augmented TAM) | - PU, PEOU, BI (from TAM)<br>- Energy Efficiency Consideration<br>- Green Investment Motivation<br>- Regulatory Constraints | Integrates energy consumption and environmental factors with tech adoption | Evaluates how firms balance energy/ resource use with technology adoption; supports policy-aligned decisions for green investment |
| UTAUT (Unified Theory of Acceptance and Use of Technology) | - Performance Expectancy<br>- Effort Expectancy<br>- Social Influence<br>- Facilitating Conditions<br>- Behavioral Intention | Emphasizes organizational and social factors; broader than TAM | Explains adoption behavior influenced by external factors (e.g., top management support, peer influence, infrastructure availability) in implementing green tech in factories |

The Unified Theory of Acceptance and Use of Technology (UTAUT) identifies four primary factors influencing online purchase intention in rural tourism contexts: (i) effort expectancy, (ii) social influence, (iii) facilitating conditions, and (iv) consumer innovativeness in adopting new technologies. Building on this, Tom Dieck and Jung (2018) developed the Mobile Augmented Technology Acceptance Model (Mobile Augmented TAM), introducing seven external dimensions that influence behavioral intention and technology usage in the context of urban heritage tourism. These dimensions include: (i) information quality, (ii) system quality, (iii) cost of use, (iv) recommendations, (v) personal innovativeness, (vi) perceived risk, and (vii) facilitating conditions. These external factors shape tourists' perceptions, resulting in varied attitudes toward the use of such applications when engaging in leisure travel or visiting cultural destinations.

The UTAUT model has been further explored in the context of sustainable technology products, reflecting a shift from conventional e-technology toward smart and eco-friendly innovations. Anser et al. (2020) extended the original model by incorporating several external factors relevant to the adoption of green household technologies. These factors include: (i) performance expectancy, (ii) effort expectancy, (iii) compatibility expectancy, (iv) hedonic motivation, (v) social pressure, (vi) sustainable innovativeness, and (vii) environmentalism. Collectively, these seven exogenous variables were found to significantly influence individuals' behavioral intention to adopt environmentally sustainable household technologies.

Anser et al. (2020) emphasized that green information technology products, such as e-books, play a vital role in raising awareness of environmental issues. This growing awareness increases consumer motivation to purchase e-books as an environmentally responsible choice. In this context, consumer knowledge becomes a key component within the UTAUT framework, helping to promote environmentally friendly technologies in support of green development. Additionally, the study found that consumers who engage in sustainable label reading behavior exhibit a stronger intention to use eco-friendly products compared to those choosing non-labeled alternatives. Therefore, the Technology Acceptance Model is not only applicable to general technology adoption but also essential for addressing environmental concerns and fostering positive attitudes toward the use of sustainable products.

## 7. INTENTIONS TO ADOPT SUSTAINABLE HOUSEHOLD TECHNOLOGY

The Unified Theory of Acceptance and Use of Technology (UTAUT), as proposed by Ahn et al. (2016), serves as the foundational framework for this study. This research develops and empirically tests an extended model that identifies key predictors of sustainable technology adoption. These predictors include consumer expectations related to technology attributes—namely, performance expectancy, effort expectancy, compatibility expectancy, and hedonic expectancy—as well as attitudes and behavioral tendencies specific to sustainable consumption, such as social pressure, sustainable innovativeness, and environmentalism. To address the research objectives, seven hypotheses were formulated based on these constructs. Notably, this study uses the term compatibility expectancy in place of UTAUT's original facilitating conditions, aligning it with the TAM framework to better represent it as a technological attribute in the current model.Performance expectancy significantly affects intention to adopt sustainable household technology.

This section presents a set of conceptual hypotheses developed from the theoretical frameworks discussed earlier—specifically TAM, EA-TAM, and UTAUT. These hypotheses aim to guide future empirical investigations into the behavioral and organizational factors that influence green innovation technology (GIT) adoption in the manufacturing sector. No primary data or statistical testing is conducted in this chapter. The following hypotheses are proposed:

H1: Perceived usefulness of green technologies positively influences behavioral intention to adopt them.

H2: Regulatory support and energy efficiency considerations positively impact firms' motivation to invest in GIT.

H3: Social influence and top management support are significant predictors of green technology adoption behavior.

H4: Facilitating conditions (e.g., infrastructure, training) moderate the relationship between intention and actual adoption.

H5: Firms with stronger CSR orientation are more likely to adopt sustainable technologies proactively.

## 8. CORPORATE ENVIRONMENTAL RESPONSIBILITY

Corporate Environmental Responsibility (CER) is the promise of businesses to operate in an environmentally sustainable manner, reducing their negative impact on the planet while promoting ecological balance. It entails embedding environmental concerns into a company's strategic planning, operational activities, and decision-making practices..Companies practicing CER focus on reducing carbon footprints, conserving natural resources, and adopting sustainable production methods. One of the key aspects of CER is pollution control and waste management. Businesses are expected to minimize emissions, properly dispose of industrial waste, and implement recycling programs to decrease environmental degradation. Many companies invest in energy-efficient technologies, switch to renewable energy sources such as solar and wind power, and design eco-friendly products that generate less waste. Sustainable supply chain management is also an essential component, ensuring that raw materials are sourced responsibly and production processes do not harm ecosystems. Compliance with environmental regulations is another crucial element of CER. Governments worldwide have established laws and policies requiring businesses to follow environmental standards, such as decreasing greenhouse gas emissions, limiting water pollution, and protecting biodiversity.

Companies that fail to meet these standards could be subject to legal consequences, harm to brand reputation, and a decline in customer confidence. Beyond regulatory compliance, many businesses voluntarily engage inCSR efforts aimed at promoting environmental sustainability. These may include tree-planting campaigns, water conservation programs, and partnerships with environmental organizations. Through active involvement in these initiatives, organizations showcase their dedication to environmental responsibility. stewardship and gain goodwill from consumers, investors, and other stakeholders. In addition to benefiting the environment, CER also offers economic and social advantages. Sustainable business practices This approach can result in cost reductions by optimizing resource utilization and minimizing waste. Businesses that emphasize environmental responsibility are more likely to appeal to eco-conscious consumers and investors, thereby strengthening their brand reputation and gaining a competitive edge.Furthermore, employees are increasingly drawn to organizations that value sustainability, leading to better workforce engagement and retention. Overall, Corporate Environmental Responsibility is essential for businesses aiming to achieve long-term sustainability. By integrating environmental considerations into their operations, companies contribute to the well-being of the planet while also securing economic success and strengthening their relationships with stakeholders.

### 8.1 Regulatory Pressures and Institutional Drivers

Regulatory and institutional influences play a significant role in shaping the adoption of Green Innovation Technologies (GIT) in the manufacturing sector. In addition to formal policies and environmental standards, Corporate Environmental Responsibility (CER) has emerged as a critical driver of sustainable behavior within firms. While often aligned with broader Corporate Social Responsibility (CSR) goals, CER focuses more specifically on an organization's environmental performance and its strategic commitment to sustainability. CER encourages firms to go beyond compliance by adopting proactive environmental initiatives, such as eco-friendly product design, waste reduction, and energy-efficient operations. This behavior often aligns with national or international environmental frameworks, such as ISO 14001 or Science-Based Targets (SBTi), and reinforces the regulatory push for sustainability.

## 9. GREEN INNOVATION STRATEGIES FOR SUSTAINABLE DEVELOPMENT

Green innovation approaches for sustainable development focus on creating environmentally friendly solutions that promote economic growth while reducing ecological harm. These strategies include adopting utilizing renewable energy sources like solar, wind, and hydropower helps reduce reliance on fossil fuels and decrease carbon emissions. Sustainable product design plays a crucial role by using biodegradable, recyclable, and energy-efficient materials to reduce waste and environmental impact. The circular economy approach further enhances sustainability by encouraging recycling, reusing, and repurposing materials to minimize waste generation. Green supply chain management ensures responsible sourcing of raw materials, efficient logistics, and reduced carbon footprints in transportation. Energy-efficient technologies, such as smart lighting, automated systems, and AI-driven energy optimization, contribute to reducing power consumption in industries and households. Sustainable architecture and green building practices focus on eco-friendly construction materials, energy-efficient designs, and water conservation techniques to minimize resource depletion. Additionally, eco-friendly transportation solutions, including electric vehicles, hydrogen fuel technology, and improved public transit systems, help reduce air pollution and dependency on fossil fuels. In agriculture, green innovation involves precision farming, vertical farming, and organic practices that optimize land and water use while reducing chemical dependence. Water conservation technologies, such as desalination and wastewater recycling, further support sustainable resource management. Businesses also integrate corporate sustainability initiatives by investing in green technologies, setting carbon neutrality goals, and engaging in environmentally responsible practices. These strategies collectively drive sustainable development by protecting natural resources, reducing pollution, and fostering long-term economic and social well-being while ensuring a healthier planet for future generations.

## 9.1 Green Product and Process Innovation

Green product and process innovation raises to the expansion of environmentally friendly products and the implementation of sustainable manufacturing processes that reduce negative environmental impacts. These innovations help businesses minimize resource consumption, lower carbon emissions, and promote sustainability while maintaining economic growth.

- **Green Product Innovation:** Green product innovation focuses on designing and developing yields that are eco-friendly through their lifecycle—from raw material sourcing to disposal. This includes using biodegradable, recyclable, or renewable materials that reduce waste and pollution. Many companies are adopting sustainable packaging solutions, for example compostable materials and returnable containers, to minimize plastic waste. Additionally, energy-efficient appliances, electric vehicles, and organic consumer goods contribute to reducing environmental harm. Circular economy principles are often applied in product innovation, encouraging modular and repairable designs to extend product lifespan and minimize waste generation.
- **Green Process Innovation:** Green process originationincludes optimizing manufacturing and operational processes to make them more sustainable. This includes decreasing energy and water consumption, minimizing industrial waste, and dropping emissions through cleaner production methods. Companies adopt energy-efficient technologies, such as smart automation

and AI-driven resource management, to enhance efficiency. Sustainable manufacturing techniques, including lean production, closed-loop systems, and the usage of renewable energy in factories, further support environmental sustainability. Waste reduction strategies, such as upcycling and reusing industrial byproducts, also contribute to greener production processes. Green innovation strategies and sustainability outcomes are shown in Table 2.

*Table 2. Green Innovation Strategies and Sustainability Outcomes*

| Strategy Type | Key Practices | Sustainability Outcomes |
|---|---|---|
| Green Product & Process Innovation | Eco-design, cleaner production, low-carbon manufacturing | Reduced emissions, improved efficiency, sustainable branding |
| Circular Economy Strategies | Recycling, remanufacturing, waste minimization | Resource conservation, reduced landfill, lower material costs |
| Digital Green Technologies | AI, IoT, digital twins for energy/ resource optimization | Real-time monitoring, predictive maintenance, smart energy use |
| Collaborative & Supply Chain Models | Green procurement, supplier engagement, logistics innovation | Greener supply chains, compliance with regulations, shared value |

## 9.2 Green Supply Chain Practices Digital Transformation and Smart Technologies

Green supply chain practices, digital transformation, and smart technologies play a crucial role in promoting sustainability and efficiency in modern business operations. Green supply chain performs focus on reducing environmental impact by implementing eco-friendly sourcing, optimizing logistics, minimizing waste, and using energy-efficient transportation methods. Companies are adopting circular economy models, promoting recycling, and ensuring ethical sourcing of raw materials to reduce carbon footprints. Digital transformation enhances these efforts by integrating advanced technologies such as artificial intelligence (AI), blockchain, and the Internet of Things (IoT) to improve supply chain transparency, traceability, and efficiency. Smart technologies, including automation, predictive analytics, and real-time monitoring systems, help businesses reduce resource consumption, optimize inventory management, and lower emissions. These innovations enable companies to make data-driven decisions, improve operational sustainability, and meet environmental regulations. By combining green supply chain practices with digital transformation and smart technologies, businesses can attain long-term sustainability, reduce costs, and enhance their reasonable advantage while contributing to a cleaner and greener future.

## 10. THE ROLE OF INNOVATION IN ACCELERATING SUSTAINABLE DEVELOPMENT

Innovation is a key driver in advancing sustainable development by offering effective solutions to environmental, social, and economic challenges. Developments in areas such as renewable energy, green technologies, and circular economy practices enable reductions in carbon emissions, waste, and resource consumption. Cutting-edge tools like artificial intelligence (AI), the Internet of Things (IoT), and blockchain enhance sustainability by improving energy efficiency, streamlining supply chains, and promoting transparency in production and consumption processes. In agriculture, techniques like precision and vertical farming improve food security while conserving land and water. Similarly, eco-friendly transportation options—such as electric vehicles and smart urban planning—help cut pollution and reduce reliance on fossil fuels. When businesses and governments embrace innovation, they stimulate economic growth while supporting long-term environmental and social well-being. Investing in clean technologies, promoting sustainable practices, and encouraging research are essential steps in accelerating progress toward global sustainability goals and ensuring a more resilient and equitable future.

## 11. CONCLUSION

This chapter explored the critical role of green innovation technologies (GIT) in accelerating sustainable development within the manufacturing sector. It examined theoretical frameworks such as TAM, EA-TAM, and UTAUT, identified key drivers of GIT adoption, and reviewed strategic approaches to embed sustainability into manufacturing operations. While the discussion provides a comprehensive conceptual foundation, it is important to acknowledge certain limitations. The analysis is primarily literature-based and conceptual; therefore, empirical validation of the proposed hypotheses and frameworks remains a necessary next step. Future research should focus on applying these models in real-world industrial contexts, conducting cross-country comparative studies, and exploring sector-specific adoption dynamics. Particular attention should be given to small and medium enterprises (SMEs), which often face greater barriers to adopting green technologies. Additionally, there is a need to further investigate the behavioral and cultural factors that influence organizational decision-making in sustainability transitions.

## 12. POLICY IMPLICATIONS AND RECOMMENDATIONS

Policy implications from this study highlight the need for targeted incentives, regulatory clarity, and infrastructure support to promote GIT adoption in manufacturing. Governments should align policies with adoption models like TAM and UTAUT to address behavioral and organizational barriers. Special focus is needed on supporting SMEs through green financing, skill development, and technology access. Education and training programs should also be strengthened to build long-term sustainability competencies across the sector.

## REFERENCES

Agarwal, S., Agrawal, V., & Dixit, J. K. (2020). Green manufacturing: A MCDM approach. *Materials Today: Proceedings*, *26*, 2869–2874.

Ahn, M., Kang, J., & Hustvedt, G. (2016). A model of sustainable household technology acceptance. *International Journal of Consumer Studies*, *40*(1), 83–91.

Alinda, K., Tumwine, S., & Kaawaase, T. K. (2024). Environmental innovations and sustainability practices of manufacturing firms in Uganda. *Asia Pacific Journal of Innovation and Entrepreneurship*, *18*(2), 102–129.

Alyahya, M., Aliedan, M., Agag, G., & Abdelmoety, Z. H. (2022). Exploring the link between sustainable development practices, institutional pressures, and green innovation. *Sustainability*, *14*(21), 14312.

Anser, M. K., Yousaf, Z., & Zaman, K. (2020). Green technology acceptance model and green logistics operations:"to see which way the wind is blowing". *Frontiers in Sustainability*, *1*, 3.

Ashraf, S. F., Li, C., Wattoo, M. U., Murad, M., & Mahmood, B. (2024). Green horizons: Unleashing green innovation through green business strategies and competencies. *Business Strategy and the Environment*, *33*(5), 4233–4251.

Baquero, A. (2024). Unveiling the path to green innovation: The interplay of green learning orientation, knowledge management capability and manufacturing firm's capability to orchestrate resources. *Journal of Business and Industrial Marketing*, *39*(10), 2205–2221.

Bhatia, M. S., & Kumar, S. (2022). Linking stakeholder and competitive pressure to Industry 4.0 and performance: Mediating effect of environmental commitment and green process innovation. *Business Strategy and the Environment*, *31*(5), 1905–1918.

Borah, P. S., Dogbe, C. S. K., & Marwa, N. (2025). Green dynamic capability and green product innovation for sustainable development: Role of green operations, green transaction, and green technology development capabilities. *Corporate Social Responsibility and Environmental Management*, *32*(1), 911–926.

Cheng, C., Ahmad, S. F., Irshad, M., Alsanie, G., Khan, Y., Ahmad, A. Y. B., & Aleemi, A. R. (2023). Impact of green process innovation and productivity on sustainability: The moderating role of environmental awareness. *Sustainability*, *15*(17), 12945.

Enbaia, E., Alzubi, A., Iyiola, K., & Aljuhmani, H. Y. (2024). The Interplay Between Environmental Ethics and Sustainable Performance: Does Organizational Green Culture and Green Innovation Really Matter? *Sustainability*, *16*(23), 10230.

Fratta, G., Stefani, I., Tapola, S., & Saetta, S. (2024). Green Innovation Practices: A Case Study in a Foundry. *Journal of Manufacturing and Materials Processing*, *8*(3), 111.

Gupta, A., & Khanna, A. (2024). A holistic approach to sustainable manufacturing: Rework, green technology, and carbon policies. *Expert Systems with Applications*, *244*, 122943.

Ha, N. M., Nguyen, P. A., & Phung, N. B. H. (2022). Technological factors affecting green innovation: Evidence from the manufacturing sector in Vietnam. *Ho Chi Minh City Open University Journal of Science-Economics and Business Administration*, *12*(1), 3–19.

Hariadi, S., Moengin, P., & Maulidya, R. (2023). Impact of green practices through green product and service innovation: Sustainable product-service system performance model. *International Journal of Sustainable Engineering*, *16*(1), 1–15.

Hossain, M. I., Teh, B. H., Tabash, M. I., Chong, L. L., & Ong, T. S. (2024). Unpacking the role of green smart technologies adoption, green ambidextrous leadership, and green innovation behaviour on green innovation performance in Malaysian manufacturing companies. *FIIB Business Review*, 23197145231225335.

Huang, J., Yang, B., & Chen, Y. (n.d.) Green Tech Innovation in Manufacturing Via Free Trade Zones: A Machine Learning Study. *Available at SSRN* 4681066.

Huang, Y. C., & Huang, C. H. (2024). Exploring institutional pressure, the top management team's response, green innovation adoption, and firm performance: Evidence from Taiwan's electrical and electronics industry. *European Journal of Innovation Management*, *27*(3), 800–824.

Ismail, I. J. (2023). The influence of green dynamic capabilities on brand sustainability among manufacturing enterprises in Tanzania: Mediation of green technology innovation. *Technological Sustainability*, *2*(4), 388–403.

Jakhar, S. K., Bhattacharya, A., Rathore, H., & Mangla, S. K. (2020). Stakeholder pressure for sustainability: Can 'innovative capabilities' explain the idiosyncratic response in the manufacturing firms? *Business Strategy and the Environment*, *29*(6), 2635–2653.

Javed, A., Li, Q., Ejaz, S., Basit, A., Hasan, S., Zita Júlia, F., & Hossain, M. B. (2024). Green synergy: Unveiling the nexus of green supply chain practices, training and innovation for sustainable manufacturing. *Kybernetes*.

Kaur, N., Sharma, R., & Mehta, K. (9). Emerging green: Exploring strategic factors for SMEs' adoption of green technology and innovation in India. *Sustainability, Green Management, and Performance of SMEs, 165*, 186.

Khakwani, M. S., Zafar, A., Mahmood, G., & Khan, Q. M. (2024). Impact of Digital Transformation and Green Manufacturing Practices on Firm Performance with Mediating Role of Green Product Innovation: An Empirical Investigation with PLS-SEM Modeling. *Sustainable Business and Society in Emerging Economies*, *6*(1), 83–98.

Li, C., Ahmad, S. F., Ayassrah, A. Y. B. A., Irshad, M., Telba, A. A., Awwad, E. M., & Majid, M. I. (2023). Green production and green technology for sustainability: The mediating role of waste reduction and energy use. *Heliyon*, *9*(12). PMID: 38076181

Li, H., Li, Y., Sarfarz, M., &Ozturk, I. (2023).Enhancing firms' green innovation and sustainable performance through the mediating role of green product innovation and moderating role of employees' green behavior. *Economic research-Ekonomskai-straživanja, 36*(2).

Li, H., Yang, Z., Wang, H., & Li, Y. (2023). Digitalization of business models, knowledge management and green technology innovation of Chinese manufacturing enterprises: A mixed analysis based on the Haier COSMOPlat ecosystem. *Asia Pacific Business Review*, •••, 1–29.

Li, Y., Zhang, X., Hao, J., & Huang, Q. (2022). The impact of green technology innovation on global value chain upgrading in China's equipment manufacturing industry. *Frontiers in Environmental Science*, *10*, 1044583.

Lutfi, A., Alqudah, H., Alrawad, M., Alshira'h, A. F., Alshirah, M. H., Almaiah, M. A., & Hassan, M. F. (2023). Green environmental management system to support environmental performance: What factors influence SMEs to adopt green innovations? *Sustainability*, *15*(13), 10645.

Malik, I. A., & Mehraj, D., u Nissa, V., &Wani, A. K. (2025). Unveiling the Dynamics of Sustainable Development: A Holistic Examination of Green Organizational Learning, Innovation, and Performance in Indian SMEs. *Business Strategy & Development*, *8*(1), e70060.

Mukhtar, B., Shad, M. K., & Lai, F. W. (2024). Fostering sustainability performance in the Malaysian manufacturing companies: The role of green technology innovation and innovation capabilities. *Benchmarking*.

Mukhtar, B., Shad, M. K., Won, L. F., Waqas, A., & Mukhtar, Z. (2023). Role of green technology innovation to promote sustainability performance in Malaysian manufacturing solar PV industry: A conceptual framework. *Platform: A Journal of Management and Humanities, 6*(1), 36-46.

Nawab, T., &Shafiq, A. (2024). The Impact of Green Technology Adoption and Dynamic Capabilities on Green Competitive Advantage and Sustainable Development: Moderating Role of Organizational Commitment. *iRASD Journal of Energy & Environment, 5*(1), 24-36.

Nzomo, J. K., Kinyua, G. M., & Mwasiaji, E. T. (2023). Green Innovation Strategy as Antecedent of Performance Sustainability Among ISO 14001 Certified Manufacturing Firms in Kenya: Does Competitive Advantage Play a Mediating Role. *International Journal of Education and Research, 11*(8), 93–108.

Ogiemwonyi, O., & Eneizan, B. (2024, March). Environmental ethics and green practices in the manufacturing sector: The role of green innovation and environmental policy. In *Natural Resources Forum*. Oxford, UK: Blackwell Publishing Ltd.

Omar, A., Al-shari, A., & Shah, S. H. A., ErkolBayram, G., Zameer Rahman, E., & Valeri, M. (2024). Green manufacturing practices and SMEs' sustainable performance: A moderated mediation mechanisms of green innovation and managerial discretion. *European Business Review, 36*(4), 588–609.

Popoola, O. A., & Popoola, G. O. (2024). Drivers of eco-innovation among manufacturing firms in Nigeria. In *Innovation, entrepreneurship and the informal economy in Sub–Saharan Africa: A sustainable development agenda* (pp. 217–248). Springer Nature Switzerland.

Rashid, N., Jabar, J., Yahya, S., & Shami, S. (2015). Dynamic eco innovation practices: A systematic review of state of the art and future direction for eco innovation study. *Asian Social Science, 11*(1), 8.

Richnák, P., & Fidlerová, H. (2022). Impact and potential of sustainable development goals in dimension of the technological revolution industry 4.0 within the analysis of industrial enterprises. *Energies, 15*(10), 3697.

Rusmayadi, G., Salawati, U., Haslinah, A., & Judijanto, L. (2023). The effect of investment in green technology and renewable technology adoption on energy efficiency and carbon emissions reduction in Indonesian manufacturing companies. *West Science Interdisciplinary Studies, 1*(11), 1175–1183.

Shaban, N., Afza, T., Ehsan, S., & Danish, R. Q. (2024). *Leveraging Green Innovation to Foster Sustainable Development through Green Dynamic Capabilities*. Research Journal for Societal Issues.

Shahzad, M., Qu, Y., Rehman, S. U., & Zafar, A. U. (2022). Adoption of green innovation technology to accelerate sustainable development among manufacturing industry. *Journal of Innovation & Knowledge*, *7*(4), 100231.

Singh, R. K., & Joshi, H. T. (2024). Greening the supply chain: Institutional pressures, data-driven innovations, and the road to circular sustainability. *Business Strategy and the Environment*, *33*(6), 6029–6044.

Siyal, A. W., Chen, H., Shahzad, F., & Bano, S. (2023). Investigating the role of institutional pressures, technology compatibility, and green transformation in driving manufacturing industries toward green development. *Journal of Cleaner Production*, *428*, 139416.

Sun, J., Xie, X., Zhou, M., & Yan, L. (2023). How to drive green innovation of manufacturing SMEs under open innovation networks–the role of innovation platforms' relational governance. *Management Decision*.

Thi Ngoc Thuyen, T., &NhuBich, L. (2024). Green innovation practices: A case study of Vietnamese manufacturing companies. *Cogent Business & Management*, *11*(1), 2333603.

Tu, Y., Lu, L., & Wang, S. (2024). Environmental regulations, GHRM and green innovation of manufacturing enterprises: Evidence from China. *Frontiers in Environmental Science*, *12*, 1308224.

Wang, M., & Han, J. (2024).A Study on Promoting Green Production and Sustainable Development of the Manufacturing Industry through Digital Innovation. *Information Systems and Economics, 5*(4).

Wang, X., Zhou, J., & Maitlo, Q. (2022). Effect of green technology innovation on the upgrading of the manufacturing value chain: Evidence from China. *Frontiers in Environmental Science*, *10*, 994323.

Wei, X., Jiang, F., Chen, Y., & Hua, W. (2024). Towards green development: The role of intelligent manufacturing in promoting corporate environmental performance. *Energy Economics*, *131*, 107375.

Xu, N., Shahzad, F., & Hu, R. (2025). Unveiling environmental excellence: The confluence of green Industrial Internet of Things, circular economy practices and dynamic capabilities in manufacturing firms. *Journal of Manufacturing Technology Management*, *36*(2), 479–503.

Xu, X., Imran, M., Ayaz, M., & Lohana, S. (2022). The mediating role of green technology innovation with corporate social responsibility, firm financial, and environmental performance: The case of Chinese manufacturing industries. *Sustainability, 14*(24), 16951.

Yang, B. (2024). Enterprise Green Technology Innovation Strategy Based on Environmental Responsibility. *Academic Journal of Business & Management, 6*(1).

Zhang, T. J., Zhou, J. Y., Wang, M., Ren, K., Imran, M., & Wang, R. (2022). Cultivation mechanism of green technology innovation in manufacturing enterprises under environmental regulations in China. *Frontiers in Environmental Science, 10*, 926896.

Zhang, W., Ye, S., Mangla, S. K., Emrouznejad, A., & Song, M. (2024). Smart platforming in automotive manufacturing for NetZero: Intelligentization, green technology, and innovation dynamics. *International Journal of Production Economics, 274*, 109289.

Zhu, Y., Zhang, H., Siddik, A. B., Zheng, Y., & Sobhani, F. A. (2023). Understanding corporate green competitive advantage through green technology adoption and green dynamic capabilities: Does green product innovation matter? *Systems, 11*(9), 461.

# Chapter 7 Integrating Artificial Intelligence in Education With a Strategic Framework for Ethical and Inclusive Innovation

**Raed Atef**
https://orcid.org/0009-0004-0012-4940
*United Arab Emirates University, UAE*

## ABSTRACT

*This chapter proposes a comprehensive framework for integrating Artificial Intelligence (AI) in education, emphasizing ethical governance, innovation, and equity. The framework addresses key dimensions such as digital literacy, scalability, accessibility, and responsible AI adoption aligned with ethical principles. It highlights the need for inclusive policies that ensure transparency, accountability, and fairness while promoting lifelong learning and social justice. The framework also outlines implications for institutions, communities, and policymakers aiming to balance technological advancement with human-centered education. Limitations include the lack of empirical validation and contextual variation, indicating the need for future studies to test the model in diverse educational settings.*

## INTRODUCTION

The rapid advancement of artificial intelligence (AI) has profoundly reshaped various domains, including industry, healthcare, education, and governance. As this

DOI: 10.4018/979-8-3373-7584-7.ch007

transformative technology continues to evolve, its integration into education presents immense opportunities for innovation, efficiency, and personalized learning. However, this progress also raises complex ethical challenges, necessitating the establishment of robust governance frameworks (Awashreh & Mohamed, 2024). Therefore, the intersection of AI governance, innovation, and ethical education is critical to ensuring that AI technologies are utilized both effectively and responsibly, fostering environments that respect human values, equity, and inclusivity (Rashid & Kausik, 2024).

In particular, AI holds the potential to revolutionize educational practices by offering adaptive learning systems, automating administrative tasks, and providing insights through data analytics. These innovations, however, promise to enhance educational outcomes by tailoring learning experiences to individual needs, increasing access to quality education, and supporting educators in their roles (Awashreh, 2024 a). Yet, alongside these transformative possibilities come significant risks, including privacy violations, algorithmic bias, and the erosion of critical human skills. Without proper governance, these risks could undermine the very foundations of ethical education, leading to unequal opportunities and societal disparities. Thus, the need for a balanced approach to AI governance in education becomes imperative (Wang et al., 2024).

In addressing this need, AI governance refers to the policies, principles, and practices that guide the development, deployment, and oversight of AI technologies. Effective governance frameworks must strike a balance between fostering innovation and ensuring accountability. To achieve this balance, a multi-stakeholder approach is required, involving policymakers, educators, technologists, and the broader community. Specifically, in education, AI governance must prioritize transparency, fairness, and inclusivity while simultaneously fostering innovation that enhances learning experiences and outcomes (Cancela-Outeda, 2024).

Moreover, ethical education must form the cornerstone of AI governance strategies. This involves integrating ethical considerations into AI systems and educating students and stakeholders about the broader implications of AI technologies. By doing so, ethical education ensures that individuals are equipped with the critical thinking skills and moral frameworks necessary to navigate the complexities of AI-driven societies. In addition, it promotes a culture of responsibility among AI developers and users, encouraging the creation of technologies that prioritize human dignity and well-being (Abulibdeh, Zaidan & Abulibdeh, 2024).

As such, societies increasingly rely on AI to shape educational policies and practices, making the need for cohesive governance frameworks ever more pressing. To address this critical need, this study explores the convergence of AI governance and ethical education (Alonso-Rodríguez, 2024). By emphasizing the importance of innovation guided by moral and social imperatives, it aims to demonstrate how aligning AI technologies with ethical values can create a future where AI not only enhances educational systems but also contributes to a more equitable and just society. To this end, the study will delve into the mechanisms of AI governance, the challenges and opportunities in ethical education, and the pathways to achieving innovation that upholds the highest standards of integrity and human welfare (Li, 2023).

Indeed, while AI integration in education has demonstrated transformative potential—such as personalized learning, administrative efficiency, and data-driven decision-making—it also introduces ethical dilemmas (Awashreh, 2024 b). For instance, issues like algorithmic bias, privacy concerns, and the risk of exacerbating educational inequities are significant challenges. Furthermore, the absence of robust AI governance frameworks compounds these problems, leaving educators and policymakers struggling to balance innovation with ethical considerations. Addressing this gap is essential to fostering equitable access and sustainable development in education, a challenge this study seeks to tackle (Al-Zahrani, 2024).

The central question for this research is: how can AI governance frameworks be designed to foster innovation while ensuring the ethical application of AI in education? To answer this, the objectives of the study are twofold:

- To explore the role of AI governance in promoting innovation within educational systems, emphasizing the integration of advanced technologies to enhance learning outcomes.
- To identify and propose ethical principles and frameworks that ensure the responsible use of AI in education, addressing concerns such as bias, privacy, and equity.

Consequently, this study addresses the critical intersection of AI governance, innovation, and ethical education. As AI continues to shape education, understanding how governance frameworks can enable innovation while safeguarding ethical standards is vital for shaping future educational policies and practices. By providing insights into the responsible integration of AI into education, this research can benefit educators, policymakers, and students alike, ensuring equitable and sustainable advancements in learning environments.

Ultimately, the significance of this study lies in its theoretical and practical contributions. Theoretically, it enriches the academic discourse on AI governance and ethics, offering a comprehensive understanding of the challenges and opportunities in educational innovation. Practically, the study provides actionable recommendations for designing governance frameworks that balance technological progress with ethical imperatives, equipping stakeholders with the tools to navigate the complexities of

AI in education. This dual contribution underlines the study's relevance in shaping the future of education in the era of AI (Goosen & Mugumo, 2024).

The structure of this book chapter reflects its comprehensive approach. The introduction provides an overview of the significance of AI in education, emphasizing the need for effective governance and ethical considerations. Subsequently, section (2) outlines the literature review and key concepts such as AI governance, innovation, and ethical education, while highlighting existing frameworks and challenges. Next section (3), the methods section details the secondary data analysis approach, including the sources of data and the analytical techniques employed. Following this, the result presented in section (4) and discussion section (5) presents the findings, analyzing the interconnections between AI governance, innovation in education, and ethical education. Section (6) conclude, the chapter introduces a cohesive model that integrates these components, followed by practical implications, suggestions for future research directions, and a call for a balanced approach to AI integration in education.

## LITERATRURE REVIEW

The integration of artificial intelligence (AI) into education has garnered significant scholarly attention due to its transformative potential in reshaping traditional pedagogical models, curriculum delivery, and administrative processes. This shift reflects broader trends in the digital transformation of education, where AI serves not only as a tool for efficiency but as a catalyst for systemic change (Dayal, Verma & Sehgal, 2023). A growing body of literature underscores the ability of AI to enhance educational outcomes by enabling personalized learning experiences, automating repetitive tasks, and providing valuable insights through data analytics. These capabilities are particularly relevant in an era where educators are increasingly tasked with addressing diverse learner needs and improving institutional performance under resource constraints (Das, Malaviya & Singh, 2023).

For instance, adaptive learning systems represent a key innovation in personalized education. Such systems utilize real-time performance data to dynamically adjust content delivery, pacing, and instructional strategies based on individual student profiles. This promotes a tailored educational experience that aligns with learners' unique cognitive abilities, learning styles, and preferences, thereby potentially improving engagement and academic achievement (Leelavathi & Surendhranatha, 2024). Moreover, adaptive technologies support formative assessment processes by identifying learning gaps and providing targeted feedback, which can significantly enhance the learning trajectory of students over time (Lim, Gottipati & Cheong, 2024).

Similarly, AI-driven tools—such as chatbots, virtual teaching assistants, and predictive analytics platforms—are revolutionizing administrative operations in educational institutions. These tools streamline processes such as responding to student inquiries, scheduling appointments, monitoring academic progress, and managing recordkeeping, thereby allowing educators and administrative staff to redirect their efforts toward enhancing instructional quality and student engagement. The deployment of such tools exemplifies how AI can reduce administrative burdens and optimize institutional resources (Davar, Dewan & Zhang, 2025).

These advancements, as noted by various researchers, signify a paradigm shift in how education is delivered, accessed, and managed in the digital age. The convergence of AI technologies with educational practices is redefining the roles of both teachers and learners, fostering new forms of interaction, and enabling more inclusive and data-informed educational ecosystems (Grubaugh & Levitt, 2023). However, while the promise of AI in education is vast, the risks associated with its unchecked deployment highlight the urgent need for robust governance mechanisms that balance technological innovation with ethical imperatives (Kamalov et al., 2023). Without appropriate oversight, AI could exacerbate existing inequalities, compromise privacy, and introduce systemic biases into educational environments.

Moreover, a recurring theme in the literature is the ethical dilemmas arising from the widespread use of AI technologies in education. As educational institutions increasingly rely on AI systems for decision-making and instructional support, scholars have identified several critical concerns, including algorithmic bias, privacy violations, and the potential erosion of human agency in learning processes (Zhai, Wibowo & Li, 2024). Algorithmic bias, for example, occurs when AI systems inadvertently perpetuate or exacerbate existing social inequities due to flawed or unrepresentative training data. These biases can manifest in various forms, such as unequal access to learning opportunities, skewed predictive assessments, or the reinforcement of stereotypes, leading to discriminatory practices that disadvantage marginalized groups (Al Saadi & Awashreh, 2024).

Privacy concerns are equally prominent. The collection, storage, and analysis of vast amounts of student data—ranging from academic records to behavioral patterns—raise significant ethical and legal questions about consent, data ownership, and the risk of misuse. Educational institutions must navigate complex issues related to data governance, particularly in ensuring transparency and accountability in how student data is used and protected. Failure to address these concerns may erode trust between institutions, learners, and the broader community (Awashreh & Bremananth, 2025).

Furthermore, critics argue that the over-reliance on AI in education could undermine essential human skills, such as critical thinking, emotional intelligence, and interpersonal communication. As students and educators become increasingly dependent on automated systems, there is a risk of devaluing human judgment and creativity in the learning process (Al Saadi & Awashreh, 2025). This concern is particularly salient in disciplines that emphasize dialogic learning, collaborative problem-solving, and moral reasoning—areas where human interaction remains irreplaceable. These challenges underscore the necessity of developing governance frameworks that address ethical issues while enabling the responsible and equitable integration of AI in education (Mogavi et al., 2024).

To address these challenges, the concept of AI governance has emerged as a focal point in policy and academic discourse. AI governance encompasses the policies, principles, and practices guiding the development and use of AI technologies. In the context of education, effective AI governance frameworks must not only ensure technical compliance but also promote values such as equity, inclusivity, and social responsibility (Papagiannidis, Mikalef & Conboy, 2025). Numerous studies have highlighted that effective governance requires a delicate balance between fostering innovation and ensuring accountability, transparency, and fairness (Awashreh & Ramachandran, 2025). Without such balance, educational systems may inadvertently amplify inequalities or become overly reliant on technologies that lack human oversight and ethical grounding.

In practice, educational AI governance must involve a multi-stakeholder approach, bringing together policymakers, educators, technologists, students, parents, and community representatives. This inclusive approach ensures that diverse perspectives inform the development and implementation of AI policies, aligning technological solutions with societal values and educational goals (Mogavi et al., 2024). Specific governance strategies should include clear guidelines for data usage, mechanisms for stakeholder consultation, and continuous monitoring of AI system impacts. Moreover, research emphasizes that transparency is crucial—not only in terms of AI system design and functionality but also in ensuring that stakeholders understand how decisions are made and the implications of those decisions. Transparent AI systems foster accountability and allow for meaningful public scrutiny (Awashreh & Ramachandran, 2025)

Fairness and inclusivity are equally critical pillars of governance. Scholars advocate for frameworks that proactively address disparities in access to AI-enabled resources and ensure that educational technologies serve all students equitably, regardless of socioeconomic background, geographic location, or learning ability (Cheong, 2024). This includes designing AI systems that are culturally sensitive, linguistically diverse, and adaptable to varied learning environments. Only through comprehensive and ethically informed governance can the educational sector harness the full potential of AI while safeguarding the rights and interests of all stakeholders (Berson, Berson & Luo, 2025).

In addition to governance frameworks, ethical education emerges as another cornerstone of the scholarly discourse on AI governance in education, underscoring the dual necessity of embedding ethical considerations into AI systems and cultivating a culture of ethical awareness among all stakeholders (Awashreh, 2024 b). The literature reveals a consensus that technological innovation alone is insufficient for ensuring the responsible deployment of AI; it must be accompanied by a strong ethical foundation embedded across institutional, curricular, and policy dimensions. Researchers argue that ethical education involves equipping students, educators, and policymakers with the knowledge and critical thinking skills required to assess the societal, psychological, and philosophical implications of AI (Awashreh & Al Ghunaimi, 2025). This involves not only understanding how AI functions but also interrogating the values and assumptions underlying its design and application.

By integrating ethical literacy into formal education curricula, institutions can empower individuals to engage meaningfully with the moral complexities inherent in AI-driven societies. Ethical literacy includes the ability to question the fairness of algorithmic decisions, evaluate the impact of data collection on privacy, and recognize how AI systems may affect social dynamics. Furthermore, it instills a sense of civic responsibility and encourages future professionals to uphold ethical standards in the development and use of AI technologies. This proactive approach to ethics education is especially crucial in preparing future generations to become both critical users and responsible designers of AI technologies.

Ethical education also extends beyond users to encompass the developers and designers of AI systems. As creators of tools that significantly influence human behavior and institutional processes, developers must be guided by principles that prioritize human dignity, social equity, and psychological well-being. Scholars have proposed a range of ethical frameworks intended to shape the development of AI technologies. Among the most commonly cited are the principles of accountability, explainability, transparency, and non-maleficence. Accountability ensures that the developers and deployers of AI are held responsible for the consequences of their systems. Explainability and transparency require that AI decision-making processes be understandable to stakeholders, thereby facilitating trust and informed engagement. Non-maleficence, a principle rooted in bioethics, mandates that AI systems should do no harm—ensuring they do not inadvertently reinforce social biases, marginalize vulnerable populations, or contribute to adverse psychological outcomes (Lottu et al., 2024).

Additionally, the literature draws increasing attention to the urgent need for cohesive, well-structured AI governance frameworks as educational systems become progressively dependent on AI technologies to shape policies, curricula, assessments, and student services. The integration of AI into decision-making processes without proper regulatory oversight may result in fragmented, inconsistent, or even harmful outcomes. Researchers have noted that piecemeal or reactive governance approaches can exacerbate the very challenges they aim to mitigate—such as the proliferation of algorithmic bias, inadequate privacy safeguards, and a lack of stakeholder accountability—ultimately undermining the potential benefits of AI in education (Awashreh, 2024b).

One prominent recommendation across the literature is the adoption of a global perspective in developing AI governance frameworks. Given the transnational nature of digital technologies, scholars argue for enhanced international collaboration and knowledge-sharing to foster consensus on core ethical principles and regulatory standards. This global alignment would facilitate the creation of shared protocols for data governance, system interoperability, and ethical auditing, ensuring that AI technologies adhere to consistent quality and safety benchmarks across contexts. At the same time, researchers caution that such frameworks must remain adaptable to local realities. Effective governance must be sensitive to the cultural, economic, political, and pedagogical specificities of different regions. Without contextual adaptability, globally imposed governance models risk becoming misaligned with local needs, undermining both their legitimacy and their effectiveness.

This dual emphasis—on global harmonization and local relevance—is seen as essential for building governance models that are both comprehensive and context-sensitive. Frameworks must reflect a shared ethical vision while accommodating diverse educational traditions and sociocultural landscapes. For example, what constitutes fair access to AI in one country might differ significantly from another based on infrastructural capacities, legal frameworks, and public attitudes toward technology.

In short, the expanding literature on AI in education underscores both the profound opportunities and the complex challenges associated with its integration. Scholars repeatedly emphasize the need for governance frameworks that strike a balance between enabling innovation and upholding ethical values. Key areas of concern include algorithmic bias, data privacy, transparency, equity of access, and the potential erosion of essential human capacities such as empathy, communication, and critical thinking. Effective governance mechanisms are essential not only to mitigate these risks but to create an enabling environment in which AI can contribute to more inclusive, efficient, and responsive educational systems (Farahani, 2024).

Moreover, the integration of ethical education into broader governance strategies serves as a vital reinforcement, strengthening the capacity of all stakeholders to responsibly engage with AI. By fostering ethical awareness and ethical reasoning skills, education systems can build a foundation for lifelong learning and moral resilience in the face of technological change. As the discourse on AI governance and ethical education continues to evolve, scholars call for future research to explore innovative frameworks and pedagogical approaches that align technological progress with deeply rooted societal values. This includes investigating the role of interdisciplinary collaboration, public-private partnerships, and participatory policy-making in shaping the future of AI in education. Ultimately, these efforts aim to ensure that AI not only advances efficiency and personalization but also contributes to a more equitable, just, and human-centered educational landscape (Akinrinola et al., 2024).

## METHODOLOGY

### Research Approach

This study adopts a secondary data analysis methodology, utilizing existing literature, reports, and datasets to explore the intersection of AI governance, innovation, and ethical education. Secondary data sources include peer-reviewed journal articles, policy documents, international standards, and case studies that examine AI integration in education (Cheong et al., 2023). This approach enables a comprehensive understanding of the topic by leveraging diverse perspectives and evidence from established research (Ofosu-Ampong, 2024).

### Research Procedures

Authors use key words in questions to search for relevant articles of interest. By searching Google, they obtain relevant secondary data from peer-reviewed journals, which is then synthesized, summarized, and analyzed to assist in writing the book chapter.

### Data Collection

In order to explore the implications of AI in education, peer-reviewed articles from databases can provide valuable theoretical insights and empirical findings, particularly on AI governance and ethical education. By consulting policy reports and case studies, one can analyze the data to gain a deeper understanding of how AI can be integrated into educational systems while maintaining ethical standards and addressing societal needs.

### Constructing Comprehensive Framework

The study will focus on constructing a comprehensive framework that integrates AI governance, innovation in education, and ethical education, highlighting the interrelationships between these critical components as suggested by Roshanaei, Olivares

& Lopez (2023). The first component of the proposed framework, AI governance, establishes the necessary ethical principles for AI development and deployment. These principles—transparency, accountability, fairness, and inclusivity—are fundamental to ensuring that AI systems are designed and implemented responsibly. Additionally, the regulatory frameworks identify existing standards and propose adaptable policies that can guide the integration of AI into educational settings, allowing for flexibility and responsiveness to technological advancements. Multi-stakeholder collaboration is also emphasized, as it promotes engagement between policymakers, educators, technologists, and community members to ensure that AI implementation is informed by diverse perspectives and addresses the needs of all stakeholders (Singhal et al., 2024).

The second component, innovation in education, focuses on harnessing the potential of AI to transform learning environments (Tan, 2023). Technological advancements in AI can provide personalized learning experiences, adaptive teaching methods, and more efficient administrative processes. Data-driven insights enable educational institutions to enhance decision-making, improve student outcomes, and streamline operations. However, ensuring the scalability and accessibility of these innovations is critical to ensure that AI tools are available to a wide range of learner populations, particularly those from underserved communities.

The third component, ethical education, plays a crucial role in preparing students and stakeholders to engage responsibly with AI technologies. Ethical literacy, which integrates critical thinking and ethical decision-making into curricula, equips individuals with the tools to navigate an AI-driven society. Responsible AI design encourages developers to create technologies that align with human-centered values, ensuring that AI systems prioritize societal well-being. Finally, addressing issues of equity and inclusion is vital for ensuring that AI-enhanced educational opportunities are accessible to all, mitigating disparities that may arise due to socioeconomic or geographic factors. Together, these components form a cohesive framework that balances the need for technological innovation with the imperative of ethical responsibility and governance (Fu & Weng, 2024). By fostering a collaborative approach and focusing on accessibility, fairness, and inclusivity, this framework aims to guide the responsible integration of AI into education, ensuring that it benefits all learners while upholding fundamental ethical principles. Below is a simple table (1) summarizing the Components of the Framework.

*Table 1. Components of the Framework*

| Component | Key Focus Areas |
|---|---|
| AI Governance | - Principles and Policies: Ethical principles (transparency, accountability, fairness, inclusivity). |
| | - Regulatory Frameworks: Standards and adaptable policies for AI integration. |
| | - Stakeholder Collaboration: Engagement of policymakers, educators, technologists, and communities. |
| Innovation in Education | - Technological Advancements: AI for personalized learning, adaptive teaching, and efficiency. |
| | - Data-Driven Insights: AI analytics to improve decision-making in education. |
| | - Scalability and Accessibility: Ensuring innovations are scalable and accessible to diverse populations. |
| Ethical Education | - Ethical Literacy: Critical thinking and ethical decision-making in curricula. |
| | - Responsible AI Design: Aligning AI technologies with human-centered values. |
| | - Equity and Inclusion: Addressing disparities for equitable access to education. |

This concise table highlights the core components and their respective focus areas in the framework.
(Sources: developed by researchers, 2024)

The interactions within the proposed framework further emphasize the interconnectedness of AI governance, innovation, and ethical education, ensuring that these components work in tandem to promote responsible AI integration in education. In this context, the governance-innovation nexus underscores the importance of creating governance frameworks that not only encourage technological innovation but also ensure that these innovations align with ethical principles and societal needs. Governance structures must provide flexibility for AI development while maintaining strict adherence to foundational ethical guidelines (Goosen et al., 2024). This balance, therefore, allows for progress without compromising the values of transparency, fairness, and inclusivity. Similarly, the governance-ethics nexus highlights the need for effective governance that incorporates ethical considerations into AI policies. Policies should not only govern the technical aspects of AI but also promote a culture of responsibility and accountability (Awashreh & Al Ghunaimi, 2025 b). By embedding ethics into governance frameworks, institutions can, in turn, ensure that AI systems are developed and deployed in ways that prioritize societal well-being and uphold human dignity, fostering public trust and ensuring long-term success.

Furthermore, the innovation-ethics nexus reinforces the idea that AI innovations must be designed with ethical principles at the forefront. Technological advancements should prioritize inclusivity, privacy, and fairness in both their design and application. Ensuring that AI tools are ethically aligned ensures, as a result, that these innovations benefit all learners, without reinforcing existing inequalities or creating new risks (Alvarez et al., 2024). This nexus highlights the critical need for responsible innovation, ensuring that the benefits of AI in education are distributed equitably while minimizing potential harms. In sum, these interwoven interactions in the framework emphasize the need for a holistic approach to AI in education—one that fosters innovation within an ethically governed environment and ensures that technological advancements are implemented in a way that benefits society as a whole. Thus, the framework provides a comprehensive model for integrating governance, innovation, and ethics in the evolving landscape of AI education. Table (2) summarizing the Interactions in the Framework.

*Table 2. Interactions in the Framework*

| Interaction | Description |
|---|---|
| **Governance-Innovation Nexus** | Governance frameworks encourage innovation while ensuring compliance with ethical principles and societal needs. |
| **Governance-Ethics Nexus** | Governance integrates ethical considerations into AI policies, fostering responsibility and accountability. |
| **Innovation-Ethics Nexus** | AI innovations align with ethical principles, prioritizing inclusivity, privacy, and fairness. |

(Sources: developed by researcher, 2025)

Table (1) captures the essence of the dynamic relationships within the framework in a clear and concise format. For the whole picture, Figure 1 draw a comprehensive framework

*Figure 1. Components and Interactions*

Figure (1) Components and Interactions

## RESULTS

The results of this study highlight the critical role of AI governance in fostering innovation within educational systems. Effective governance frameworks encourage technological advancements while ensuring ethical principles, such as fairness, transparency, and inclusivity, are upheld to benefit students, educators, and institutions. Figure (2) present the resuslts is simple way

*Figure 2. presesnt the resuslt major secition*

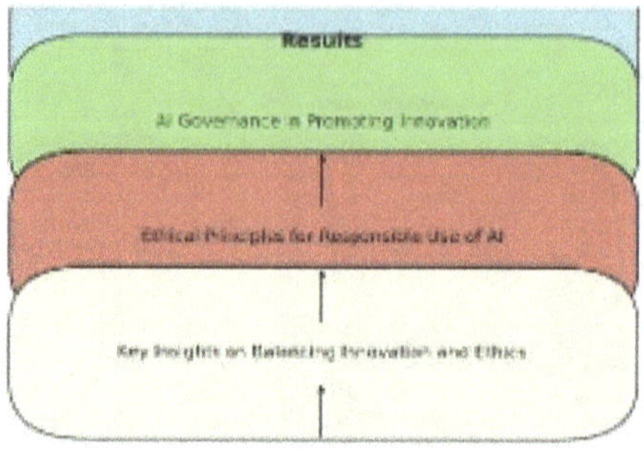


Figure 2: presesnt the resuslt major secition

## Role of AI Governance in Promoting Innovation in Education

AI governance plays a pivotal role in balancing technological innovation with responsible use within educational systems. Through the analysis of existing frameworks and practices, it becomes clear that effective AI governance encourages innovation while ensuring that the development and application of AI technologies align with ethical principles and societal needs. In this context, AI governance fosters a conducive environment for transformative educational practices, particularly in adaptive learning, administrative processes, and data-driven decision-making (David et al., 2024).

One of the key areas where AI governance has a significant impact is in promoting adaptive learning. Governance frameworks that emphasize transparency, fairness, and accountability are essential in facilitating the development of adaptive learning systems. By personalizing learning experiences to suit individual needs, AI technologies enhance learning outcomes. Moreover, collaboration between educators, technologists, and policymakers under governance policies further maximizes the potential of AI to revolutionize educational practices (Abdelkader et al., 2024).

Additionally, AI governance plays an important role in automating administrative tasks, thereby improving operational efficiency within educational institutions. Strong governance frameworks guide the use of AI-powered systems, allowing educators to focus more on teaching rather than time-consuming administrative duties. This shift enables better resource allocation, leading to more productive educational environments that benefit both educators and students alike (Igbokwe, 2023).

Furthermore, AI governance is crucial in driving data-driven decision-making within education. Governance frameworks promote the ethical and responsible use of data analytics to guide educational decisions. By ensuring that data-driven tools are used with integrity, AI governance helps educational institutions make informed decisions, improve student outcomes, and identify gaps in the curriculum. This approach enables a more tailored and personalized learning experience, resulting in more effective educational strategies. In summary, AI governance serves as a cornerstone in integrating innovative AI technologies into education. Through its emphasis on fairness, transparency, and ethical data use, it ensures that AI's role in education is both transformative and responsible, with significant benefits for students, educators, and institutions (Papagiannidis, Mikalef & Conboy, 2025).

## Ethical Principles and Frameworks for the Responsible Use of AI in Education

The implementation of AI in education requires robust ethical principles to prevent potential misuse and mitigate risks such as algorithmic bias and privacy violations. In light of these challenges, it is essential to establish ethical guidelines that not only promote innovation but also ensure that AI technologies are used responsibly and equitably within educational systems. These ethical principles provide a foundation for balancing technological advancement with societal needs, ensuring that AI's integration into education is both effective and fair (Tahir, Amanat & Awan, 2024).

One critical principle is transparency and accountability, which ensures that AI algorithms and processes are open to scrutiny. By making AI systems more transparent, educational institutions can build trust among students, educators, and other stakeholders. It is important for schools and universities to offer clear guidelines about how AI technologies are used in the classroom and how decisions, particularly those that affect student outcomes, are made. Moreover, ensuring the accountability of both AI developers and educational institutions is crucial in safeguarding privacy, security, and fairness, ultimately leading to more responsible AI implementation (Cheong, 2024).

Another essential principle is fairness and inclusivity, which mandates that AI systems should not reinforce biases. Governance frameworks must ensure that AI algorithms are regularly audited for bias and adjusted accordingly to promote fairness across all demographic groups. This is particularly important for marginalized or underrepresented groups, as AI systems should not worsen existing educational disparities. By incorporating these principles into AI governance frameworks, educational institutions can create environments where every student, regardless of background, has equitable access to learning opportunities (Schwartz et al., 2024).

Additionally, privacy and data protection are vital considerations in the ethical implementation of AI in education. Student data is sensitive, and AI governance frameworks must prioritize privacy to prevent misuse of personal information. Ensuring compliance with global data protection regulations, such as GDPR, is essential in safeguarding student information. Moreover, governance frameworks must establish clear guidelines for the ethical use of student data in personalized learning and analysis, maintaining the privacy and security of this valuable resource (Huang, 2023).. In summary, ethical principles play a crucial role in guiding the integration of AI into educational systems. By focusing on transparency, accountability, fairness, inclusivity, privacy, and data protection, AI governance can prevent the misuse of AI technologies and ensure that their application benefits all students, promoting a more ethical and just educational environment.

## Key Insights on Balancing Innovation with Ethical Standards

From the analysis, several key insights emerge regarding the integration of AI in education. One of the primary insights is the need for innovation with responsibility. The intersection of AI governance, innovation, and ethics emphasizes that technological advancements in AI must be aligned with ethical principles. While innovations such as personalized learning and AI-based administrative tools hold immense potential, their deployment must prioritize ethical considerations such as equity, transparency, and privacy. A governance framework that encourages responsible innovation will ensure that AI tools contribute to improved educational outcomes without exacerbating existing societal inequalities, helping to create a fairer educational landscape (Lim et al., 2023).

In addition to innovation, collaborative governance models play a vital role in the success of AI integration in education. The multi-stakeholder approach to AI governance ensures that all relevant parties—policymakers, educators, technologists, students, and the broader community—collaborate to design and implement AI solutions that meet diverse needs and concerns. This inclusive model is crucial for addressing the unique challenges faced by different educational contexts, ensuring that AI systems are developed in ways that benefit all learners, regardless of their background or location (OECD, 2023).

Equally important is the focus on ethical education as a foundation for the responsible use of AI. Integrating ethical thinking into the curriculum is paramount in helping students and educators navigate the complexities of AI in educational settings. By equipping learners with the knowledge to critically evaluate AI technologies, educational systems can foster a culture of responsibility and ensure that future generations are prepared to engage with AI in an ethically sound manner. This not only supports the responsible development of AI but also prepares students to become active, ethical participants in the evolving digital world (Isiaku et al., 2024).

The results of this study underscore the importance of AI governance in promoting innovation within educational systems while maintaining ethical integrity. Establishing robust frameworks that emphasize transparency, fairness, and inclusivity is key to harnessing the full potential of AI technologies. Such frameworks ensure that AI can enhance learning outcomes, streamline administrative functions, and promote equitable access to education. Moreover, the integration of ethical principles within these frameworks safeguards privacy, minimizes biases, and promotes the well-being of all students.

In the evolving landscape of AI in education, the challenge lies in creating flexible governance frameworks that balance technological innovation with societal needs. These frameworks must not only foster innovation but also ensure that innovations serve societal needs, promote equity, and uphold human dignity. This study offers a comprehensive approach to balancing these factors and contributes to the ongoing conversation about the best ways to integrate AI into educational systems for the benefit of all stakeholders, ensuring that AI is used to improve educational practices while maintaining a strong ethical foundation (Awashreh, 2025 c).

## DISUCSSION

The integration of Artificial Intelligence (AI) into education offers a transformative opportunity to enhance learning outcomes and bridge educational disparities. In the U.S., the focus is on ensuring equitable access to AI tools, particularly for underserved communities, through government grants and private funding (Lin et al., 2023). However, disparities in funding and access remain significant challenges, highlighting the need for targeted policies to ensure AI benefits all students (Jindal et al., 2023). Moreover, AI governance frameworks must align with ethical and educational goals, incorporating transparency, accountability, fairness, and inclusivity to build trust (Cheong, 2024).

In addition, the complexity of implementing AI governance across diverse educational systems requires adaptable frameworks addressing issues like data privacy, algorithmic bias, and digital literacy. Collaboration among policymakers, educators, and technologists is essential to meet the unique needs of all learners (OECD, 2023). Furthermore, balancing governance and innovation is crucial to fostering creativity while ensuring alignment with societal values (Abulibdeh, Zaidan & Abulibdeh, 2024). Ethical principles must be embedded to ensure AI contributes to better educational outcomes while promoting fairness (Awashreh, 2025).

Moreover, ethical education is vital in preparing students and educators to navigate AI technologies responsibly, fostering a culture of ethical engagement (Isiaku et al., 2024). While AI has the potential to enhance personalized learning and administrative efficiency, it also faces challenges related to scalability, accessibility, and digital literacy. Therefore, investments in infrastructure and digital skills are necessary for widespread AI adoption (Kamalov et al., 2023).

Additionally, localized, flexible AI governance frameworks are key, particularly for underserved communities. Public-private partnerships can ensure innovation aligns with ethical principles (United Arab Emirates, 2024). Longitudinal and case studies will also be crucial for evaluating the long-term impact of AI policies on educational outcomes and equity (Ou, 2024). In summary, integrating AI into education requires balancing governance, innovation, and ethics to address challenges like resource constraints and regional disparities. Therefore, future research should focus on longitudinal studies to assess AI's long-term impact on educational practices and its potential to transform learning experiences worldwide (Dwivedi et al., 2023).

**For implication**, the proposed framework's interactions between AI governance, innovation, and ethical education have significant implications for society, academia, and institutions, shaping the future landscape of AI integration in education. For society, the governance-innovation nexus ensures that AI advancements benefit all individuals, particularly marginalized groups, by upholding ethical principles such as inclusivity, fairness, and transparency. By embedding ethical guidelines into AI policies and technologies, society stands to gain from innovations that not only drive economic and technological progress but also foster equitable access to educational opportunities. The prioritization of ethical principles ensures that AI tools are deployed responsibly, preventing the reinforcement of existing societal inequalities and minimizing new risks. This holistic approach to AI can, therefore, contribute to the creation of a more just and inclusive society, where technology serves to empower rather than marginalize vulnerable populations (Sargiotis, 2024).

In academia, the governance-ethics nexus has profound implications for how institutions develop and implement AI-related curricula and research. By incorporating ethical considerations into AI policies, academia can cultivate a culture of responsibility and accountability, ensuring that AI technologies are studied and developed with a strong sense of societal impact. Furthermore, integrating AI ethics into educational programs helps prepare future generations of students to make informed, responsible decisions about the design and use of AI technologies. Academia can thus play a critical role in shaping the ethical standards that guide AI development, promoting interdisciplinary research that considers the social, economic, and cultural implications of AI (Camilleri, 2023).

For institutions, the innovation-ethics nexus calls for a careful balancing act between technological progress and ethical responsibility. Educational institutions must not only adopt AI innovations but also ensure that these innovations are aligned with ethical principles that prioritize privacy, inclusivity, and fairness. This means that institutions must develop policies that govern the deployment of AI technologies in a way that is both technically effective and ethically sound (Al-Zahrani & Alasmari, 2024). By doing so, they ensure that AI is used to enhance educational practices—such as personalized learning and adaptive teaching—while safeguarding against potential harm to students and society. Moreover, fostering stakeholder collaboration between policymakers, educators, technologists, and communities can help institutions navigate the complex ethical landscape surrounding AI and ensure that these technologies are deployed in ways that align with the values of the broader society (Herane, 2024). In short, the framework's emphasis on the interconnections between governance, innovation, and ethics provides a roadmap for institutions, academia, and society to collectively navigate the challenges and opportunities presented by AI in education. By ensuring that AI technologies are developed and implemented with a focus on ethical principles, these sectors can work together to create a more inclusive, accountable, and responsible future for education and beyond.

To enhance AI integration in education, here are actionable recommendations and practical steps addressing scalability, accessibility, and digital literacy, alongside strategies for implementing the framework across diverse contexts:

1. To ensure scalability, the following recommendations should adapt
   - Develop modular AI solutions that scale with user growth.
   - Foster public-private partnerships to create affordable AI tools for diverse institutions.
   - Invest in AI infrastructure, such as high-speed internet and cloud services.
   - **Implementation Steps:**
   - Conduct needs assessments to identify scalability challenges.
   - Choose flexible, modular AI tools.
   - Create scalable educator training programs.
2. To ensure accessibility, the following recommendations should adapt
   - Ensure affordable access through government subsidies or incentives.
   - Adapt AI tools for low-resource environments, prioritizing mobile solutions.
   - Design AI systems that are culturally and linguistically customizable.
   - **Implementation Steps:**
     - Target regions with low infrastructure for AI access.
     - Host workshops for educators on optimizing AI in resource-limited settings.
     - Collaborate on creating multilingual, culturally relevant AI tools.
3. For digital literacy, the following recommendations should adapt
   - Integrate digital literacy into the core curriculum for both students and educators.
   - Provide ongoing professional development for educators.

- Support marginalized communities with AI-focused digital literacy programs.
- **Implementation Steps:**
  - Work with curriculum developers to embed digital literacy.
  - Establish continuous professional development for teachers.
  - Launch outreach programs to promote digital literacy in underserved areas.

4. Implementing the Framework Across Educational Contexts
   - **Recommendations:**
   - Customize AI governance frameworks to local contexts, considering infrastructure and cultural factors.
   - Pilot AI programs before broader implementation.
   - Engage diverse stakeholders in the design and rollout of AI solutions.
   - **Implementation Steps:**
     - Develop AI adoption plans specific to each region's resources and needs.
     - Start with pilot programs, adjusting based on real-world feedback.
     - Form advisory boards with key stakeholders to ensure alignment with local priorities.

By addressing scalability, accessibility, and digital literacy, AI can be successfully integrated into diverse educational systems. Tailoring governance frameworks to local contexts, along with involving all stakeholders, ensures a sustainable, equitable model for AI in education that fosters innovation while upholding ethical standards.

To evaluate the success and impact of the AI governance framework in real-world educational settings, the following specific metrics or indicators can be used:

1. Scalability Metrics
   - Adoption Rate: Measures the percentage of educational institutions actively

     implementing AI-based tools within a defined timeframe, reflecting the pace of systemic AI integration.
   - Growth in Usage: Tracks the increase in the number of active users—including students, educators, and administrators—interacting with AI tools, indicating user acceptance and reliance.
   - Infrastructure Expansion: Assesses investments in foundational AI infrastructure such as broadband connectivity, cloud computing, and smart devices, and the proportion of institutions with access to these essential resources.

- Cost Efficiency: Evaluates the reduction in the average cost of AI tools and services, especially for low-income or underserved institutions, highlighting progress toward equitable scalability.

2. Accessibility Metrics
    - Access to AI Tools: Quantifies the percentage of students and educators in marginalized, remote, or underfunded areas who have reliable access to AI-powered educational platforms and resources.
    - Financial Accessibility: Measures the number of institutions benefiting from government or private subsidies, grants, or funding schemes for AI implementation and assesses how these supports influence adoption capacity.
    - Device Compatibility: Tracks the proportion of institutions using AI tools that function effectively on existing hardware, such as mobile devices or budget-friendly computers, ensuring technological inclusivity.
    - Language and Cultural Adaptation: Assesses the availability of AI tools in local languages and their alignment with regional or cultural learning contexts, which enhances relevance and usability.
3. Digital Literacy Metrics
    - Digital Literacy Improvement: Measures the increase in students' and educators' understanding of digital tools, AI basics, data privacy, and responsible technology use, often via standardized assessments.
    - Professional Development Participation: Calculates the percentage of educators engaging in ongoing training related to AI integration, pedagogy enhancement, and ethical use, contributing to skilled implementation.
    - Increased Confidence in Technology Use: Gathers survey-based data on the perceived confidence of educators and learners in applying AI tools, revealing psychological and behavioral readiness.
    - Community Engagement: Tracks the number of community-led or school-facilitated programs—such as workshops and digital awareness campaigns—aimed at fostering inclusive digital literacy, especially in vulnerable regions.
4. Impact on Learning Outcomes
    - Student Performance: Analyzes quantitative improvements in academic performance (e.g., test scores, grades) pre- and post-introduction of AI tools, illustrating their academic value.
    - Engagement and Retention: Monitors student engagement indicators (e.g., participation in AI-based learning modules, completion rates), and retention trends over time.

- Personalized Learning Outcomes: Evaluates the effectiveness of AI in enabling customized educational experiences by tracking student progress along individualized learning paths and measuring improvements in learning efficiency.

5. Stakeholder Satisfaction and Engagement
    - Stakeholder Feedback: Collects and analyzes feedback from students, teachers, and administrators regarding AI tool usability, relevance, and effectiveness in enhancing learning and administrative tasks.
    - Stakeholder Involvement: Measures the frequency and depth of stakeholder consultations or involvement in the planning, development, and evaluation phases of AI initiatives.
    - Collaboration Levels: Assesses the number and quality of partnerships formed between schools, policymakers, tech developers, and NGOs to support and refine AI integration efforts.
6. Governance and Ethical Standards
    - Compliance with Ethical Guidelines: Tracks the adherence of institutions to nationally or internationally recognized AI ethics standards—including data privacy, nondiscrimination, and fairness in algorithms.
    - Transparency: Measures how transparently institutions communicate AI decision-making processes, including public access to policies, algorithmic logic explanations, and data use disclosures.
    - Incident Reporting: Monitors the frequency and nature of reported ethical concerns or algorithmic biases and evaluates the responsiveness and efficacy of institutional mechanisms in addressing them.
7. Long-Term Sustainability
    - Continued Funding and Investment: Assesses ongoing financial support from public or private sources to maintain and expand AI initiatives, ensuring projects are not short-lived or donor-dependent.
    - Adaptability and Evolution: Evaluates how AI systems and governance frameworks adapt to rapid changes in educational demands, technological innovation, and policy shifts, ensuring long-term relevance.
    - Institutional Integration: Measures the extent to which AI is embedded into the regular teaching, learning, and administrative functions—rather than being treated as an add-on or experiment.

These metrics provide a comprehensive way to evaluate the effectiveness, equity, and sustainability of AI in educational environments. Regular assessment using these indicators will help ensure the framework is meeting its goals and can guide further adjustments or improvements.

## Theoretical Contribution

This study makes several significant theoretical contributions to the evolving discourse on Artificial Intelligence (AI) in education by offering an integrated framework that aligns governance, innovation, and ethics as central pillars of AI deployment in educational systems. Theoretically, the framework advances the understanding of how AI can be harnessed not only as a technological tool but also as a socio-educational catalyst guided by ethical imperatives and governance structures tailored to local contexts.

First, the study enriches the AI governance literature by proposing a dynamic and adaptive governance model rooted in ethical accountability and contextual flexibility. Unlike static, top-down models, this study emphasizes the co-creation of governance frameworks involving diverse stakeholders—governments, educators, communities, and private sector actors—thus contributing to the theory of distributed governance in digital education ecosystems.

Second, the research contributes to educational innovation theory by positioning AI not merely as an enhancer of instructional delivery but as an enabler of systemic transformation through scalable, accessible, and inclusive practices. By embedding the principles of modular design, infrastructure equity, and cultural adaptability, the study bridges the gap between innovation theory and practical scalability in educational reform, particularly in underserved settings.

Third, this work adds depth to ethical theory in educational technology, introducing the "governance-innovation-ethics nexus" as a novel conceptual lens. This nexus offers a theoretical foundation for understanding how ethical frameworks must evolve in parallel with technological capabilities and how such alignment ensures responsible AI integration. It builds on normative ethical models (e.g., virtue ethics, deontology) and translates them into operationalized guidelines tailored for educational institutions.

Fourth, the study expands the theory of socially responsive education systems by articulating how AI implementation can serve as a vehicle for addressing broader societal disparities. Through the integration of equity metrics, culturally responsive AI design, and digital literacy development, the study offers a theoretical model for how educational technologies can support social justice aims.

Lastly, by advocating for longitudinal, multi-dimensional evaluation metrics, the study contributes to evaluation theory in education technology. It moves beyond short-term effectiveness assessments to propose a comprehensive framework that incorporates impact, sustainability, stakeholder engagement, and ethical compliance over time, thus offering scholars and practitioners a robust tool for evaluating the transformative potential of AI in education. In sum, the proposed framework offers a theoretical synthesis that fills key gaps in the literature across governance, innovation, and ethics in educational AI. It sets the stage for future empirical research and interdisciplinary dialogue, serving as a foundational model for the responsible integration of AI into global education systems.

## CONCLUSION

This study underscores the critical importance of AI governance in fostering innovation while upholding ethical standards within educational systems. By aligning AI technologies with robust ethical frameworks and governance structures, educational institutions can unlock the full potential of AI, ensuring that equity, transparency, and accountability are prioritized. The findings highlight the need for flexible and adaptive regulatory frameworks capable of addressing key challenges such as algorithmic bias, data privacy, and digital divides. Moreover, promoting ethical literacy and encouraging responsible AI design ensures that technological advancements align with societal values and respect human dignity. The study also emphasizes the significance of localized approaches that take into account cultural, economic, and technological contexts to ensure equitable AI integration across diverse educational environments.

The interdependent relationships between governance, innovation, and ethics form the foundation of a comprehensive approach to AI in education, guaranteeing that future educational systems remain inclusive, ethically sound, and technologically advanced. The proposed framework integrates these elements to ensure that AI technologies are not only innovative but also aligned with core ethical principles that serve society's best interests. This holistic approach aims to create a responsible and inclusive AI landscape that benefits individuals, educational institutions, and society as a whole. The synergies between the governance-innovation, governance-ethics, and innovation-ethics nexuses are vital in ensuring that AI is deployed in ways that enhance educational outcomes while minimizing potential ethical risks and societal harm.

However, there are several avenues for further research that can deepen our understanding of AI's integration into education and its broader societal implications. First, empirical studies could explore how the proposed framework is being applied in real-world educational contexts, including case studies and longitudinal research to assess the effectiveness of various governance models and their impact on AI innovation and ethical outcomes. Second, research could investigate the influence of cultural and regional differences on AI governance and ethical standards, particularly in diverse educational systems across the globe. Understanding how these factors shape AI deployment could inform more localized, context-sensitive approaches to AI integration. Furthermore, research on the long-term societal impacts of AI in education, with a focus on equity, access, and social mobility, is crucial. Investigating whether AI technologies are contributing to reducing educational disparities or exacerbating inequalities could provide important insights. Finally, there is a need to develop new ethical frameworks that specifically address emerging AI technologies, such as deep learning and neural networks, to ensure their responsible use in educational settings.

In conclusion, the proposed framework offers a solid foundation for the responsible integration of AI into education. However, ongoing research is essential to refine and adapt these principles in practice, ensuring that the transformative potential of AI is realized in a manner that benefits all learners and promotes societal well-being. By continuing to investigate these areas, we can ensure that AI's role in education evolves in an ethical, inclusive, and responsible manner, with long-term positive outcomes for both individuals and society.

## REFERENCES


Abdelkader, A. A. M., Hassan, H., & Abdelkader, M. (2024). The role of artificial intelligence in designing higher education courses: Benefits and challenges. In Lytras, M. D., Alkhaldi, A., Malik, S., Serban, A. C., & Aldosemani, T. (Eds.), *The evolution of artificial intelligence in higher education* (pp. 83–97). Emerald Publishing Limited., DOI: 10.1108/978-1-83549-486-820241005

Abulibdeh, A., Zaidan, E., & Abulibdeh, R. (2024). Navigating the confluence of artificial intelligence and education for sustainable development in the era of industry 4.0: Challenges, opportunities, and ethical dimensions. *Journal of Cleaner Production, 437*, 140527. DOI: 10.1016/j.jclepro.2023.140527

Akinrinola, O., Okoye, C. C., Ofodile, O. C., & Ugochukwu, C. E. (2024). Navigating and reviewing ethical dilemmas in AI development: Strategies for transparency, fairness, and accountability. *GSC Advanced Research and Reviews*, 18(3), 050-058. https://doi.org/DOI: 10.30574/gscarr.2024.18.3.0088

Al Saadi, A., & Awashreh, R. (2024). Enhancing the performance of translation graduates through training: A proposed practical model. In Mansour, N., & Bujosa Vadell, L. M. (Eds.), *Finance and law in the metaverse world* (pp. 219–229). Springer., DOI: 10.1007/978-3-031-67547-8_19

Al-Zahrani, A. M., & Alasmari, T. M. (2024). Exploring the impact of artificial intelligence on higher education: The dynamics of ethical, social, and educational implications. *Humanities & Social Sciences Communications, 11*, 912. DOI: 10.1057/s41599-024-03432-4

Alonso-Rodríguez, A. M. (2024). Towards an ethical framework for artificial intelligence in education. *Teoría de la Educación. Revista Interuniversitaria, 36*(1), 31821. Advance online publication. DOI: 10.14201/teri.31821

Alsaadi, A., & Awashreh, R. (2025). Practical university training impact on job performance of translation graduates in Oman. *Forum for Linguistic Studies, 7*(2), 786–796. DOI: 10.30564/fls.v7i2.8306

Alvarez, J. M., Colmenarejo, A. B., & Elobaid, A.. (2024). Policy advice and best practices on bias and fairness in AI. *Ethics and Information Technology, 26*, 31. DOI: 10.1007/s10676-024-09746-w

Awashreh, R. (2024a). Omani private universities: Debates between progress in human development but weak education quality. *The International Journal of Educational Organization and Leadership, 32*(1), 1–15. DOI: 10.18848/2329-1656/CGP/v32i01/1-15

Awashreh, R. (2024b). Be aware: Navigating challenges in AI-driven higher education. *The International Journal of Interdisciplinary Educational Studies*, *20*(1), 203–218. DOI: 10.18848/2327-011X/CGP/v20i01/203-218

Awashreh, R. (2025). Navigating leadership dynamics: Insights and strategies across domains. In *Optimizing leadership and governance in higher education* (pp. 203–232). IGI Global., DOI: 10.4018/979-8-3693-3534-5.ch010

Awashreh, R., & Al Ghunaimi, H. (2025). Rethinking the PhD: Aligning higher education with market needs and practical skills. *Forum for Linguistic Studies*, *7*(2), 254–264. DOI: 10.30564/fls.v7i2.7942

Awashreh, R., & Al Ghunaimi, H. (2025b). Bridging cultural gaps: Enhancing student motivation and academic integrity in Oman's universities. *Forum for Linguistic Studies*, *7*(2), 265–279. DOI: 10.30564/fls.v7i2.8300

Awashreh, R., & Bremananth, R. (2025). A study on ethical implementation of AI in collegiate studies using fuzzy implication. *Pakistan Journal of Life and Social Sciences*, *23*(1), 00317. Advance online publication. DOI: 10.57239/PJLSS-2025-23.1.00317

Awashreh, R., & Mohamed, Y. (2024). Comparative study of leadership perceptions in government and education sectors: Insights from the UAE and Oman. *The International Journal of Organizational Diversity*, *24*(2), 109–123. DOI: 10.18848/2328-6261/CGP/v24i02/109-123

Awashreh, R., & Ramachandran, B. (2024). Can artificial intelligence dominate and control human beings? *International Research Journal of Multidisciplinary Scope*, *5*(4), 427–438. DOI: 10.47857/irjms.2024.05i04.01569

Berson, I. R., Berson, M. J., & Luo, W. (2025). Innovating responsibly: Ethical considerations for AI in early childhood education. *AI and the Brain of the Child*, *1*(2). Advance online publication. DOI: 10.1007/s44436-025-00003-5

Camilleri, M. A. (2023). Artificial intelligence governance: Ethical considerations and implications for social responsibility. *Expert Systems: International Journal of Knowledge Engineering and Neural Networks*. Advance online publication. DOI: 10.1111/exsy.13406

Cancela-Outeda, C. (2024). The EU's AI act: A framework for collaborative governance. *Internet of Things : Engineering Cyber Physical Human Systems*, *27*, 101291. DOI: 10.1016/j.iot.2024.101291

Chanda, T. C., Sain, Z. H., Shogbesan, Y., & Phiri, E. V. (2024). Digital literacy in education: Preparing students for the future workforce. *International Journal of Research, 11*(8), 327–344. DOI: 10.5281/zenodo.13347718

Cheong, B. C. (2024). Transparency and accountability in AI systems: Safeguarding wellbeing in the age of algorithmic decision-making. *Frontiers in Human Dynamics, 6*, 1421273. DOI: 10.3389/fhumd.2024.1421273

Cheong, H.-I., Lyons, A., Houghton, R. W., & Majumdar, A. (2023). Secondary qualitative research methodology using online data within the context of social sciences. *International Journal of Qualitative Methods, 22*(2), 16094069231180160. DOI: 10.1177/16094069231180160

Das, A., Malaviya, S., & Singh, M. (2023). The impact of AI-driven personalization on learners' performance. *International Journal on Computer Science and Engineering, 11*(8), 15–22. DOI: 10.26438/ijcse/v11i8.1522

Davar, N. F., Dewan, M. A. A., & Zhang, X. (2025). AI chatbots in education: Challenges and opportunities. *Information (Basel), 16*(3), 235. DOI: 10.3390/info16030235

David, A., Yigitcanlar, T., Desouza, K., Li, R. Y. M., Cheong, P. H., Mehmood, R., & Corchado, J. (2024). Understanding local government responsible AI strategy: An international municipal policy document analysis. *Cities (London, England), 155*, 105502. DOI: 10.1016/j.cities.2024.105502

Dayal, G., Verma, P., & Sehgal, S. (2023). A comprehensive review on the integration of artificial intelligence in the field of education. In *Leveraging AI and emotional intelligence in contemporary business organizations* (pp. 331–349). IGI Global., DOI: 10.4018/979-8-3693-1902-4.ch020

Dwivedi, Y. K., Kshetri, N., Hughes, L., Slade, E. L., Jeyaraj, A., Kar, A. K., Baabdullah, A. M., Koohang, A., Raghavan, V., Ahuja, M., Albanna, H., Albashrawi, M. A., Al-Busaidi, A. S., Balakrishnan, J., Barlette, Y., Basu, S., Bose, I., Brooks, L., Buhalis, D., & Wright, R. (2023). Opinion paper: "So what if ChatGPT wrote it?" Multidisciplinary perspectives on opportunities, challenges and implications of generative conversational AI for research, practice and policy. *International Journal of Information Management, 71*, 102642. DOI: 10.1016/j.ijinfomgt.2023.102642

Farahani, M. Sh. (2024). *Artificial intelligence and inequality: Challenges and opportunities*. Qeios., DOI: 10.32388/7HWUZ2

Fu, Y., & Weng, Z. (2024). Navigating the ethical terrain of AI in education: A systematic review on framing responsible human-centered AI practices. *Computers and Education: Artificial Intelligence*, *7*, 100306. DOI: 10.1016/j.caeai.2024.100306

Goosen, W., & Mugumo, V. P. (2024). A framework for the application of AI in higher education in association with APPETD and Swiss Institute for Management and Innovation. In *Proceedings of the International Conference on Medical Imaging, Electronic Imaging, Information Technologies, and Sensors (MIEITS 2024)*. SPIE. https://doi.org/DOI: 10.1117/12.3030740

Grubaugh, S., & Levitt, G. (2023). Artificial intelligence and the paradigm shift: Reshaping education to equip students for future careers. *The International Journal of Social Sciences and Humanities Invention*, *10*(6), 7931–7941. DOI: 10.18535/ijsshi/v10i06.02

Herane, M. (2024, January 16). AI in education, balancing innovation with ethics. *Higher Education Digest*. Retrieved from https://www.highereducationdigest.com/ai-in-education-balancing-innovation-with-ethics/

Huang, L. (2023). Ethics of artificial intelligence in education: Student privacy and data protection. *Science Insights Education Frontiers*, *16*(2), 2577–2587. DOI: 10.15354/sief.23.re202

Igbokwe, I. C. (2023). Application of artificial intelligence (AI) in educational management. *International Journal of Scientific and Research Publications*, *13*(3), 300. DOI: 10.29322/IJSRP.13.03.2023.p13536

Isiaku, L., Muhammad, A. S., Kefas, H. I., & Ukaegbu, F. C. (2024). Enhancing technological sustainability in academia: Leveraging ChatGPT for teaching, learning, and evaluation. *Quality Education for All*, *1*(1), 385–416. DOI: 10.1108/QEA-07-2024-0055

Jindal, M., Chaiyachati, K. H., Fung, V., Manson, S. M., & Mortensen, K. (2023). Eliminating health care inequities through strengthening access to care. *Health Services Research*, *58*(Suppl 3), 300–310. DOI: 10.1111/1475-6773.14202 PMID: 38015865

Kamalov, F., Santandreu Calonge, D., & Gurrib, I. (2023). New era of artificial intelligence in education: Towards a sustainable multifaceted revolution. *Sustainability*, *15*(16), 12451. DOI: 10.3390/su151612451

Kamalov, F., Santandreu Calonge, D., & Gurrib, I. (2023). New era of artificial intelligence in education: Towards a sustainable multifaceted revolution. *Sustainability*, *15*(16), 12451. DOI: 10.3390/su151612451

Kamalov, F., Santandreu Calonge, D., & Gurrib, I. (2023). New era of artificial intelligence in education: Towards a sustainable multifaceted revolution. *Sustainability, 15*(16), 12451. DOI: 10.3390/su151612451

Leelavathi, R., & Surendhranatha, R. C. (2024). ChatGPT in the classroom: Navigating the generative AI wave in management education. *Journal of Research in Innovative Teaching & Learning*. Advance online publication. https://doi.org/DOI: 10.1108/JRIT-01-2024-0017

Li, N. (2023). Ethical considerations in artificial intelligence: A comprehensive discussion from the perspective of computer vision. *SHS Web of Conferences*, 179(1), 04024. https://doi.org/DOI: 10.1051/shsconf/202317904024

Lim, T., Gottipati, S., & Cheong, M. L. F. (2023). Ethical considerations for artificial intelligence in educational assessments. In *Creative AI tools and ethical implications in teaching and learning* (pp. 32–79). IGI Global., DOI: 10.4018/979-8-3693-0205-7.ch003

Lim, T., Gottipati, S., & Cheong, M. L. F. (2024). Educational technologies and assessment practices: Evolution and emerging research gaps. In *Reshaping learning with next generation educational technologies*. IGI Global., DOI: 10.4018/979-8-3693-1310-7

Lin, C. C., Huang, A. Y. Q., & Lu, O. H. T. (2023). Artificial intelligence in intelligent tutoring systems toward sustainable education: A systematic review. *Smart Learning Environments, 10*, 41. DOI: 10.1186/s40561-023-00260-y

Lottu, O., Jacks, B. S., Ajala, O. A., & Okafor, E. S. (2024). Towards a conceptual framework for ethical AI development in IT systems. *World Journal of Advanced Research and Reviews, 21*(3), 408–415. DOI: 10.30574/wjarr.2024.21.3.0735

Mogavi, R. H., Deng, C., Kim, J. J., Zhou, P., Kwon, Y. D., Metwally, A. H. S., Tlili, A., Bassanelli, S., Bucchiarone, A., Gujar, S., Nacke, L. E., & Hui, P. (2024). ChatGPT in education: A blessing or a curse? A qualitative study exploring early adopters' utilization and perceptions. *Computers in Human Behavior: Artificial Humans, 2*(1), 100027. DOI: 10.1016/j.chbah.2023.100027

OECD. (2023). *OECD digital education outlook 2023: Towards an effective digital education ecosystem*. OECD Publishing., DOI: 10.1787/9872e201-

Ofosu-Ampong, K. (2024). Artificial intelligence research: A review on dominant themes, methods, frameworks, and future research directions. *Telematics and Informatics Reports, 14*, 100127. DOI: 10.1016/j.teler.2024.100127

Ou, S. (2024). Transforming education: The evolving role of artificial intelligence in students' academic performance. *International Journal of Education and Humanities, 13*(2), 163–173. DOI: 10.54097/cc1x7r95

Papagiannidis, E., Mikalef, P., & Conboy, K. (2025). Responsible artificial intelligence governance: A review and research framework. *The Journal of Strategic Information Systems, 34*(2), 101885. DOI: 10.1016/j.jsis.2024.101885

Rashid, A. B., & Kausik, M. A. K. (2024). AI revolutionizing industries worldwide: A comprehensive overview of its diverse applications. *Hybrid Advances, 7*, 100277. DOI: 10.1016/j.hybadv.2024.100277

Roshanaei, M., Olivares, H., & Lopez, R. (2023). Harnessing AI to foster equity in education: Opportunities, challenges, and emerging strategies. *Journal of Intelligent Learning Systems and Applications, 15*, 123–143. DOI: 10.4236/jilsa.2023.154009

Sargiotis, D. (2024). Fostering ethical and inclusive AI: A human-centric paradigm for social impact. SSRN *Electronic Journal*. https://doi.org/DOI: 10.2139/ssrn.4879372

Schwartz, R., Vassilev, A., Greene, K., Perine, L., Burt, A., & Hall, P. (2024). *Towards a standard for identifying and managing bias in artificial intelligence* (NIST Special Publication 1270). National Institute of Standards and Technology. https://nvlpubs.nist.gov/nistpubs/SpecialPublications/NIST.SP.1270.pdf

Singhal, A., Neveditsin, N., Tanveer, H., & Mago, V. (2024). Toward fairness, accountability, transparency, and ethics in AI for social media and health care: Scoping review. *JMIR Medical Informatics, 12*, e50048. DOI: 10.2196/50048 PMID: 38568737

Tahir, M., Amanat, I., & Awan, S. M. (2024). Ethical considerations and challenges in the integration of artificial intelligence in education: A systematic review. *Journal of Education and Management Studies, 3*(4). Advance online publication. DOI: 10.69565/jems.v3i4.314

Tan, S. (2023). Harnessing artificial intelligence for innovation in education. In *Learning intelligence: Innovative and digital transformative learning strategies* (pp. 335–363). Springer., DOI: 10.1007/978-981-19-9201-8_8

United Arab Emirates. (2024). *UAE guiding principles on AI policy*. UAE Government. Retrieved from https://ai.gov.ae/wp-content/uploads/2024/10/UAE-Guiding-on-ai-policy-EN-V3.pdf

Wang, S., Wang, F., Zhu, Z., Wang, J., Tran, T., & Du, Z. (2024). Artificial intelligence in education: A systematic literature review. *Expert Systems with Applications, 252*(Part A), 124167. https://doi.org/DOI: 10.1016/j.eswa.2024.124167

Zhai, C., Wibowo, S., & Li, L. D. (2024). The effects of over-reliance on AI dialogue systems on students' cognitive abilities: A systematic review. *Smart Learning Environments*, *11*(28). Advance online publication. DOI: 10.1186/s40561-024-00316-7

Zhai, X., Chu, X., Chai, C. S., Jong, M. S. Y., Istenic, A., Spector, M., Liu, J. B., Yuan, J., & Li, Y. (2021). A review of artificial intelligence (AI) in education from 2010 to 2020. *Complexity*, *2021*, 8812542. Advance online publication. DOI: 10.1155/2021/8812542

# Chapter 8
# Mapping Health Integrating Spatial Data Infrastructure With Visual Learning Techniques for Smart Healthcare

**Munir Ahmad**
https://orcid.org/0000-0003-4836-6151
*Survey of Pakistan, Pakistan*

## ABSTRACT

*The convergence of Spatial Data Infrastructure (SDI) and visual learning represents a pivotal shift toward smarter, more responsive healthcare systems. This chapter explores how integrating structured spatial data with visual tools enhances health operations, decision-making, and community engagement. It highlights emerging innovations such as AI-powered geovisualization and AR/VR for immersive communication, offering real-time insights into spatial health dynamics. Realizing this potential demands interdisciplinary collaboration and ethical safeguards. By embedding spatial intelligence into healthcare, systems can achieve more equitable, informed, and resilient outcomes.*

## INTRODUCTION

The global healthcare sector is facing the challenge of fast digitalization and data-driven innovation. The utilization of intelligent technologies in these systems is increasingly gaining traction due to their potential, both in terms of streamlining

DOI: 10.4018/979-8-3373-7584-7.ch008

service delivery and patient outcomes and ensuring the efficiency of the health dynamics planning. Among them, Spatial Data Infrastructure (SDI) and learning methods in visual ways have been strong measures to respond to the changing needs of intelligent healthcare systems. As a combination of disciplines, they provide a powerful collaboration that helps health professionals, politicians, and individuals to interpret the difficult geospatial health information using easy-to-understand graphical presentations (Adeleye et al., 2025; Ahmad et al., 2025; Ali et al., 2021). The integration of these two worlds provides a way out to more successful, fair, and data-driven healthcare ecosystems.

SDI is an end-to-end system in the form of technologies, data standards, institutional mechanisms, and policy that are aimed at facilitating the generation, maintenance, exchange, and use of geospatial data. In the healthcare context, SDI offers the critical structure for the acquisition and combination of spatial information of the healthcare infrastructure, disease incidence, population distribution, and environmental medical hazards. It enables inter-agency cooperation, enhances the data flow, not limiting it to real-time, and guarantees the availability of the most crucial spatial data at the right time and place (Agunbiade et al., 2024; Aydinoglu et al., 2025; Piyasena et al., 2023). SDI not only makes any spatial data a dynamic asset, but it also makes it an implementable resource in the strategy, resource planning, and response during emergencies in a health system.

Simultaneously, to explain complicated information more effectively, visual learning methods are implemented, which make use of visual means, e.g., maps, infographics, dashboards, diagrams, etc., and interactive simulations. In healthcare, these methods are key to transforming abstract or information-dense knowledge into easily accessible knowledge to many different audiences, such as clinicians, public health officials, patients, and community members. Visual learning is associated with improved comprehension and retention, besides encouraging inclusiveness based on making health information accessible to people with varying health literacy levels. The method is especially useful in the case of spatial data, in which geographic relationships are often visualized to offer clarification of patterns, differences, and trends that would have otherwise remained invisible.

The addition of SDI to visual learning is one of the important breakthroughs in the spatial thinking evolution in the sphere of contemporary health systems. The competence involved in thinking spatially, which is presented as learning to recognize and comprehend position-based relationships and patterns, is being acknowledged as a supreme skill set in the fields of public health, organizing of urban organizing, and emergency medicine. Whether it be following the migration of an infectious disease, locating underserved populations, or intelligently placement of new medical services, spatial thinking allows more timely and informed decision-making.

The main objective of the chapter is to explore the opportunities and challenges posed by the unification of SDI and visual learning methodology in smart healthcare. The chapter starts with creating the conceptual foundation of both SDI and visual learning, and the discussion on the synergetic integration of such components. The next section includes several critical areas of application, such as geospatial analysis and surveillance of population health, policy formulation, and community outreach. Technical, ethical, and operational issues are also covered in the chapter.

## FOUNDATIONS OF SPATIAL DATA INFRASTRUCTURE

Before engaging in an elaborate discussion concerning the relationship between SDI and visual learning methods in smart healthcare, one should have a clear idea about the basics of each of them. In this conceptualization segment, this paper displays a guiding representation of the fundamental elements, roles, and implementations of SDI and visual learning with the view towards defining in future essays their compound worth in healthcare systems.

### Components and Functions of Spatial Data Infrastructure

Spatial Data Infrastructure is a methodical pattern created to assist with the competent delivery of spatial (georeferenced) data creation, management, sharing, and use. It works on various institutional and technical levels and allows a variety of stakeholders (public health authorities, hospitals, emergency services, and research institutions) to access any relevant spatially referenced information and reuse it. SDI, in its essence, has five main aspects (Gómez et al., 2019; Mwange et al., 2018):

#### Data

Any Spatial Data Infrastructure is based on information. Spatial data in the context of healthcare is a broad range of georeferenced information required in both day-to-day operations and emergency activities. These can be the geographical location of hospitals, clinics, or testing facilities, demographic population distribution (age, gender, income), disease incidence (e.g., COVID-19 hotspots), environmental exposure (e.g., pollution concentration or distance to toxic sites), and infrastructural systems (e.g., road and transport networks).

The characteristic that makes healthcare-related spatial data unique is the fact that it has two significant focal points, not only spatial but temporal sensitivity as well. As an example, it is only with timely data, as well as a high enough degree of spatial granularity, that one can be able to track the geographical distribution of a contagious disease over both space and time to get a picture of the local spread of the disease. The quality of the spatial analysis depends on the richness and precision of this kind of data and forms part of the strategic decision-making during outbreak containment, vaccine coverage, health equity, etc.

## Standards

Data standards in a complex and multi-agency healthcare ecosystem are necessary in a way that spatial details do not exist across all types of sources, but can be brought together, and would have a consistent way to be analyzed. These standards are grouped into the technical and semantic ones. Technical standards refer to uniformity of data formats (examples include GeoJSON, GML) (Frozza & Mello, 2020)Coordinate reference systems (examples include WGS84 and UTM), and geospatial metadata schema (examples include ISO 19115), which creates the ability to map, share, and query data within the available platforms. In their turn, semantic standards specify healthcare-specific terminologies and ontologies (e.g., SNOMED CT, HL7 standards), which enable the spatial health data attributes to be interpreted precisely.

Deviations in such standards make the cross-platform analysis and even integration of regional data difficult or even impossible. As a simple example, a mismatch in projections across datasets or a difference in health terminology may lead to incorrect visualizations or poor policy conclusions. This way, standards play an essential part in promoting the interoperability that is important in an integrated smart health system.

## Access Mechanisms

The access mechanisms include the interface and infrastructure to enable spatial health data discovery and reuse. These are a geospatial data portal, APIs, and web-based GIS. Health geoportals, dashboard systems, or integrated e-health platforms are the means commonly used to implement such mechanisms in the healthcare industry (Budi & Sutanta, 2023; Koshkarev et al., 2008; Maguire & Longley, 2005). As an example, in times of flight outbreaks, real-time dashboards with the distribution of cases, hospital capacities, and testing coverage keep the authorities and the general population equally in the know about the situation at hand. Equally, APIs enable researchers and developers to retrieve spatial data programmatically to analyze data, create mobile health tools using APIs, or create their visualization tools.

Accessibility of spatial health data should be open, secure, and user-friendly, and therefore, transparency, data-driven decision-making, and collaboration across institutions should grow. This needs, however, to be pegged against privacy and ethical concerns, particularly when information is about identifiable people or when it captures sensitive health occurrences.

## Polices and Governance

The institutional and Legal Framework is the most sensitive component of the SDI, arguably, especially in the area of healthcare, where ethical, regulatory, and legal norms converge. There are rules and regulatory systems that determine the ownership of data, subjects that can access it, and the scale of that access and its uses. Key aspects of SDI governance are between the agencies sharing data (e.g., ministries of health, research institutions, emergency responders), legal conformance with privacy regulations like HIPAA or GDPR, and institutional responsibility of data stewardship. It also entails setting up the process of data anonymization, encryption, and consent, where sensitive information tends to be at the individual level in information involving individual levels of health information (Ahmad & Ali, 2023; J. Sjoukema et al., 2020; J. W. Sjoukema et al., 2017). The governance should also deal with the risks of data misuse, cybersecurity threats, and biases in data representation. When there is weak governance, even the best SDI systems may turn out to be a liability instead of an asset, particularly in politically charged environments or in crisis-prone contexts.

## Technologies

The technological aspect of SDI is the locomotive of efficient administration of spatial data by going through the whole lifecycle, beginning with the acquisition to the publication. The crucial element in this technological infrastructure is systems and tools that support the collection, processing, analysis, retention, and representation of geospatial information, which are essential to the development of smart healthcare. Maps and spatial analysis Mapping and spatial analysis are based on Geographic Information System (GIS) and provide a picture to a decision-maker showing how patterns in health are distributed across a given spatial domain, and analyze those patterns. Such systems play a pivotal role in procedures such as determining where underserved areas are and developing models of disease dissemination to determine the most desirable location of new healthcare structures. In addition to GIS, the Global Positioning Systems (GPS) provide accurate geolocation functionalities, which are critical to asset tracking, field survey organization, as well as the spatial accuracy of the health facilities and service provision.

The environmental and epidemiological surveillance revolution takes place using remote sensing information, based on satellite data, and using drones. This is particularly useful in surveillance in areas that directly affect the health of the people, including air quality, land use change, and urban heat islands. Spatial databases and cloud computing, e.g., PostGIS and Google Earth Engine, have transformed the scale at which spatial information can be stored and accessed. The technologies enable real-time processing of data, huge storage capacity, and the possibility to share data collaboratively, and various stakeholders involved can read and use the same sets of data simultaneously.

In addition to conventional instruments, SDI is quickly acquiring new capacities through the involvement of emerging technologies. Geospatial analytics with artificial intelligence increases predictive modeling and decision support capabilities by revealing health data complex spatial patterns. Such tools as augmented reality and 3D visualization provide an opportunity to transform the delivery and interaction with spatial health information, providing immersive experiences and simulations as well as training and outreach to the general population. The advanced technologies in the smart healthcare systems are not just instruments of efficient data management but enhance spatial intelligence to the level of a strategic resource, which allows proactive planning, dynamic response, and provision of personalized care. A combination of these elements enables SDI to serve as a strong backbone of spatial intelligence within healthcare and help to support a diversity of applications, ranging from disease mapping and healthcare logistics.

## Types of Visual Learning Techniques in Healthcare

Visual learning is a cognitive perception process of getting information through the use of visual tools that express complex information in simple forms. Visual learning techniques assist with simplification in communication and enable more engagement, especially in healthcare, where data is usually multidimensional, dynamic, and located between multiple geographical locations. The important visual learning tools involve:

- Spatial data analysis and visualization always resort to maps as another relatively strong tool to visualize the geographical distribution of health-related phenomena (Maurya et al., 2022; Menon et al., 2021; Noon & Hankins, 2001). Public health Maps have been very popular in the field of public health to show hotspots of diseases, map underserved areas where people lack adequate access to health care of any sort, or map the spread of infectious diseases. As an example, choropleth maps could present the vaccination coverage by administrative district, whereas the point maps could be deployed to find clinics, pharmacies, or reported cases of disease. Such geographical representations help the health authorities to identify trends, distribute resources more fairly, and prioritize interventions depending on geographic requirements. Maps also have significant benefits in the field of spatial epidemiology, assisting with the longitudinal study of clusters of diseases over time; they are therefore tools of major interest in surveillance, trend analysis.

- Charts as well as graphs supplement spatial maps by providing quantitative comparisons, graphical representations of trends that are not grounded in a specific geographical location, yet are essential to provide insights into overall patterns. Bar graphs may be used to compare the prevalence of cases by area or age group, pie charts may show the proportional distribution of the people with various kinds of diseases, and histograms can show the prevalence of a health event, such as hospital admissions or the proportion of people with a specific disease immunized. Line graphs are especially useful in visualizing a time series or data, like how many cases of COVID-19 have been experienced per week or maternal mortality rates per month, which enables health professionals to keep track of changes and observe irregularities. These visualizations render huge volumes of data into a manageable format to facilitate effective communication of the main results to policymakers, practitioners, and citizens.
- The ability of interactive dashboards offers a dynamic platform that integrates several visual data presentations, including maps, graphs, indicators, and filters, into one interface. Dashboards find more and more applications in health information systems to show current statistics, hospital bed state, monitoring immunization campaigns, or the distribution of a pandemic with reference to regions (Dowding et al., 2015; Iftikhar et al., 2019; Zhuang et al., 2022). This interactivity enables users to navigate the data by zooming in on a particular place or filtering it by demographic variables, or switching indicators. This type of dashboard can provide actionable intelligence to the decision-makers and frontline health workers, particularly in rapidly shifting situations such as disease outbreaks or disaster management.
- Visual learning in the healthcare profession through simulations and animations introduces the aspect of time and behavior. Simulations allow recreating disease outbreak evolution in different intervention configurations, including lockdowns, vaccination campaigns, or the management of vectors through computational models. It is possible to visualize patient flow through a hospital or the performance of emergency medical services in case of a mass casualty through animations. These instruments are especially helpful in training skills, strategic plans, and communicating to the masses. They enable health professionals to look forward, experiment with policy options using a virtual world, and optimize their reactions to what they see visualized and what they hear.

All of these methods address various spheres of health communication, including statistical reporting and strategic scenario planning, and usually work best when tailored to user understanding and involvement.

## Relevance in Healthcare Contexts

One of the most important uses of SDI can be found in epidemiology and disease surveillance. Offering the geospatial basis of tracking, management, and prediction of the propagation of diseases, SDI complements the structure of the health surveillance system of the populace with both instant and past-based information. Epidemiologists and decision-makers can decode intricate patterns of space and time of disease transmission through visual interpretations of interactive heat maps and time-lapse animations. As an example, in the context of the COVID-19 pandemic, heat maps showing a concentration of cases by neighborhood or district allowed local governments to quickly draw and focus attention on high-risk areas, to prevent them promptly. Besides being used by professionals, such visual products were also useful in informing the general population, thus improving how people adhere to health recommendations.

It is the spatial analysis that helps greatly in planning and managing healthcare facilities. Through combined demographic data of the population, transportation facilities, and available healthcare resources, SDI assists the planners in determining the underserved populations and distributes the resources more efficiently. Real-time picture dashboards and other visual tools can depict the capacity of facilities as well as their bed occupancy in ICUs and medical supplies provided in regions. The information given in these dashboards improves transparency and situational awareness among health administrators and in times of crisis, like in the case of pandemics, natural disasters, or any mass vaccination campaigns. They can also be used to future-proof healthcare systems by strategically locating new hospitals, mobile clinics, or telehealth hubs using spatial need.

Intuitive visual representation of health information also promotes health literacy and the connection of people with their community. Missed Complicated data, including such examples as disease prevalence, environmental risks, or vaccination progress, can be changed into easy-to-read maps and infographics that can appeal to non-professional readers. An illustration of such application can be given as the maps showing air quality in communities or incidence of dengue fever to assist people in realizing their local situation of risk and take adequate preventive action. These tools not only enhance personal health behavior, but they also enhance civic participation, which translates to communities demanding improved services as well as protection of their environment. This way, the visual tools can connect data and public behavior.

The visual and spatial teaching tools and equipment are becoming an important part of training and capacity building in the health sector to build the core competencies of the medical fraternity and the health workers. The spatial concepts to be taught using simulations, animations, and interactive learning platforms are particularly the disease diffusion patterns, the accessibility of health services, and the environmental determinants of health. As an example, a spatial simulation might provide a trainee the opportunity to discover how cholera outbreaks spread across the lines of water supply or to investigate how the topography affects response times of ambulances. These tools not only develop spatial literacy but also ensure the development of critical thinking, scenario planning, and decision-making skills in contexts of real-life health situations.

SDI and visual learning methods are an interconnected accelerator to smarter medical care. SDI makes spatial data findable, interoperable, and operational, and visual learning methods convert that information into knowledge that could act as an actionable driver in encouraging the participation of all levels of the health system, in learning and making decisions. Figure 1 shows a typical workflow of SDI-enabled visual mapping.

*Figure 1. Workflow of SDI-Enabled Visual Mapping*

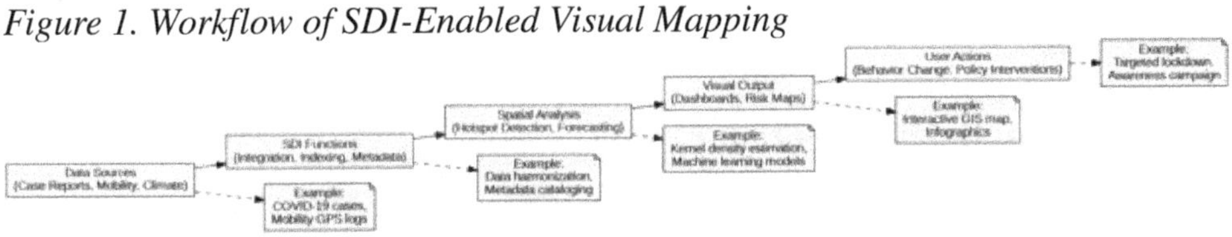


## SYNERGISTIC INTEGRATION

The convergence between the SDI and visual learning techniques embraces a paradigm shift in the management, interpretation, and communication of spatially driven health information in the healthcare system. Although SDI offers the basic structure for the collection, handling, and distribution of geospatial health information, visual teaching approaches offer a window through which this information becomes recognized, useful, and effective. Their convergence helps turn healthcare systems into active intelligence engines; smart, speedy, and more inclusive decision-making processes.

## Conceptual Framework of Integration

To apprehend the relationship between the synergy of SDI and visual learning in intelligent healthcare, we would hypothesize a three-layered integration model. Figure 2 shows a flowchart-based conceptual diagram to depict the progression from raw data (Data Layer), through analysis (Processing and Analysis Layer), to visualized outputs (Visualization and Learning Layer).

### Data Layer (SDI Core)

This is the core of spatial health intelligence. It consists of quality-verified and standardized geospatial data of importance to the field of public health, such as disease incidence maps, population demographics, health facilities location, environmental risk areas (e.g. flood flood-prone and pollution-intensive areas), and so on. This layer is powerful because it subscribes to the aspects of SDI, which include data standards, frameworks of metadata, and secure methods of accessibility. These components guarantee consistency, interoperability, discoverability, and accessibility of data when it comes to the health sector and governance level. The data layer is considered the raw material required in carrying out any type of spatial analysis or visualization.

### Processing and Analysis Layer

The next stage, which is very crucial after the gathering of spatial data and its structuring, is that of processing and analytical transformation. Such a layer accesses the highly potent instruments, which are Geographic Information Systems (GIS), remote sensing applications, spatial databases (e.g., PostGIS), and even high-end modeling algorithms to extract knowledge. The interoperability mechanisms at SDI allow a frictionless integration of datasets with varied origins- assembly of epidemiological records, climate variables, socio-economic data, and infrastructure maps into a single analytic system. As a result of this integration, the health professionals can be able to perform spatial risk assessment, disease modeling, detection of hot spots, accessibility, and scenario prediction. This level is a data-to-intelligence transformation.

### Visualization and Learning Layer

The model has the visualization and learning layer as its top. In this case, the processed products are made interactive and consumable in digestible forms to address different user needs. Some of those include the maps that show the progression of diseases, dashboards that depict real-time capacity within hospitals, animations that represent the spread of the virus, and even emergency response simulations. Such visual resources allow many different goals to be achieved, including supporting policy decisions, educating health workers, and building social awareness and involvement. Noteworthy, this layer democratizes data, making it artfully easy to comprehend and perform actions based on the result depicted of complex analysis translated into a simplified visual representation understandable by non-users, thus filling the barrier that exists between data science and human comprehensibility.

*Figure 2. Three-Layered Conceptual Framework Integrating SDI and Visual Learning*

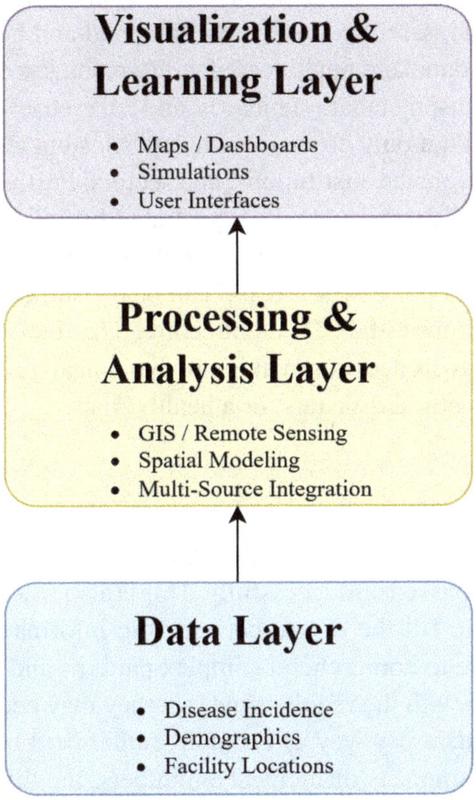

## Enhancing the Health Data Lifecycle

Combining SDI and visual learning can improve all facets of the health data lifecycle (data acquisition through interpretation) because they fill the divide between spatial thinking and human interpretation.

### Data Pipeline Optimization

SDI is important in the optimization of the preliminary phases of the health data lifecycle, especially data acquisition, standardization, storage, and sharing. SDI makes it easy to homogenize various health data sources, including epidemiological surveys in the field, satellite-based environmental and health surveillance, mobile health (mHealth) data, and health care facility management information by specifying common formats, metadata standards, and data retrieval methods. These standardized mechanisms not only do away with data silos but also permit interoperability throughout the agencies, institutions, and sectors. Furtherly, SDI would fit the deployment of real-time streams of data generated by IoT-connected devices, e.g., wearable health trackers, biosensors, and ambulance GPS extension. The given data sources are timely and place-specific and can be consumed continuously and indexed as a spatial location in the SDI architecture. This facilitates swift spatial analysis and can assist in swift decision-making in dynamically changing situations such as disease clusters, natural disasters, or a health crisis.

### Visual Applications

The importance of data after its collection and processing is the ability of this data to be interpreted and passed on successfully. This is also where the use of visual learning tools comes in to fill the divide between big information and decision-making. Users can be able to comprehend complex patterns and relations within a short time, in comparison with the regular time that they may need to look through the textual or numerical data. By way of example, rather than being manually interpreted by row and column sets of incidence numbers, the disease officials can visually recognize through the map plotting interface where outbreaks are forming or where vaccination rates are dropping in real-time throughout the region. The tools can increase an understanding of health to broad audiences (decision-makers, field workers, and general citizenry) as information is displayed in a contextually relevant and intuitive manner. The democratization of data not only increases the speed of response but also enhances collaborative decision-making, transparency, and decision-making maturity.

## Feedback and Engagement Loop

Alongside the top-down use of data sharing, other visual tools and geospatial Web-based platforms are also vehicles of bottom-up involvement. Participation in GIS-based applications and interactive dashboards engages communities and citizens to provide insights into local knowledge, record local health events, and raise environmental or infrastructural issues. This can establish a feedback loop through which community entries, like the report on water quality, symptoms of local outbreaks, or difficulty of access, can be geotagged, validated, and reintroduced into the SDI. These forms of two-way communication enhance not only the granularity and relevance of spatial analysis but also trust and collaboration between the authorities in health and citizens. This kind of cyclical exchange over time helps to strengthen the resilience and responsiveness of the health system so that both top-down analytics and bottom-up knowledge are used in terms of planning, resource allocations, and policy formulations.

The combination of visual learning and SDI forms a logical ecosystem that links spatial information with the minds of humans. It enables any user (epidemiologists, urban planners, community health workers, or ordinary citizens) to get timely and location-specific insight in intuitive formats. The synergy is not merely a technological improvement, but a thinking shift towards more knowledgeable, engaged, and fairer healthcare systems.

# APPLICATIONS AND BENEFITS IN SMART HEALTHCARE

A combination of SDI and visual learning methods opens up disruptive trends in the design, delivery, and management of intelligent healthcare systems. This integration would support better execution and analysis since geospatial intelligence could be shared with visual modes that people could understand easily, leading to better situational awareness, sound decision-making, community participation, and bolstering of the social infrastructure of public health. Its practical effects in breadth and depth are illuminated in the following thematic areas. Tables 1 and 2 show complementary functions of SDI and visual learning across the health data lifecycle.

*Table 1. Applications and Benefits of SDI*

| Thematic Area | SDI Contribution | Visual Learning Contribution | Outcome |
|---|---|---|---|
| Geospatial Analysis | Spatial datasets and GIS tools | Maps, overlays, and comparative visuals | Identify disease clusters and service gaps |
| Decision Support | Integrated spatial models and real-time data | Interactive dashboards and scenario viewers | Inform strategic health interventions |
| Community Engagement | Open-access health geoportals | Dashboards, risk maps, participatory interfaces | Empower informed citizen participation |
| Education & Training | Spatial datasets and case-based learning environments | Simulations, animated visuals, geovisual storytelling | Build spatial literacy and preparedness |
| Public Health Surveillance | Real-time data from the field and health systems | Time-series maps, alert dashboards | Detect and monitor threats in real time |
| Policy Development | Aggregated spatial evidence for policy modeling | Visual policy impact simulations and briefing materials | Enable evidence-based, equitable policymaking |

## Geospatial Analysis

Geospatial analysis is one of the most basic SDI usages in the sphere of health-care because it consists of the study of spatial patterns of health-related data and spatial interrelationships. Geospatial analysis is beneficial when coupled with visual learning tools like heat maps, spatial overlays, and interactive choropleth maps to provide a diagnosis and planning tool.

### Disease Clustering

Spatial clustering methodology has been significant in determining the geographic clustering as well as the time evolution of disease outbreaks (Webster et al., 2021). Through kernel density estimation, spatial autocorrelation (e.g., Moran's I), scan statistics (e.g., SaTScan), and other methods, the public health officials can detect statistically significant clusters of diseases such as dengue, malaria, COVID-19, and cholera. These clusters usually suggest the spots of increased transmission risk, which can be coupled with either the environment (e.g., stagnant water collection, inadequate sanitation), pattern of mobility, or even density.

The geovisualizations of such clusters, e.g., interactive heatmaps or animated time series maps, can be very revealing in terms of both making sense and taking action. They enable the health authorities to monitor the evolution of outbreaks in near real-time, focus testing or mass vaccination campaigns, and trigger specific responses, including fogging in mosquito-prone environs, sending out emergency medical services, and so on. This can further improve forecasting and early warning by means of integration with meteorological data.

## Service Coverage and Accessibility

Spatial accessibility models play a very imperative role in determining the supply and demand of healthcare services in various geographical locations. Planners can assess the distances that people have to travel to access necessary amenities through the use of such tools as network analysis, travel-time modeling, or catchment area delineation (e.g., through the use of the two-step floating catchment area method) (Drake et al., 2021; Ouma et al., 2021). Such analysis indicates service deserts, geospatial regions where people cannot reach certain locations easily due to their distances or deficiency of the transport infrastructure, or those with limited access to facilities.

Stakeholders are able to determine the underserved rural areas quickly or peri-urban slums, or isolated communities quickly through visual maps of the coverage zones. Such data is invaluable when it comes to ensuring that the building of new healthcare installations, including clinics, field hospitals, or mobile medicine units, is placed accordingly. Also, such maps may complement emergency planning activities, such as the most efficient ambulance routes, medicine supply chains, or the recruitment of outreach teams in cases of pandemics or natural disasters.

## Spatial Inequalities

Multilayered spatial analysis of public health inequalities can be realized with the use of a combination of health, demographic, environmental, and socioeconomic datasets. Placing indicators like level of income, air pollution, housing status, and disease occurrence over one another can enable the analysts to establish systematic discrepancies in health outcomes and risk of exposure. Such inequalities are usually entangled with some of the social determinants of health, which include race, gender, education, and geographic location (Jia et al., 2022; Lee, 2022).

These multidimensional patterns can be displayed with interactive spatial dashboards or inequality atlases, highlighting those communities that receive a twofold or threefold burden, including high incidence of a disease, lack of access to healthcare, and exposure to environmental risks. These are significant insights into evidence-based policymaking and resource governing. They enable the decision-makers to formulate equity-based interventions, including subsidies for vulnerable populations or awareness programs, or built-in urban planning interventions to reduce exposure to health hazards, such as pollution or heat islands.

## Decision Support

Healthcare decision-making problems usually include the interpretation of large amounts of complicated information to choose the best and fairest interventions. The data-driven decision support systems (DSS) with SDI and interactive visual tools can help to assess alternatives and predict results.

### Scenario Modeling

With the visual tools enabled by SDI, stakeholders (including health planners, emergency managers, and policymakers) are made to navigate through the various courses of action that public health measures can take before their real-life execution. They combine real-time and past geospatial data, epidemiology trends, and infrastructure data in simulation environments.

As an illustrative example, planners will be able to test a scenario in which they will increase the coverage of the vaccination in a given district and monitor what effect the increase will have an effect on the rate of infections. Similarly, movement or expansion of hospitals can also be simulated using the population density and accessibly related variables to determine whether the services would be delivered better. These simulations facilitate evidence-based decision-making, lessen trial-and-error during policy enforcement, and enable preemptive changes to a morphing environment, the most important being in a constantly changing environment, such as a pandemic or a disaster area.

### Resources Allocation

One of the main uses of SDI in public health is through the use of the tool in effective and fair resource allocation. Overlaying the maps of the disease burden with the information related to the health infrastructure, the logistics network, and the availability of supplies, the decision-makers can mark where the medical resources are required the most and where the shortages in provision exist.

SDI-fed real-time dashboards have the potential to show real-time availability of ventilators or oxygen tanks, map vaccine storage units, and find the location of moving ambulances or areas of mobile units. When used in pandemic or crisis environments, such dashboards can facilitate balancing of logistical activities so that there is a quick and specific delivery of the life-saving materials such as protective gear (PPE), vaccines, or make-shift hospitals. This geospatially-informed allocation decreases waste, generates better results, and aids adaptive response strategies in case the situation changes quickly.

### Intervention Planning

SDI can support spatial risk mapping to help in the development and implementation of public health operations. By combining the data of the environment, demographics, and infrastructure, the planners could define high-risk areas, flood-prone regions, heat islands, air pollution lines, or high densities of informal settlements.

These risk zones can be mapped to facilitate the proactive planning of interventions to be deployed in the future and results in these maps are described and displayed as risk zones that could allow proactive implementation of targeted health interventions, i.e. the monsoon season would allow preventive health campaign in flood areas, or air quality monitoring and respiratory care clinics in air pollution locations. Geospatial tools are also used to design evacuation routes and temporary care centers in disaster-prone areas (geared according to the needs of people at risk e.g., elderly, disabled, or children). Such spatial knowledge guarantees the planning of public health in a resilience perspective, being sensitive to the variations of geography and risk distribution.

## Community Engagement

Open, participatory visualizations would open up access to health information, democratize the process and enable community participation, and enable people to make informed choices and contribute to the community health choices.

### Public Dashboards

The dashboards are smart, SDI-driven portals that bring priority health data to the people in a location-based fashion, e.g., shots on target, disease incidence rates, maternal health indicators, or environmental alerts. The application of these dashboards is frequently incorporated into maps, trend graphs, risk indicators, as well as alerts, in this manner enabling the user to familiarize themselves with the health hazards around them.

A citizen, in his/her turn, can check the COVID-19 infection rate in his/her neighborhood, observe the presence of vaccination sites, or review the air quality index (AQI) before going outside. These dashboards will encourage individuals to make informed personal choices, will aid behavior adaptation (mask-wearing, vaccination, and missing high-risk areas), and will lead to increased trust and transparency between the community and health officials since complex spatial data will be visible and available in real-time.

### Risk Maps

Geospatial risk mapping is extremely important to convey visually the exposure to health risks, such as, amongst others, the spread of vector-borne diseases, industrial pollution, insecure drinking water sources, or high temperature areas. Such maps are frequently overlaid with environmental and infrastructural data to show the geographical location of the threats to specific populations.

As an example, households can use mosquito breeding hotspot maps of hotspots during the monsoon to implement specific forms of prevention (e.g., fogging, net use). The groundwater contamination areas detected with the help of SDI can cause local reactions in water treatment. Risk maps enable community awareness and precautionary measures since they present risks in a spatial and visual form that is empowering at the community level, particularly among those populations who are vulnerable or have low literacy levels.

### Participatory Platforms

Through SDI, participatory geospatial platforms can be used to achieve two-way communication between citizens and health authorities. Community members can report locally focused health (e.g., emergent symptoms, vector outbreaks, or public health sanitation concerns) through geotagged mobile applications or reporting tools via SMS or through web portals.

Such inputs are instantly displayed on SDI-linked dashboards or maps accessible to public health officials so that in-time tracking and reaction are enabled. This forms a bottom-up movement of data that complements the official monitoring and surveillance to enhance situational awareness and community-based interventions. These types of participatory instruments do more than increase data richness and coverage, offering an opportunity to develop public ownership and enhance social accountability and resonate with the principle of inclusive and responsive health governance.

## Education and Training

Students and healthcare professionals require skills in understanding spatial awareness and analysis. The combination of SDI and visual learning enables immersive and interactive learning in education and capacity building.

## Simulations

Spatial simulations provide a high-fidelity, hands-on setting in which health care practitioners, emergency responders, and planners can experience and practice complicated public health situations in the virtual world. These can be in the form of an epidemic outbreak response, mass casualty, or natural disasters such as floods or earthquakes. Using SDI-merged data, a realistic simulation of the population density, infrastructure, disease transmission, and environmental risk factors can be modeled. Players can make decisions on the spot, e.g., triage of a hospital on the fly, routing evacuations, allocating resources, and see the results in real time.

These simulation tools are vital in preparedness planning and skills development in the health sector because they are the best ways of improving operational preparedness, decision-making under conditions of uncertainty, and spatial awareness.

## Visual Storytelling

Maps, infographics, and animations enable one to demonstrate a visual story about complicated spatial and epidemiological data, and in the form of understandable stories, make it interesting and less vulnerable to misunderstandings. Large datasets can be condensed into powerful narratives by being transformed into animated disease progression maps, timelines of vaccine rollout out or maps with layers of health and environmental indicators.

The tools are particularly more useful in public education and advocacy campaigns, donor reporting, and academic knowledge translation. To take one example, showing how a cholera outbreak spread throughout a city following a flood on an animated map can effectively convey the case as to why water sanitation infrastructure is needed. Visual storytelling reinforces the message contained in the available policies, helps retain information in memory, and fills the gap between science and popular perception.

## Curriculum Integration

The medical, nursing, and public health curricula can incorporate geospatial data instruments and SDI-empowered platforms in their coursework to promote geo-literacy among health care professionals of the future. An example of such activities includes the work with GIS-based case studies, analysis of spatial patterns of disease, or simulations of the interventions in the sphere of public health based on real-world data.

Through such integration, the learners are assisted in acquiring the knowledge of the core competencies in spatial mapping, epidemiological mapping, diversity in hot spots, and decision support analysis. This not only helps them to become better skilled in conceptualizing problems with health inequities and environmental determinants but also enables them in being able to apply evidence-based understanding of data to their work in clinical practice and in the community at large.

## Public Health Surveillance

Spatially-enabled data plays a key role in providing adequate time to respond to a threat in terms of effective public health surveillance. SDI is important in facilitating surveillance systems, whereas visual tools facilitate the clarity of findings, which are communicated promptly.

### Real-Time Dashboards

Real-time dashboards are dynamic, ever-changing interfaces that combine real-time data feeds of hospitals, diagnostic laboratories, field-based surveillance teams, and IoT health-related devices, even social media feeds. These dashboards, powered by SDIs, can create a centralized situational awareness for the public health authorities.

The indicators of new infections, number of available hospital beds, vaccination levels, emergency calls, and environmental health indicators are presented in geospatial format (usually with options to filter by time, location, or populations). In health emergency operations centers and epidemic intelligence systems, real-time dashboards are critical in that they allow proactive decision-making, organize resources, and facilitate open communication with the population.

### Outbreak Tracking

Animated spatiotemporal visualization helps in tracking the outbreak and provides a vital insight into the progress, speed, and direction of the disease spread, irrespective of administrative boundaries. By applying the historical case data and geocoded repositories with the infection reports, a time animation heat map or circulation map can display the spread of a disease like measles, COVID-19, or cholera by population.

Such visual tools can aid not only in finding superspreading events, transmission corridors, and high-risk areas by epidemiologists, but also help in communicating with the population and in media briefings by making the dynamics of the disease easier to understand and compelling to follow. Outbreak monitoring, when successful within the SDI systems, allows evidence-based quarantine measures, controls at borders, and community-level response activities.

## Early Warning Systems

SDI-enabled early warning systems combine space analytics and real-time health surveillance to identify aberrant health occurrences before they become total mishaps. For example, as the number of respiratory complaints reported through the emergency rooms in a given area goes up suddenly (plotted geospatially), a color-coded message on the dashboard is set off.

These alerts are commonly informed by pre-determined thresholds, statistical models of statistical anomaly detection, or by machine learning approaches of pattern recognition. The presentation of such warnings based on easily comprehensible visual indicators, traffic light color scales, flashing areas, or hazardous slope mapping allows the authorities to act in advance to coordinate the resources to respond, raise awareness, or conduct other special probes. The specific value of this visual early warning capability is to track vector-borne diseases, environmental health hazards, and climate-sensitive diseases.

*Table 2. Complementary Functions of SDI and Visual Learning Across the Health Data Lifecycle*

| Health Data Stage | Role of SDI | Role of Visual Learning |
|---|---|---|
| Data Acquisition | Collects spatial data from multiple sources | Not applicable |
| Data Integration | Harmonizes formats and ensures interoperability | Not applicable |
| Spatial Analysis | Enables geospatial modeling and clustering | Enhances understanding of patterns via visual interpretation |
| Interpretation & Decision | Provides structured access and real-time data pipelines | Dashboards and visual tools simplify data for fast decisions |
| Communication & Engagement | Facilitates data sharing via portals and APIs | Communicates data to the public/ stakeholders through intuitive visuals |
| Feedback and Updates | Ingests user-generated and local health data | Engages users and gathers insights for refining visualization |

## Evidence-Based Policymaking

Health policy must be conducted well, backed up by strong evidence. A combination of SDI with visual learning adds value in the development of the policy because complex sets of data will be understandable by the decision-makers as well as the citizens.

## Spatial Policy Modeling

The ability to be able to model spatial policy through SDI-integrated platforms allows decision makers to be able to run simulations on the impact of policy changes within a geographic area. As an example, potential decision options like closing a small-town clinic, changing the location of a vaccination site, or a change of nature of emergency transport routes can be presented as what-if mapping scenarios, which would disclose their expected consequences on service coverage, travel time, or health outcomes of the population.

These models put into use population density, infrastructure patterns, health demand patterns, and area of epidemiological risks to predict real-life impacts. Spatial policy modeling simultaneously assists health planners in preventing unintended holes in service coverage and makes public health policy based on the data, equitable, and spatially conscious because it supports decision-making only in situations when there are possible service gaps that might fall short of the service.

## Planning for Equity

The equity plannings of geospatial visualizations include the layers of health data and indicators of social vulnerability, including poverty level, ethnicity, age, disability, environmental exposure, and access to transportation. It is a multidimensional spatial analysis that shows any type of inequality in service allocation, disease prevalence, or environmental health risks, especially in the marginalized rural, peri-urban, or slum areas.

Such visual tools help health agencies to prioritize their investment in the area of greatest need, use mobile health units, or focus their health communication in a manner conducive to equity and representation in access to health services. Therefore, spatial decision support tools can contribute to the shift, like rights-based and equity-centered planning in the context of public health.

## Public Communication

Spatial storytelling as a form of public communication increases transparency, accountability, and involvement of the population in the health policy. The visual communication of policy outcomes can be seen through interactive maps, animated timelines, infographics, and community dashboards, describing what outcomes to expect or how many cases of illness can be reduced by a vaccination program, or how much faster they will receive treatment via a new clinic site, and so on.

This visual mode of government intervention makes the intensive information more approachable and closer to ordinary people, encouraging trust in health officials and soliciting community input. Geospatial tools facilitate democratic governance and active citizens who make a difference by contributing to the visibility of the rationality behind interventions, thus demystifying the decision-making process.

## CHALLENGES, LIMITATIONS, AND ETHICAL CONSIDERATIONS

Although SDI, coupled with visual learning strategies, has good prospects to be made beneficial in smart healthcare, implementing the same would not come without its fair share of problems. These barriers are technical, ethical, institutional, and socio-economic, and should be identified and overcome to have a responsible, equitable, and sustainable use. This section looks at various and ambiguous limitations and ethical issues that may impede or complicate the implementation of integrated geospatial-visual systems within a healthcare setting. Figure 3 shows the abstract of challenges in SDI integration.

*Figure 3. Challenges in SDI Integration*

## Technical Limitations

The first broad area of challenges is the technical area, and mainly the area of data integration, interoperability, and infrastructure-readiness.

- Health data can come from a variety of sources electronic health records (EHRs), epidemiological surveys, mobile health apps, and environmental sensors, and satellite imagery. They are heterogeneous, and incorporating them under an integrated SDI framework is a complicated process involving a variety of differences in terms of formats, temporal scales, resolution, and completeness. Incorrect georeferencing or metadata mismatch, or inconsistency, can decrease the precision of the analysis and degrade the visualization results.

- The healthcare system is still highly siloed, with proprietary software or closed data architecture being a critical step in cross-platform interoperability despite the development of geospatial standards (e.g., OGC, HL7, ISO 19115). This fragmentation may impede the ability to collaborate in spatial analysis or real-time data sharing between the departments or agencies.
- Assessment of any technological block is too scarce to support strong GIS platforms, cloud services, or experienced people qualified to manage SDI systems in the resource-constrained environment. Poor bandwidth or server power can also become a hindrance to interactive dashboards and simulation applications.

## Privacy and Data Ethics

Ethical contours of spatial health data visualization are deep, with their significant effect when personal health data is combined and crosses over with geographic identifiers.

- Making the health data at an individual level (e.g., HIV status, cases of infection, or genetic risk) visible on maps can, even when anonymous, reveal individuals or communities to prejudice, discrimination, or even damage. When phenomena of high spatial resolution are combined with demographic layers, a re-identification may follow.
- The visual applications are often constructed using secondary data sources, so one wonders how informed consent was obtained to use such information or visualize the same. Data sources, the purpose of visualization, and limitations should be disclosed to use the information ethically.
- Based on the graphics, the visuals may mislead without any malice unless they are created responsibly. Being too focused on particular risk areas, using an incorrect scale, and the omission of contextual information may strengthen stereotypes or distort the perception of the public.

These risks can only be mitigated by using ethical design principles and stringent compliance with data protection laws (e.g., HIPAA, GDPR) and the design of methods to anonymize geospatial data.

## Digital Divide and Equitable Access

Though visual tools are useful in increasing understanding, they might not be fairly distributed since there is a digital divide.

- Populations in rural or low-income locations may not be connected with access to high-speed internet, modern devices, or geospatial software and platforms to access web-based health dashboards or spatial learning applications.
- Visible inequality in visual or digital or health literacy can have the effect of barring particular groups (e.g., older people, people with disabilities, or linguistically marginalized groups) from adequately interpreting geospatial visualizations even when digital access is available.
- A lot of visualization tools are developed without the service of universal design, which means that impaired individuals with their impairments or the constraints of the mind are locked out. Making sure that it is accessible (e.g., alt text, voice-overs, multilingual support) is important, as well, to engage fairly.

What is needed to bridge the digital gap is investment in digital infrastructure, training people to use technology, and designing inclusively, ensuring accessibility and equality.

## Institutional and Policy Issues

At the governmental level, there are potential challenges inherent to the adoption of integrated SDI-visual learning systems in the sphere of healthcare on the basis of institutional and policy-related issues.

- The health and geospatial information is typically handled under various ministries or departments (e.g., Health, Environment, Urban Planning), which makes it dysfunctional, lacks a clear mandate, and causes silos of data, thus making it difficult to integrate.
- A lack of policy frameworks focuses on the usage of geospatial data in healthcare, especially on the aspects of data-sharing protocols, cross-sectoral interoperability, and some ethical principles, which are observed in many countries.
- The majority of SDI and visualization undertakings are project-themed and receive no permanent financial support or institutional facilitation. Such systems can miss a long-term impact without the built-in mechanisms of maintenance, training, and scaling.

- The hesitancy of institutions towards embracing new technologies, as well as a lack of well-trained GIS experts, data ethicists, and visualization designers to work in the health sector, restricts innovation and scalability.

The solution to such institutional pitfalls is elaborated national policies, mechanisms of interagency cooperation, capacity-building initiatives, and long-term investment plans in geospatial innovations in health. Figure 4 depicts the ethical considerations in AI-driven decision-making.

*Figure 4. Ethical Considerations in AI-Driven Decision-Making*

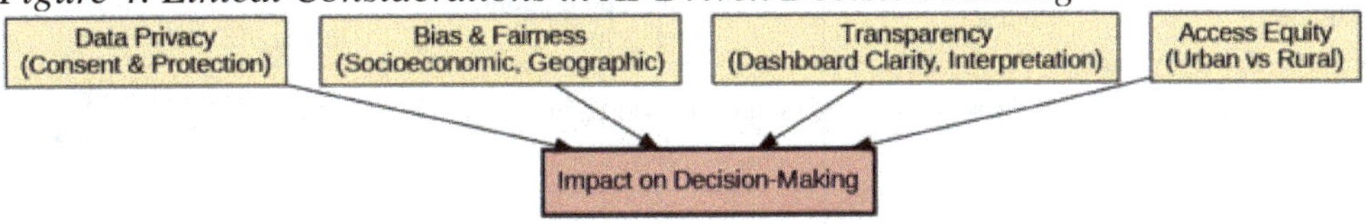


The possibilities of SDI and visual learning in the healthcare system are immense, but the way these gains can be realized successfully is by first mitigating their risk factors ahead of time. This includes drawing up ethical governance of data models, investing in fair infrastructure, and building multi-sectoral collaboration. We can make sure that the benefits of spatial intelligence and visual learning reach every community by incorporating principles of privacy, accessibility, and institutional accountability into implementation strategies, making not only intelligent but also fair, smart healthcare systems. Table 3 summarizes the major challenges, their consequences on smart healthcare outcomes, and possible mitigation pathways to guide responsible implementation.

*Table 3. Challenges, Impacts, and Mitigation Strategies for SDI*

| Challenge Domain | Key Challenge | Impact on Smart Healthcare | Mitigation Strategy |
|---|---|---|---|
| Technical | Data integration from heterogeneous sources | Reduced data accuracy, poor interoperability | Adopt open standards (OGC, HL7), metadata harmonization |
| Technical | Limited interoperability across platforms | Inhibits cross-sector collaboration and decision-making | Develop interoperable SDI frameworks and APIs |
| Technical | Infrastructure constraints | Poor performance of real-time visual tools | Cloud migration, scalable GIS architecture, technical capacity building |

continued on following page

*Table 3. Continued*

| Challenge Domain | Key Challenge | Impact on Smart Healthcare | Mitigation Strategy |
|---|---|---|---|
| Ethical & Privacy | Risk of individual re-identification through spatial data | Violates patient privacy, legal non-compliance | Data anonymization, spatial resolution limits, and ethical review mechanisms |
| Ethical & Privacy | Biased or misleading visualizations | Public misunderstanding, policy misdirection | Adhere to ethical visualization guidelines, reviewed by experts |
| Digital Divide | Inequitable access to digital health tools | Exclusion of marginalized populations | Invest in digital infrastructure, promote inclusive design |
| Digital Divide | Low visual and digital literacy | Misinterpretation of risk information, poor public engagement | Community education, multilingual and visual literacy-friendly tools |
| Institutional & Policy | Fragmented data governance | Redundant efforts, inefficient systems | Establish cross-sector data-sharing protocols and governance bodies |
| Institutional & Policy | Absence of legal and ethical frameworks | Legal uncertainty, lack of accountability | Develop spatial health data policy and regulatory frameworks |
| Institutional & Policy | Project-based implementation with no continuity | System obsolescence, wasted resources | Secure long-term funding, institutionalize within health systems |

## CONCLUSION

Combining SDI and visual learning methods is a radical move to a more intelligent, reactive, and fair healthcare environment. With spatial thinking occupying the center stage in the modern health systems, a structured data environment and the communicative powers of the visual tools can significantly benefit the operations, decision-making, and community outreach in healthcare.

As we move forward, developing trends in the field of AI-augmented geovisualization, predictive spatial analytics, and augmented and virtual reality (AR/VR) use in providing immersive communication in the field of public health would transform how health data can be interpreted and acted upon. Such technologies have the potential to provide high-resolution, real-time understanding of spatial health dynamics, allowing proactive response to challenges such as disease outbreaks as well as infrastructure planning.

Nevertheless, their amazing capabilities can be achieved only through a strong cross-disciplinary cooperation between geographers, data scientists, epidemiologists, health professionals, and policymakers. Multidisciplinary collaborations are not only necessary to create inclusive systems but also to create regulatory and ethical models that guarantee privacy, equity of data, and data access.

At this point, it is easy to conclude that the intersection of SDI with visual learning in smart healthcare brings enormous positive implications: an increase in geospatial understanding, the ability to effectively communicate with the stakeholders, informed decision-making, and citizen empowerment. In a bid to operationalize this vision, the healthcare systems should embark on capacity building, the development of interoperability standards, a community engagement mechanism, and cross-sector alliances. Such intentional integration and strategic planning are the only ways through which smart healthcare can actually tap into the potential of spatial intelligence in terms of improved health outcomes and sustainable communities.

## REFERENCES


Adeleye, V. M., Ashinze, P., Okeoyo, T., El Nabbout, V., Phiri, E. C., Gautam, G., Chukwunonso, C., Adebayo, A. A., Ali, H., & Monsurat, E. O. (2025). Advancing public health through Spatial Data Infrastructures: A review of global practices, governance and policy recommendations. *Discover Public Health*, *22*(1), 1–11. DOI: 10.1186/S12982-025-00563-0/FIGURES/2

Agunbiade, M., Akindeju, O., Elias, P., Olajide, O., & Agama, F. (2024). Transit-Oriented Development and Spatial Data Infrastructure in African Cities. *GeoJournal Library*, (Part F3316), 147–161. DOI: 10.1007/978-3-031-58726-9_9

Ahmad, M., & Ali, A. (2023). A Review of Governance Frameworks for National Spatial Data Infrastructure. In Correia, A., & Agua, P. B. (Eds.), *Innovation, Strategy, and Transformation Frameworks for the Modern Enterprise* (pp. 186–207). IGI Global., DOI: 10.4018/979-8-3693-0458-7.ch008

Ahmad, M., Ali, A., & Hussain, H. (2025). Data Analytics and Decision Making in Healthcare Using Spatial Data Infrastructure: The Case of Pakistan. In Vijit, C., Prashant, S., Anandhi, R., & Divya, A. (Eds.), *Improving Healthcare Quality and Patient Engagement*. IGI Global Scientific Publishing., DOI: 10.4018/979-8-3693-8552-4.ch004

Ali, A., Imran, M., Jabeen, M., Ali, Z., & Mahmood, S. A. (2021). Factors influencing integrated information management: Spatial data infrastructure in Pakistan. *Information Development*, *39*(2), 213–234. DOI: 10.1177/02666669211048483

Aydinoglu, A. C., Bovkir, R., Sisman, S., & Kara, A. (2025). Enhancing the National Spatial Data Infrastructure to Support 3D Real Estate Valuation: A Case Study of GIS-Supported Scoring of 3D Residential Units Based on Expert Opinion. *Transactions in GIS*, *29*(2), e70018. DOI: 10.1111/TGIS.70018

Budi, S., & Sutanta, H. (2023). Worldwide Status of Geoportal and Geospatial Data Completeness at National Geoportals. *IOP Conference Series. Earth and Environmental Science*, *1276*(1). Advance online publication. DOI: 10.1088/1755-1315/1276/1/012071

Dowding, D., Randell, R., Gardner, P., Fitzpatrick, G., Dykes, P., Favela, J., Hamer, S., Whitewood-Moores, Z., Hardiker, N., Borycki, E., & Currie, L. (2015). Dashboards for improving patient care: Review of the literature. *International Journal of Medical Informatics*, *84*(2), 87–100. DOI: 10.1016/J.IJMEDINF.2014.10.001 PMID: 25453274

Drake, C., Nagy, D., Nguyen, T., Kraemer, K. L., Mair, C., Wallace, D., & Donohue, J. (2021). A comparison of methods for measuring spatial access to health care. *Health Services Research, 56*(5). Advance online publication. DOI: 10.1111/1475-6773.13700 PMID: 34250592

Frozza, A. A., & Mello, R. dos S. (2020). JS4Geo: A canonical JSON Schema for geographic data suitable to NoSQL databases. *GeoInformatica, 24*(4). Advance online publication. DOI: 10.1007/s10707-020-00415-w

Gómez, P. M., García, M. P., Seco, G. G., Santiago, A. R., & Johnson, C. T. (2019). The Americas' spatial data infrastructure. *ISPRS International Journal of Geo-Information, 8*(10). Advance online publication. DOI: 10.3390/ijgi8100432

Iftikhar, A., Bond, R., McGilligan, V., McShane, A., Leslie, S. J., Knoery, C., & Peace, A. (2019). Role of dashboards in improving decision making in healthcare: Review of the literature. *ECCE 2019 - Proceedings of the 31st European Conference on Cognitive Ergonomics: "'Design for Cognition,'"* 215–219. https://doi.org/DOI: 10.1145/3335082.3335109;CSUBTYPE:STRING:CONFERENCE

Jia, P., Wang, Y., Yang, M., Wang, L., Yang, X., Shi, X., Yang, L., Wen, J., Liu, Y., Yang, M., Xin, J., Zhang, F., Jiang, L., Chi, C., Zhang, L., Ma, X., Ma, X., Zhao, L., & Li, W. (2022). Inequalities of spatial primary healthcare accessibility in China. *Social Science & Medicine, 314*, 115458. DOI: 10.1016/J.SOCSCIMED.2022.115458 PMID: 36279792

Koshkarev, A. V., Antipov, A. N., Batuyev, A. R., Yermoshin, V. V., & Karakin, V. P. (2008). Geo-portals as part of spatial data infrastructures: Russian Academy-supported resources and geoservices. *Geography and Natural Resources, 29*(1). Advance online publication. DOI: 10.1016/j.gnr.2008.04.005

Lee, S. (2022). Spatial and Socioeconomic Inequalities in Accessibility to Healthcare Services in South Korea. *Healthcare 2022, Vol. 10, Page 2049, 10*(10), 2049. https://doi.org/DOI: 10.3390/HEALTHCARE10102049

Maguire, D. J., & Longley, P. A. (2005). The Emergence of Geoportals and their Role in Spatial Data Infrastructures. In *Computers, Environment and Urban Systems* (Vol. 29, Issue 1 SPEC.ISS., pp. 3–14). https://doi.org/DOI: 10.1016/j.compenvurbsys.2004.05.012

Maurya, S. P., Ohri, A., & Gaur, S. (2022). *Relevance of Spatio-temporal Data Visualization Techniques in Healthcare System*. 59–78. https://doi.org/DOI: 10.1007/978-981-16-9476-9_3

Menon, A., Aishwarya, M. S., Maria Joykutty, A., Av, A. Y., & Av, A. Y. (2021). Data Visualization and Predictive Analysis for Smart Healthcare: Tool for a Hospital. *TENSYMP 2021 - 2021 IEEE Region 10 Symposium*. https://doi.org/DOI: 10.1109/TENSYMP52854.2021.9550822

Mwange, C., Mulaku, G. C., & Siriba, D. N. (2018). Reviewing the status of national spatial data infrastructures in Africa. *Survey Review*, *50*(360), 191–200. DOI: 10.1080/00396265.2016.1259720

Noon, C. E., & Hankins, C. T. (2001). Spatial data visualization in healthcare: Supporting a facility location decision via GIS-based market analysis. *Proceedings of the Hawaii International Conference on System Sciences*, 149. https://doi.org/DOI: 10.1109/HICSS.2001.926573

Ouma, P., Macharia, P. M., Okiro, E., & Alegana, V. (2021). *Methods of Measuring Spatial Accessibility to Health Care in Uganda BT - Practicing Health Geography: The African Context*. Practicing Health Geography.

Piyasena, N. M. P. M., Vithanage, P. A. D. V., & Witharana, S. L. (2023). A Review of Sri Lanka's National Spatial Data Infrastructure (SL-NSDI) with the Aim of Enhancing Its Functionalities. In de Vries, W. T., Rudiarto, I., & Piyasena, N. M. P. M. (Eds.), *Geospatial Science for Smart Land Management: An Asian Context* (1st ed., p. 17). CRC Press., DOI: 10.1201/9781003349518-15

Sjoukema, J., Bregt, A. K., & Crompvoets, J. (2020). Understanding governance dynamics: The governing system of spatial data infrastructures. *International Journal of Spatial Data Infrastructures Research*, •••, 15.

Sjoukema, J. W., Bregt, A., & Crompvoets, J. (2017). Evolving spatial data infrastructures and the role of adaptive governance. *ISPRS International Journal of Geo-Information*, *6*(8). Advance online publication. DOI: 10.3390/ijgi6080254

Webster, A. J., Gaitskell, K., Turnbull, I., Cairns, B. J., & Clarke, R. (2021). Characterisation, identification, clustering, and classification of disease. *Scientific Reports*, *11*(1). Advance online publication. DOI: 10.1038/s41598-021-84860-z PMID: 33686097

Zhuang, M., Concannon, D., & Manley, E. (2022). A Framework for Evaluating Dashboards in Healthcare. *IEEE Transactions on Visualization and Computer Graphics*, *28*(4), 1715–1731. DOI: 10.1109/TVCG.2022.3147154 PMID: 35213306

## KEY TERMS AND DEFINITIONS

**Community Engagement:** The active involvement of individuals, groups, and organizations in decision-making processes, planning, and actions that affect their community, ensuring their voices, needs, and knowledge are considered.

**Geographic Information System (GIS):** A computer-based system that captures, stores, analyzes, and visualizes geographic data to support decision-making and spatial problem-solving.

**Participatory Platforms:** Digital or physical tools that enable stakeholders, including the public, to contribute ideas, share data, collaborate, and influence decision-making processes.

**Real-Time Dashboards:** Interactive digital interfaces that display up-to-the-minute data and visualizations, enabling users to monitor, track, and respond to changing conditions instantly.

**Spatial Data Analysis:** The process of examining geographic data to identify patterns, relationships, and trends, often using statistical, computational, or visualization methods.

**Spatial Data Infrastructure (SDI):** A coordinated framework of technologies, policies, standards, and human resources designed to collect, store, manage, share, and use spatial (geographic) data efficiently across organizations and sectors.

**Spatial Inequalities:** Uneven distribution of resources, services, and opportunities across different geographic areas, often reflecting underlying social, economic, or environmental disparities.

# Compilation of References


Abdelkader, A. A. M., Hassan, H., & Abdelkader, M. (2024). The role of artificial intelligence in designing higher education courses: Benefits and challenges. In Lytras, M. D., Alkhaldi, A., Malik, S., Serban, A. C., & Aldosemani, T. (Eds.), *The evolution of artificial intelligence in higher education* (pp. 83–97). Emerald Publishing Limited., DOI: 10.1108/978-1-83549-486-820241005

Abdullah, W. (2024). Artificial Intelligence for Achieving Sustainable Development Goals: Applications, Techniques and Progress. [Zagazig University]. *International Journal of Computers and Informatics*, *5*, 117–128.

Abulibdeh, A., Zaidan, E., & Abulibdeh, R. (2024). Navigating the confluence of artificial intelligence and education for sustainable development in the era of industry 4.0: Challenges, opportunities, and ethical dimensions. *Journal of Cleaner Production*, *437*, 140527. DOI: 10.1016/j.jclepro.2023.140527

Adeleye, V. M., Ashinze, P., Okeoyo, T., El Nabbout, V., Phiri, E. C., Gautam, G., Chukwunonso, C., Adebayo, A. A., Ali, H., & Monsurat, E. O. (2025). Advancing public health through Spatial Data Infrastructures: A review of global practices, governance and policy recommendations. *Discover Public Health*, *22*(1), 1–11. DOI: 10.1186/S12982-025-00563-0/FIGURES/2

Adenle, A. A., De Steur, H., Mwongera, C., Rola-Rubzen, F., de Barcellos, M. D., Vivanco, D. F., Timilsina, G. R., Possas, C., Alders, R., Chertow, M., Poons, S., & Scholes, B. (2023). *Global UN 2030 agenda: How can Science, Technology and Innovation accelerate the achievement of Sustainable Development Goals for All?* PLOS Sustainability and Transformation.

Adewoyin, M. A., Adediwin, O., & Audu, A. J. (2025). Artificial intelligence and sustainable energy development: A review of applications, challenges, and future directions. *International Journal of Multidisciplinary Research and Growth Evaluation*, *6*(2), 196–203.

Agarwal, S., Agrawal, V., & Dixit, J. K. (2020). Green manufacturing: A MCDM approach. *Materials Today: Proceedings*, *26*, 2869–2874.

Agunbiade, M., Akindeju, O., Elias, P., Olajide, O., & Agama, F. (2024). Transit-Oriented Development and Spatial Data Infrastructure in African Cities. *GeoJournal Library*, (Part F3316), 147–161. DOI: 10.1007/978-3-031-58726-9_9

Ahmad, M., & Ali, A. (2023). A Review of Governance Frameworks for National Spatial Data Infrastructure. In Correia, A., & Agua, P. B. (Eds.), *Innovation, Strategy, and Transformation Frameworks for the Modern Enterprise* (pp. 186–207). IGI Global., DOI: 10.4018/979-8-3693-0458-7.ch008

Ahmad, M., Ali, A., & Hussain, H. (2025). Data Analytics and Decision Making in Healthcare Using Spatial Data Infrastructure: The Case of Pakistan. In Vijit, C., Prashant, S., Anandhi, R., & Divya, A. (Eds.), *Improving Healthcare Quality and Patient Engagement*. IGI Global Scientific Publishing., DOI: 10.4018/979-8-3693-8552-4.ch004

Ahmad, U., Aman, A., Khan, A. A., & Ali, S. E. A. (2025). Optimizing crowdfunding for mineral resources of Dutch economy: The role of fintech in achieving sustainable development goals through artificial intelligence. *Resources Policy*, *100*, 105413.

Ahn, M., Kang, J., & Hustvedt, G. (2016). A model of sustainable household technology acceptance. *International Journal of Consumer Studies*, *40*(1), 83–91.

Ajmal, C. S., Yerram, S., Abishek, V., Nizam, V. M., Aglave, G., Patnam, J. D., & Srivastava, S. (2025). Innovative Approaches in Regulatory Affairs: Leveraging Artificial Intelligence and Machine Learning for Efficient Compliance and Decision-Making. *The AAPS Journal*, *27*(1), 22. PMID: 39776314

Akinrinola, O., Okoye, C. C., Ofodile, O. C., & Ugochukwu, C. E. (2024). Navigating and reviewing ethical dilemmas in AI development: Strategies for transparency, fairness, and accountability. *GSC Advanced Research and Reviews*, 18(3), 050-058. https://doi.org/DOI: 10.30574/gscarr.2024.18.3.0088

Al Saadi, A., & Awashreh, R. (2024). Enhancing the performance of translation graduates through training: A proposed practical model. In Mansour, N., & Bujosa Vadell, L. M. (Eds.), *Finance and law in the metaverse world* (pp. 219–229). Springer., DOI: 10.1007/978-3-031-67547-8_19

Ali, A., Imran, M., Jabeen, M., Ali, Z., & Mahmood, S. A. (2021). Factors influencing integrated information management: Spatial data infrastructure in Pakistan. *Information Development*, *39*(2), 213–234. DOI: 10.1177/02666669211048483

Alijoyo, F. A., Aziz, T. S. A., Omer, N., Yusuf, N., Kumar, M. D., Ramesh, A. V. N., & El-Ebiary, Y. A. B. (2025). Personalized marketing: Leveraging AI for culturally aware segmentation and targeting. *Alexandria Engineering Journal*, *119*, 8–21.

Alinda, K., Tumwine, S., & Kaawaase, T. K. (2024). Environmental innovations and sustainability practices of manufacturing firms in Uganda. *Asia Pacific Journal of Innovation and Entrepreneurship*, *18*(2), 102–129.

Alonso-Rodríguez, A. M. (2024). Towards an ethical framework for artificial intelligence in education. *Teoría de la Educación. Revista Interuniversitaria*, *36*(1), 31821. Advance online publication. DOI: 10.14201/teri.31821

Alqahtani, N., & Wafula, Z. (2025). Artificial intelligence Integration: Pedagogical strategies and policies at leading universities. *Innovative Higher Education*, *50*(2), 665–684.

Al-Raeei, M. (2024). Artificial intelligence for climate resilience: Advancing sustainable goals in SDGs 11 and 13 and its relationship to pandemics. *Discover Sustainability*, *5*(1), 513.

Al-Raeei, M. (2025). The smart future for sustainable development: Artificial intelligence solutions for sustainable urbanization. *Sustainable Development*, *33*(1), 508–517.

Alsaadi, A., & Awashreh, R. (2025). Practical university training impact on job performance of translation graduates in Oman. *Forum for Linguistic Studies*, *7*(2), 786–796. DOI: 10.30564/fls.v7i2.8306

Alvarez, J. M., Colmenarejo, A. B., & Elobaid, A.. (2024). Policy advice and best practices on bias and fairness in AI. *Ethics and Information Technology*, *26*, 31. DOI: 10.1007/s10676-024-09746-w

Alyahya, M., Aliedan, M., Agag, G., & Abdelmoety, Z. H. (2022). Exploring the link between sustainable development practices, institutional pressures, and green innovation. *Sustainability*, *14*(21), 14312.

Al-Zahrani, A. M., & Alasmari, T. M. (2024). Exploring the impact of artificial intelligence on higher education: The dynamics of ethical, social, and educational implications. *Humanities & Social Sciences Communications*, *11*, 912. DOI: 10.1057/s41599-024-03432-4

Alzboon, M. S., Al-Shorman, H. M., Alka'awneh, S. M. N., Saatchi, S. G., Alqaraleh, M. K. S., Samara, E. I. M., & Haija, A. A. A. (2025). The Role of Perceived Trust in Embracing Artificial Intelligence Technologies: Insights from SMEs. In *Intelligence-Driven Circular Economy: Regeneration Towards Sustainability and Social Responsibility—Volume 2* (pp. 1–15). Springer Nature Switzerland.

Amuda, Y. J. (2025). Artificial intelligence for food production among smallholder farmers: Towards achieving sustainable development goals (SDGs) in Nigeria. *Journal of Ecohumanism*, *4*(1), 175–185.

Anser, M. K., Yousaf, Z., & Zaman, K. (2020). Green technology acceptance model and green logistics operations:"to see which way the wind is blowing". *Frontiers in Sustainability*, *1*, 3.

Arévalo, P., & Jurado, F. (2024). Impact of artificial intelligence on the planning and operation of distributed energy systems in smart grids. *Energies*, *17*(17), 4501.

Arini, D., & Nursa'ban, M. (2024). Contribution of Artificial Intelligence (AI) in Education to Support the Achievement of Sustainable Development Goals (SDGs) 2030. *Jurnal Penelitian Pendidikan IPA, 10*(SpecialIssue), 39-45.

Aroba, O. J., & Rudolph, M. (2024). Systematic literature review on the application of precision agriculture using artificial intelligence by small-scale farmers in Africa and its societal impact. *Journal of Infrastructure. Policy and Development*, *8*(13), 8872.

Ashraf, S. F., Li, C., Wattoo, M. U., Murad, M., & Mahmood, B. (2024). Green horizons: Unleashing green innovation through green business strategies and competencies. *Business Strategy and the Environment*, *33*(5), 4233–4251.

Awashreh, R. (2024a). Omani private universities: Debates between progress in human development but weak education quality. *The International Journal of Educational Organization and Leadership*, *32*(1), 1–15. DOI: 10.18848/2329-1656/CGP/v32i01/1-15

Awashreh, R. (2024b). Be aware: Navigating challenges in AI-driven higher education. *The International Journal of Interdisciplinary Educational Studies*, *20*(1), 203–218. DOI: 10.18848/2327-011X/CGP/v20i01/203-218

Awashreh, R. (2025). Navigating leadership dynamics: Insights and strategies across domains. In *Optimizing leadership and governance in higher education* (pp. 203–232). IGI Global., DOI: 10.4018/979-8-3693-3534-5.ch010

Awashreh, R., & Al Ghunaimi, H. (2025). Rethinking the PhD: Aligning higher education with market needs and practical skills. *Forum for Linguistic Studies*, *7*(2), 254–264. DOI: 10.30564/fls.v7i2.7942

Awashreh, R., & Al Ghunaimi, H. (2025b). Bridging cultural gaps: Enhancing student motivation and academic integrity in Oman's universities. *Forum for Linguistic Studies*, *7*(2), 265–279. DOI: 10.30564/fls.v7i2.8300

Awashreh, R., & Bremananth, R. (2025). A study on ethical implementation of AI in collegiate studies using fuzzy implication. *Pakistan Journal of Life and Social Sciences*, *23*(1), 00317. Advance online publication. DOI: 10.57239/PJLSS-2025-23.1.00317

Awashreh, R., & Mohamed, Y. (2024). Comparative study of leadership perceptions in government and education sectors: Insights from the UAE and Oman. *The International Journal of Organizational Diversity*, *24*(2), 109–123. DOI: 10.18848/2328-6261/CGP/v24i02/109-123

Awashreh, R., & Ramachandran, B. (2024). Can artificial intelligence dominate and control human beings? *International Research Journal of Multidisciplinary Scope*, *5*(4), 427–438. DOI: 10.47857/irjms.2024.05i04.01569

Aydinoglu, A. C., Bovkir, R., Sisman, S., & Kara, A. (2025). Enhancing the National Spatial Data Infrastructure to Support 3D Real Estate Valuation: A Case Study of GIS-Supported Scoring of 3D Residential Units Based on Expert Opinion. *Transactions in GIS*, *29*(2), e70018. DOI: 10.1111/TGIS.70018

Bagiyam, D., Blessy Doe, M., & Aravindan, J. S. (2024). *Navigating complexities through unveiling sustainability challenges in AI using a bibliometric approach*. IGI Global., DOI: 10.4018/979-8-3693-3282-5.ch014

Bai, C., & Sarkis, J. (2020). A supply chain transparency and sustainability technology appraisal model for blockchain technology. *International Journal of Production Research*, *58*(7), 2142–2162. DOI: 10.1080/00207543.2019.1708989

Baig, M. A. A., Huang, J., & Xu, J. (2024). AI for United Nations sustainable development goals: AI for UNSDGs.

Balan, A. (2024). Examining the ethical and sustainability challenges of legal education's AI revolution. *International Journal of the Legal Profession*, *31*(3), 1–26. DOI: 10.1080/09695958.2024.2421179

Baquero, A. (2024). Unveiling the path to green innovation: The interplay of green learning orientation, knowledge management capability and manufacturing firm's capability to orchestrate resources. *Journal of Business and Industrial Marketing, 39*(10), 2205–2221.

Barbedo, J. G. A. (2025). A review of artificial intelligence techniques for wheat crop monitoring and management. *Agronomy (Basel), 15*(5), 1157.

Barney, J. (1991). Firm resources and sustained competitive advantage. *Journal of Management, 17*(1), 99–120.

Bassey, K., Stephen, A., & Juliet, A. (2024). AI-enhanced lifecycle assessment of renewable energy systems. *Engineering Science & Technology Journal, 5*(7), 2082–2099. DOI: 10.51594/estj.v5i7.1254

Batool, A., Zowghi, D., & Bano, M. (2025). AI governance: A systematic literature review. *AI and Ethics*, •••, 1–15.

Batty, M. (2018). *Inventing future cities*. MIT Press.

Bender, E. M., Gebru, T., McMillan-Major, A., & Shmitchell, S. (2021). On the dangers of stochastic parrots: Can language models be too big? *Proceedings of the 2021 ACM Conference on Fairness, Accountability, and Transparency*, 610–623. https://doi.org/DOI: 10.1145/3442188.3445922

Berson, I. R., Berson, M. J., & Luo, W. (2025). Innovating responsibly: Ethical considerations for AI in early childhood education. *AI and the Brain of the Child, 1*(2). Advance online publication. DOI: 10.1007/s44436-025-00003-5

Bhatia, M. S., & Kumar, S. (2022). Linking stakeholder and competitive pressure to Industry 4.0 and performance: Mediating effect of environmental commitment and green process innovation. *Business Strategy and the Environment, 31*(5), 1905–1918.

Bhattasali, T., & Savarimuthu, X. (2021). *Technological innovations for environmental sustainability*. CRC., DOI: 10.1201/9781003055020-08

Boatemaa, R., Asare, S. O., Akabadin, S. C., Agyabeng, V., & Addy, A. (2024). The role of AI in Enhancing Disease Surveillance and Outbreak Response in Developing Countries. *Ghana Journal of Nursing and Midwifery, 1*(4), 16–29.

Bocean, C. G. (2025). Sustainable Development in the Digital Age: Harnessing Emerging Digital Technologies to Catalyze Global SDG Achievement. *Applied Sciences (Basel, Switzerland), 15*(2), 816.

Borah, P. S., Dogbe, C. S. K., & Marwa, N. (2025). Green dynamic capability and green product innovation for sustainable development: Role of green operations, green transaction, and green technology development capabilities. *Corporate Social Responsibility and Environmental Management, 32*(1), 911–926.

Bousdekis, A., Apostolou, D., & Mentzas, G. (2024). Artificial intelligence applications for increasing resource efficiency in industrial production. *Sustainability, 13*(12), 6689. DOI: 10.3390/su13126689

Brynjolfsson, E., & McAfee, A. (2014). The second machine age: Work, progress, and prosperity in a time of brilliant technologies. WW Norton & company.

Budi, S., & Sutanta, H. (2023). Worldwide Status of Geoportal and Geospatial Data Completeness at National Geoportals. *IOP Conference Series. Earth and Environmental Science, 1276*(1). Advance online publication. DOI: 10.1088/1755-1315/1276/1/012071

Camilleri, M. A. (2023). Artificial intelligence governance: Ethical considerations and implications for social responsibility. *Expert Systems: International Journal of Knowledge Engineering and Neural Networks.* Advance online publication. DOI: 10.1111/exsy.13406

Cancela-Outeda, C. (2024). The EU's AI act: A framework for collaborative governance. *Internet of Things : Engineering Cyber Physical Human Systems, 27*, 101291. DOI: 10.1016/j.iot.2024.101291

Carayannis, E. G., Dumitrescu, R., Falkowski, T., Papamichail, G., & Zota, N. R. (2025). Enhancing SME Resilience through Artificial Intelligence and Strategic Foresight: A Framework for Sustainable Competitiveness. *Technology in Society*, •••, 102835.

Cassettari, L., Bendato, I., Mosca, M., & Mosca, R. (2017). Energy resources intelligent management using online real-time simulation: A decision support tool for sustainable manufacturing. *Applied Energy, 190*, 841–851.

Chanda, T. C., Sain, Z. H., Shogbesan, Y., & Phiri, E. V. (2024). Digital literacy in education: Preparing students for the future workforce. *International Journal of Research, 11*(8), 327–344. DOI: 10.5281/zenodo.13347718

Cheng, C., Ahmad, S. F., Irshad, M., Alsanie, G., Khan, Y., Ahmad, A. Y. B., & Aleemi, A. R. (2023). Impact of green process innovation and productivity on sustainability: The moderating role of environmental awareness. *Sustainability, 15*(17), 12945.

Cheng, T. C. E., Lai, K. H., & Lun, Y. H. V. (2023). Integration of artificial intelligence in sustainable manufacturing: A systematic literature review. *Journal of Manufacturing Systems*, *67*, 10–25. DOI: 10.1016/j.jmsy.2023.01.004

Chen, P., & Dagestani, A. A. (2023). What lies about circular economy practices and performance? Fresh insights from China. *Journal of Cleaner Production*, *416*, 137893. DOI: 10.1016/j.jclepro.2023.137893

Chen, T., Jason Leong, K., Yee, M., Baitsegi, O., Palanisamy, L., & Ramasamy, R. K. (2023). Hybrid Project Management between Traditional Software Development Lifecycle and Agile Based Product Development for Future Sustainability. *Sustainability*.

Cheong, B. C. (2024). Transparency and accountability in AI systems: Safeguarding wellbeing in the age of algorithmic decision-making. *Frontiers in Human Dynamics*, *6*, 1421273. DOI: 10.3389/fhumd.2024.1421273

Cheong, H.-I., Lyons, A., Houghton, R. W., & Majumdar, A. (2023). Secondary qualitative research methodology using online data within the context of social sciences. *International Journal of Qualitative Methods*, *22*(2), 16094069231180160. DOI: 10.1177/16094069231180160

Chien, F., Ajaz, T., Andlib, Z., Chau, K. Y., Ahmad, P., & Sharif, A. (2021). The role of technology innovation, renewable energy and globalization in reducing environmental degradation in Pakistan: A step towards sustainable environment. *Renewable Energy*, *177*, 308–317.

Cho, H., & Ackom, E. (2025). Artificial Intelligence (AI)-driven approach to climate action and sustainable development. *Nature Communications*, *16*(1), 1228. PMID: 39890783

Clark, G. (2007). *A farewell to alms: A brief economic history of the world*. Princeton University Press.

Coral, J.S., & Papell, G.T. (2012). Sustainable technology innovation course. Constructive and community-oriented learning postgraduate education.

Danladi, S., Prasad, M. S. V., Modibbo, U. M., Ahmadi, S. A., & Ghasemi, P. (2023). Attaining sustainable development goals through financial inclusion: Exploring collaborative approaches to Fintech adoption in developing economies. *Sustainability*, *15*(17), 13039.

Das, A., Malaviya, S., & Singh, M. (2023). The impact of AI-driven personalization on learners' performance. *International Journal on Computer Science and Engineering*, *11*(8), 15–22. DOI: 10.26438/ijcse/v11i8.1522

Davar, N. F., Dewan, M. A. A., & Zhang, X. (2025). AI chatbots in education: Challenges and opportunities. *Information (Basel), 16*(3), 235. DOI: 10.3390/info16030235

Dave, V. (2024). A systematic literature review of the effect/contribution of artificial intelligence technology towards achieving the sustainable development goals.

David, A., Yigitcanlar, T., Desouza, K., Li, R. Y. M., Cheong, P. H., Mehmood, R., & Corchado, J. (2024). Understanding local government responsible AI strategy: An international municipal policy document analysis. *Cities (London, England), 155*, 105502. DOI: 10.1016/j.cities.2024.105502

Dayal, G., Verma, P., & Sehgal, S. (2023). A comprehensive review on the integration of artificial intelligence in the field of education. In *Leveraging AI and emotional intelligence in contemporary business organizations* (pp. 331–349). IGI Global., DOI: 10.4018/979-8-3693-1902-4.ch020

Dhar, N., & Mallick, B. (2025). *Re-thinking posthumanism across the global south: An introduction*. https://doi.org/DOI: 10.3726/b22159

Dong, L. (2023). Strengthening Sustainability in Agile Education: Using Client-Sponsored Projects to Cultivate Agile Talents. *Sustainability*.

Dowding, D., Randell, R., Gardner, P., Fitzpatrick, G., Dykes, P., Favela, J., Hamer, S., Whitewood-Moores, Z., Hardiker, N., Borycki, E., & Currie, L. (2015). Dashboards for improving patient care: Review of the literature. *International Journal of Medical Informatics, 84*(2), 87–100. DOI: 10.1016/J.IJMEDINF.2014.10.001 PMID: 25453274

Drake, C., Nagy, D., Nguyen, T., Kraemer, K. L., Mair, C., Wallace, D., & Donohue, J. (2021). A comparison of methods for measuring spatial access to health care. *Health Services Research, 56*(5). Advance online publication. DOI: 10.1111/1475-6773.13700 PMID: 34250592

Dunleavy, P., & Margetts, H. (2025). Data science, artificial intelligence and the third wave of digital era governance. *Public Policy and Administration, 40*(2), 185–214.

Dwivedi, Y. K., Kshetri, N., Hughes, L., Slade, E. L., Jeyaraj, A., Kar, A. K., Baabdullah, A. M., Koohang, A., Raghavan, V., Ahuja, M., Albanna, H., Albashrawi, M. A., Al-Busaidi, A. S., Balakrishnan, J., Barlette, Y., Basu, S., Bose, I., Brooks, L., Buhalis, D., & Wright, R. (2023). Opinion paper: "So what if ChatGPT wrote it?" Multidisciplinary perspectives on opportunities, challenges and implications of generative conversational AI for research, practice and policy. *International Journal of Information Management, 71*, 102642. DOI: 10.1016/j.ijinfomgt.2023.102642

Ebirim, W., Montero, D.J., Ani, E.C., Ninduwezuor-Ehiobu, N., Usman, F.O., & Olu-lawal, K.A. (2024). THE ROLE OF AGILE PROJECT MANAGEMENT IN DRIVING INNOVATION IN ENERGY-EFFICIENT HVAC SOLUTIONS. *Engineering Science & Technology Journal.*

Ebrahim, T. Y. (2020). Clean and sustainable technology innovation. *Current Opinion in Environmental Sustainability.*

Elias, O., Esebre, S. D., Abijo, I., Timothy, A. M., Babayemi, T. D., Makinde, E. O., & Fatoki, I. E. (2024). Harnessing artificial intelligence to optimize financial technologies for achieving sustainable development goals. *World J. Adv. Res. Rev, 23*, 616–625.

Eliseo, M. A., Junior, L. C., & Silveira, I. F. (2025). A Comprehensive and Structured Maturity Model for Measuring AI Adoption Levels in Industry 4.0. *CLEI Electronic Journal, 28*(1), 3–1.

Enbaia, E., Alzubi, A., Iyiola, K., & Aljuhmani, H. Y. (2024). The Interplay Between Environmental Ethics and Sustainable Performance: Does Organizational Green Culture and Green Innovation Really Matter? *Sustainability, 16*(23), 10230.

Esteva, A., Kuprel, B., Novoa, R. A., Ko, J., Swetter, S. M., Blau, H. M., & Thrun, S. (2017). Dermatologist-level classification of skin cancer with deep neural networks. *Nature, 542*(7639), 115–118. DOI: 10.1038/nature21056 PMID: 28117445

Făgără an, C., Cristea, C., Cristea, M., Popa, O., & Pîslă, A. (2023). Integrating Sustainability Metrics into Project and Portfolio Performance Assessment in Agile Software Development: A Data-Driven Scoring Model. *Sustainability.*

Farahani, M. Sh. (2024). *Artificial intelligence and inequality: Challenges and opportunities*. Qeios., DOI: 10.32388/7HWUZ2

Farmanesh, P., Solati Dehkordi, N., Vehbi, A., & Chavali, K. (2025). Artificial Intelligence and Green Innovation in Small and Medium-Sized Enterprises and Competitive-Advantage Drive Toward Achieving Sustainable Development Goals. *Sustainability, 17*(5), 2162.

Fazal, A., Ahmed, A., & Abbas, S. (2025). Importance of artificial intelligence in achieving sustainable development goals through financial inclusion. *Qualitative Research in Financial Markets, 17*(2), 432–452.

Filgueiras, F. (2025). Artificial intelligence and governance challenges in Latin America–the game between decolonization and dependence. In *Handbook on Governance and Data Science* (pp. 198–221). Edward Elgar Publishing.

Floridi, L., Cowls, J., Beltrametti, M., Chatila, R., Chazerand, P., Dignum, V., & Vayena, E. (2018). AI4People—an ethical framework for a good AI society: Opportunities, risks, principles, and recommendations. *Minds and Machines*, *28*, 689–707. PMID: 30930541

Fornasiero, R., Kiebler, L., Falsafi, M., & Sardesai, S. (2025). Proposing a maturity model for assessing artificial intelligence and big data in the process industry. *International Journal of Production Research*, *63*(4), 1235–1255.

Fratta, G., Stefani, I., Tapola, S., & Saetta, S. (2024). Green Innovation Practices: A Case Study in a Foundry. *Journal of Manufacturing and Materials Processing*, *8*(3), 111.

Freeman, R. E. (1984). *Strategic management: A stakeholder approach.* Pitman.

Frozza, A. A., & Mello, R. dos S. (2020). JS4Geo: A canonical JSON Schema for geographic data suitable to NoSQL databases. *GeoInformatica*, *24*(4). Advance online publication. DOI: 10.1007/s10707-020-00415-w

Fukuyama, K. (1997). Technological incentives of firms under the environmental regulations. *Proceedings of the 1997 IEEE International Conference on Systems, Man, and Cybernetics*, 1, 815–820. https://doi.org/DOI: 10.1109/icsmc.1997.626198

Fu, Y., & Weng, Z. (2024). Navigating the ethical terrain of AI in education: A systematic review on framing responsible human-centered AI practices. *Computers and Education: Artificial Intelligence*, *7*, 100306. DOI: 10.1016/j.caeai.2024.100306

Garg, T., Kumar, U., Yadav, H., & Jain, A. (2024, April). Fostering Sustainable Growth via the Fusion of Artificial Intelligence and Computer Vision. In *International Conference on Sustainable Development through Machine Learning, AI and IoT* (pp. 102-109). Cham: Springer Nature Switzerland.

Gautam, K., Kumari, A., Kumari, A., & Saini, A. (2020). AI's role in sustainable energy. *International Journal of Psychosocial Rehabilitation*, *24*(7), 11396–11398. DOI: 10.61841/v24i7/400271

Geissdoerfer, M., Savaget, P., Bocken, N. M., & Hultink, E. J. (2017). The circular economy–A new sustainability paradigm? *Journal of Cleaner Production*, *143*, 757–768.

Ghobakhloo, M., & Fathi, M. (2023). The role of artificial intelligence in sustainable supply chain management. *International Journal of Production Research*, *61*(4), 1345–1362. DOI: 10.1080/00207543.2023.2161234

Ghosh, S. S. (2024). Transforming the Indian Education Landscape: The Impact of Personalized Learning and Adaptive Technologies in Continuing Education. In *Embracing Technological Advancements for Lifelong Learning* (pp. 278-299). IGI Global.

Ghosh, S., Sarkar, S. K., & Roy, P. (2025). Application of Automation and Artificial Intelligence (AI) in Green Transportation System. In *Driving Green Transportation System Through Artificial Intelligence and Automation: Approaches, Technologies and Applications* (pp. 21–42). Springer Nature Switzerland.

Gift, M. D. M., Boopathi, S., Jayaseelan, P., Hasan, D. S., Alagarraja, K., & Senthil, T. S. (2024). *Additive manufacturing and 3D printing innovations*. IGI Global., DOI: 10.4018/979-8-3693-0968-1.ch010

Ginters, E., & Revathy, J. C. (2021). Attributes of digital technologies and related impacts on sustainability assessment. *2021 International Conference on Electrical, Communication, and Computer Engineering (ICECCE)*, 1–5. https://doi.org/DOI: 10.1109/ICECCE52056.2021.9514094

Godil, D. I., Yu, Z., Sharif, A., Usman, R., & Khan, S. A. (2021). Investigate the role of technology innovation and renewable energy in reducing transport sector CO 2 emission in China: A path toward sustainable development. *Sustainable Development*.

Gomase, G., & Gajbhiye, C. (2024). The Contribution and Challenges of Artificial Intelligence (AI)-based techniques for achieving Sustainable Development Goals.

Gómez, P. M., García, M. P., Seco, G. G., Santiago, A. R., & Johnson, C. T. (2019). The Americas' spatial data infrastructure. *ISPRS International Journal of Geo-Information*, *8*(10). Advance online publication. DOI: 10.3390/ijgi8100432

Gong, Y., Ma, F., Wang, H., Tzachor, A., Sun, W., Zhu, J., & Schandl, H. (2025). The evolution of research at the intersection of industrial ecology and artificial intelligence. *Journal of Industrial Ecology*, *29*(2), 440–457.

Goorun, Y., Marais, S., & Nicolls, F. (2024). Robotic waste sorting using deep learning. *MATEC Web of Conferences, 406*, 10003. https://doi.org/DOI: 10.1051/matecconf/202440610003

Goosen, W., & Mugumo, V. P. (2024). A framework for the application of AI in higher education in association with APPETD and Swiss Institute for Management and Innovation. In *Proceedings of the International Conference on Medical Imaging, Electronic Imaging, Information Technologies, and Sensors (MIEITS 2024)*. SPIE. https://doi.org/DOI: 10.1117/12.3030740

Gosselink, B. H., Brandt, K., Croak, M., DeSalvo, K., Gomes, B., Ibrahim, L., . . . Manyika, J. (2024). AI in action: Accelerating progress towards the Sustainable Development Goals. *arXiv preprint arXiv:2407.02711*.

Grubaugh, S., & Levitt, G. (2023). Artificial intelligence and the paradigm shift: Reshaping education to equip students for future careers. *The International Journal of Social Sciences and Humanities Invention*, *10*(6), 7931–7941. DOI: 10.18535/ijsshi/v10i06.02

Gupta, K., & Singh, N. (2024a). A systematic review of literature on greenwashing. Sustainability Development through Green Economics, 114, 75–90. https://doi.org/DOI: 10.1108/S1569-375920240000114005

Gupta, A., & Khanna, A. (2024). A holistic approach to sustainable manufacturing: Rework, green technology, and carbon policies. *Expert Systems with Applications*, *244*, 122943.

Gupta, K., & Singh, N. (2024b). Greenwashing perception and attitude–intention relationship towards green product purchase: A mediating model. *Environment, Development and Sustainability*, •••, 1–24. DOI: 10.1007/s10668-024-05486-5

Gupta, K., & Singh, N. (2024c). Visualization of global research trends and future research directions of greenwashing by using bibliometric analysis. *Environment, Development and Sustainability*, •••, 1–21. DOI: 10.1007/s10668-024-04548-y

Gupta, S. M., Güngör, A., Govindan, K., Özceylan, E., Kalaycı, C. B., & Piplani, R. (2020). Responsible & sustainable manufacturing. *International Journal of Production Research*, *58*(23), 7181–7182. DOI: 10.1080/00207543.2020.1841968

Gupta, S., Gupta, S. B., & Gupta, M. (2024). Importance of artificial intelligence in achieving sdgs in India. *International Journal of Built Environment and Sustainability*, *11*(2), 1–26.

Gupta, S., & Singh, A. (2024). Importance of Artificial Intelligence in Achieving SDGs in India. *International Journal of Built Environment and Sustainability*, *11*(2), 1–26. DOI: 10.11113/ijbes.v11.n2.1193

Hall, J., Matos, S., & Bachor, V. (2017). From green technology development to green innovation: Inducing regulatory adoption of pathogen detection technology for sustainable forestry. *Small Business Economics*, *52*, 877–889.

Ha, N. M., Nguyen, P. A., & Phung, N. B. H. (2022). Technological factors affecting green innovation: Evidence from the manufacturing sector in Vietnam. *Ho Chi Minh City Open University Journal of Science-Economics and Business Administration*, *12*(1), 3–19.

Handl, G. (2012). Declaration of the United Nations Conference on the Human Environment (Stockholm Declaration), 1972 and the Rio Declaration on Environment and Development, 1992. *United Nations Audiovisual Library of International Law, 11*(6), 1–11.

Hanna, B., Xu, G., Wang, X., & Hossain, J. (2024, August). Leveraging Artificial Intelligence for Affordable and Clean Energy: Advancing UN Sustainable Development Goal 7. In *2024 11th International Conference on Behavioural and Social Computing (BESC)* (pp. 1-9). IEEE.

Hanna, M. G., Pantanowitz, L., Jackson, B., Palmer, O., Visweswaran, S., Pantanowitz, J., & Rashidi, H. H. (2025). Ethical and bias considerations in artificial intelligence/machine learning. *Modern Pathology, 38*(3), 100686. PMID: 39694331

Hariadi, S., Moengin, P., & Maulidya, R. (2023). Impact of green practices through green product and service innovation: Sustainable product-service system performance model. *International Journal of Sustainable Engineering, 16*(1), 1–15.

Hastuty, A., Maswati, M., Saharuddin, M., Sukri, A. M., & Halik, A. (2025). Artificial intelligence: A review of the philosophy of Islamic educational science. *Journal of Research in Instructional, 5*(1), 90–102.

Herane, M. (2024, January 16). AI in education, balancing innovation with ethics. *Higher Education Digest*. Retrieved from https://www.highereducationdigest.com/ai-in-education-balancing-innovation-with-ethics/

Heras-Saizarbitoria, I., & Boiral, O. (2013). ISO 9001 and ISO 14001: Towards a research agenda on management system standards. *International Journal of Management Reviews, 15*(1), 47–65.

Hodge, B.-M. A., Palchak, D., Ela, E., & Milligan, M. (2020). Wind and solar integration in the US power system: Operational practices, challenges, and opportunities. Current Sustainable/Renewable. *Energy Reports, 7*, 1–10. DOI: 10.1007/s40518-020-00146-6

Hossain, M. I., Teh, B. H., Tabash, M. I., Chong, L. L., & Ong, T. S. (2024). Unpacking the role of green smart technologies adoption, green ambidextrous leadership, and green innovation behaviour on green innovation performance in Malaysian manufacturing companies. *FIIB Business Review*, 23197145231225335.

Huang, J., Yang, B., & Chen, Y. (n.d.) Green Tech Innovation in Manufacturing Via Free Trade Zones: A Machine Learning Study. *Available at SSRN* 4681066.

Huang, L. (2023). Ethics of artificial intelligence in education: Student privacy and data protection. *Science Insights Education Frontiers*, *16*(2), 2577–2587. DOI: 10.15354/sief.23.re202

Huang, Y. C., & Huang, C. H. (2024). Exploring institutional pressure, the top management team's response, green innovation adoption, and firm performance: Evidence from Taiwan's electrical and electronics industry. *European Journal of Innovation Management*, *27*(3), 800–824.

Iftikhar, A., Bond, R., McGilligan, V., McShane, A., Leslie, S. J., Knoery, C., & Peace, A. (2019). Role of dashboards in improving decision making in healthcare: Review of the literature. *ECCE 2019 - Proceedings of the 31st European Conference on Cognitive Ergonomics: "'Design for Cognition,'"* 215–219. https://doi.org/DOI: 10.1145/3335082.3335109;CSUBTYPE:STRING:CONFERENCE

Igbokwe, I. C. (2023). Application of artificial intelligence (AI) in educational management. *International Journal of Scientific and Research Publications*, *13*(3), 300. DOI: 10.29322/IJSRP.13.03.2023.p13536

Iorember, P. T., Hounkanrin, D. O., Diyoke, K., & Tang, C. F. (2025). Tracing financial inclusion pathway to sustainable development: The criticality of population growth and energy intensity using a machine learning approach. *African Journal of Economic and Management Studies*.

Ishak, M.S., & Saad, N.A. (2016). Research on Project Management System in the Delivery of Green Development from Stakeholders Perspective.

Isiaku, L., Muhammad, A. S., Kefas, H. I., & Ukaegbu, F. C. (2024). Enhancing technological sustainability in academia: Leveraging ChatGPT for teaching, learning, and evaluation. *Quality Education for All*, *1*(1), 385–416. DOI: 10.1108/QEA-07-2024-0055

Ismail, I. J. (2023). The influence of green dynamic capabilities on brand sustainability among manufacturing enterprises in Tanzania: Mediation of green technology innovation. *Technological Sustainability*, *2*(4), 388–403.

Jakhar, S. K., Bhattacharya, A., Rathore, H., & Mangla, S. K. (2020). Stakeholder pressure for sustainability: Can 'innovative capabilities' explain the idiosyncratic response in the manufacturing firms? *Business Strategy and the Environment*, *29*(6), 2635–2653.

Jan, A., Salameh, A. A., Rahman, H. U., & Alasiri, M. M. (2023). Can blockchain technologies enhance environmental sustainable development goals performance in manufacturing firms? Potential mediation of green supply chain management practices. *Business Strategy and the Environment*, *33*(3), 2004–2019.

Javed, A., Li, Q., Ejaz, S., Basit, A., Hasan, S., Zita Júlia, F., & Hossain, M. B. (2024). Green synergy: Unveiling the nexus of green supply chain practices, training and innovation for sustainable manufacturing. *Kybernetes*.

Jayaraman, T. (2015). The Paris Agreement on climate change: Background, analysis, and implications. *Review of Agrarian Studies*, *5*(2).

Jha, A., & Singh, S. R. (2025). Bridging the Divide: Capacity Building for AI Adoption in Developing Countries. In *AI Strategies for Social Entrepreneurship and Sustainable Economic Development* (pp. 133-150). IGI Global Scientific Publishing.

Jia, P., Wang, Y., Yang, M., Wang, L., Yang, X., Shi, X., Yang, L., Wen, J., Liu, Y., Yang, M., Xin, J., Zhang, F., Jiang, L., Chi, C., Zhang, L., Ma, X., Ma, X., Zhao, L., & Li, W. (2022). Inequalities of spatial primary healthcare accessibility in China. *Social Science & Medicine*, *314*, 115458. DOI: 10.1016/J.SOCSCIMED.2022.115458 PMID: 36279792

Jindal, M., Chaiyachati, K. H., Fung, V., Manson, S. M., & Mortensen, K. (2023). Eliminating health care inequities through strengthening access to care. *Health Services Research*, *58*(Suppl 3), 300–310. DOI: 10.1111/1475-6773.14202 PMID: 38015865

Kamalov, F., Santandreu Calonge, D., & Gurrib, I. (2023). New era of artificial intelligence in education: Towards a sustainable multifaceted revolution. *Sustainability*, *15*(16), 12451. DOI: 10.3390/su151612451

Kamble, S. S., Gunasekaran, A., & Sharma, R. (2023). Artificial intelligence techniques for sustainable reconfigurable manufacturing systems. *Machines (Basel)*, *8*(11), 152. DOI: 10.3390/machines8110152

Kamilaris, A., & Prenafeta-Boldú, F. X. (2018). Deep learning in agriculture: A survey. *Computers and Electronics in Agriculture*, *147*, 70–90. DOI: 10.1016/j.compag.2018.02.016

Kamkar, M., Leonard, K. C., Ferrer, I., Loo, S. C. J., Biddinger, E. J., Brady, D., & Serrano, J. F. (2024). Artificial Intelligence (AI) for sustainable resource management and chemical processes. *ACS Sustainable Resource Management*, *1*(2), 178–180.

Kaur, N., Sharma, R., & Mehta, K. (9). Emerging green: Exploring strategic factors for SMEs' adoption of green technology and innovation in India. *Sustainability, Green Management, and Performance of SMEs, 165*, 186.

Kazlauskaitė, R., Ziemba, E. W., Ejdys, J., Mazurek, G., Stankevičienė, J., Duong, C. D., ... & Wach, K. (2024). Leveraging artificial intelligence to meet the sustainable development goals. *Journal of Economics and Management.*, 508-583.

Kerin, A., & Pham, D. T. (2024). Digital twins and AI-powered simulations for sustainable manufacturing. *Frontiers in Sustainability*, *2*(1), 55–72. DOI: 10.3389/frsus.2024.1508647

Khakwani, M. S., Zafar, A., Mahmood, G., & Khan, Q. M. (2024). Impact of Digital Transformation and Green Manufacturing Practices on Firm Performance with Mediating Role of Green Product Innovation: An Empirical Investigation with PLS-SEM Modeling. *Sustainable Business and Society in Emerging Economies*, *6*(1), 83–98.

Khalfallah, A., & Leitão, C. (2024). Sustainable manufacturing and green processing methods. *Machines (Basel)*, *12*(11), 815. DOI: 10.3390/machines12110815

Khan, K., Khurshid, A., & Su, C. W. (2024). Is Sustainable Innovation an Impetus to Sustainable Development Goals? Evidence From the EU. *Sustainable Development*.

Khan, N., Ray, R. L., Kassem, H. S., Hussain, S., Zhang, S., Khayyam, M., Ihtisham, M., & Asongu, S. A. (2021). Potential Role of Technology Innovation in Transformation of Sustainable Food Systems. *Revista de Agricultura (Piracicaba)*.

Khapekar, S. H., Sawai, S., Agrawal, S., Wankhade, S., & Jaronde, P. (2024). *AI-driven data analytics within digital twins*. IGI Global., DOI: 10.4018/979-8-3693-1818-8.ch005

Kirikkaleli, D., Aad, S., & Kirikkaleli, N. O. (2025). Sustainable development and investment in artificial intelligence in the USA. *Humanities & Social Sciences Communications*, *12*(1), 1–7.

Kolhe, M. L. (2025). Advancing Sustainable Electrical Energy Technologies: A Multifaceted Approach Towards SDG Achievement. *Processes (Basel, Switzerland)*, *13*(1), 210.

Koshkarev, A. V., Antipov, A. N., Batuyev, A. R., Yermoshin, V. V., & Karakin, V. P. (2008). Geo-portals as part of spatial data infrastructures: Russian Academy-supported resources and geoservices. *Geography and Natural Resources*, *29*(1). Advance online publication. DOI: 10.1016/j.gnr.2008.04.005

Kothandapani, H. P. (2025). AI-Driven Regulatory Compliance: Transforming Financial Oversight through Large Language Models and Automation. *Emerging Science Research*, 12-24.

Krishna Pasupuleti, M. (2024). *Green energy revolution: AI-powered systems for sustainable power management*. National Education Services., DOI: 10.62311/nesx/7264

Kulkov, I., Kulkova, J., Rohrbeck, R., Menvielle, L., Kaartemo, V., & Makkonen, H. (2024). Artificial intelligence-driven sustainable development: Examining organizational, technical, and processing approaches to achieving global goals. *Sustainable Development*, *32*(3), 2253–2267.

Kumaran, M. S., Keerthika, V., Reddy, P. S., & Rajendra, A. (2025). Rural Ecosystem Monitoring in Food Security Analysis Based on Sustainable Agriculture: Artificial Intelligence Application. *Remote Sensing in Earth Systems Sciences*, *8*(1), 56–64.

Kumar, S. (2025). A review on new marketing management theory 6.0: A new paradigm in consumer engagement. [Kuwait chapter]. *Arabian Journal of Business and Management Review*, *14*(1), 1–5.

Lakshminarasimham, K. C. (2025). Technology Leadership for Program Success: Integrating AI and Agile Methods for Modern Enterprises. In *Integrating Blue-Green Infrastructure Into Urban Development* (pp. 489-506). IGI Global Scientific Publishing.

Lampropoulos, G., Garzón, J., Misra, S., & Siakas, K. (2024). The role of artificial intelligence of things in achieving sustainable development goals: State of the art. *Sensors (Basel)*, *24*(4), 1091. PMID: 38400249

Lawal, Y.A., Sanwoolu, J.A., Adebayo, O.T., & Olateju, O.I. (2024). Enhancing Sustainability in Project Management through Smart Technology Integration: A Case Study Approach to Green Building Projects. *Dutch Journal of Finance and Management*.

Law, R., Ye, H., & Lei, S. S. I. (2025). Ethical artificial intelligence (AI): Principles and practices. *International Journal of Contemporary Hospitality Management*, *37*(1), 279–295.

Leal Filho, W., Mbah, M. F., Dinis, M. A. P., Trevisan, L. V., de Lange, D., Mishra, A., & Aina, Y. A. (2024). The role of artificial intelligence in the implementation of the UN Sustainable Development Goal 11: Fostering sustainable cities and communities. *Cities (London, England)*, *150*, 105021.

Leal Filho, W., Ribeiro, P. C. C., Mazutti, J., Lange Salvia, A., Bonato Marcolin, C., Lima Silva Borsatto, J. M., & Viera Trevisan, L. (2024). Using artificial intelligence to implement the UN sustainable development goals at higher education institutions. *International Journal of Sustainable Development and World Ecology, 31*(6), 726–745.

Lee, S. (2022). Spatial and Socioeconomic Inequalities in Accessibility to Healthcare Services in South Korea. *Healthcare 2022, Vol. 10, Page 2049, 10*(10), 2049. https://doi.org/DOI: 10.3390/HEALTHCARE10102049

Leelavathi, R., & Surendhranatha, R. C. (2024). ChatGPT in the classroom: Navigating the generative AI wave in management education. *Journal of Research in Innovative Teaching & Learning*. Advance online publication. https://doi.org/DOI: 10.1108/JRIT-01-2024-0017

Li, H., Li, Y., Sarfarz, M., &Ozturk, I. (2023).Enhancing firms' green innovation and sustainable performance through the mediating role of green product innovation and moderating role of employees' green behavior. *Economic research-Ekonomskaistraživanja, 36*(2).

Li, N. (2023). Ethical considerations in artificial intelligence: A comprehensive discussion from the perspective of computer vision. *SHS Web of Conferences*, 179(1), 04024. https://doi.org/DOI: 10.1051/shsconf/202317904024

Li, B., Jiang, F., & Xia, H., & pan, J. (2022). Under the Background of AI Application, Research on the Impact of Science and Technology Innovation and Industrial Structure Upgrading on the Sustainable and High-Quality Development of Regional Economies. *Sustainability*.

Li, C., Ahmad, S. F., Ayassrah, A. Y. B. A., Irshad, M., Telba, A. A., Awwad, E. M., & Majid, M. I. (2023). Green production and green technology for sustainability: The mediating role of waste reduction and energy use. *Heliyon, 9*(12). PMID: 38076181

Li, H., Yang, Z., Wang, H., & Li, Y. (2023). Digitalization of business models, knowledge management and green technology innovation of Chinese manufacturing enterprises: A mixed analysis based on the Haier COSMOPlat ecosystem. *Asia Pacific Business Review*, •••, 1–29.

Limón, M. E. R., Osuna, J. H. O., Hernández, G. T., & Rico, F. N. M. (2025). AI in public administration-transformative opportunities for climate resilience and sustainable development. *Revista de Ciencias Tecnológicas, 8*(2), 1–21.

Lim, T., Gottipati, S., & Cheong, M. L. F. (2023). Ethical considerations for artificial intelligence in educational assessments. In *Creative AI tools and ethical implications in teaching and learning* (pp. 32–79). IGI Global., DOI: 10.4018/979-8-3693-0205-7.ch003

Lim, T., Gottipati, S., & Cheong, M. L. F. (2024). Educational technologies and assessment practices: Evolution and emerging research gaps. In *Reshaping learning with next generation educational technologies*. IGI Global., DOI: 10.4018/979-8-3693-1310-7

Lin, C. C., Huang, A. Y. Q., & Lu, O. H. T. (2023). Artificial intelligence in intelligent tutoring systems toward sustainable education: A systematic review. *Smart Learning Environments*, *10*, 41. DOI: 10.1186/s40561-023-00260-y

Lin, Y., Yousaf, Z., Grigorescu, A., & Popovici, N. (2025). Harnessing digital foundations and artificial intelligence synergies: Unraveling the role of digital platforms, artificial intelligence, and strategic adaptability in organizational innovativeness. *Journal of Innovation & Knowledge*, *10*(2), 100670.

Liu, J., Pham, D. T., Zhang, J., Zhou, Z., & Xu, W. (2016, June 27). Industrial cloud robotics towards sustainable manufacturing. *Proceedings of the ASME 2016 11th International Manufacturing Science and Engineering Conference*. https://doi.org/ DOI: 10.1115/msec2016-8733

Li, Y., Fan, Y., & Nie, L. (2025). Making governance agile: Exploring the role of artificial intelligence in China's local governance. *Public Policy and Administration*, *40*(2), 276–301.

Li, Y., Zhang, X., Hao, J., & Huang, Q. (2022). The impact of green technology innovation on global value chain upgrading in China's equipment manufacturing industry. *Frontiers in Environmental Science*, *10*, 1044583.

Lottu, O., Jacks, B. S., Ajala, O. A., & Okafor, E. S. (2024). Towards a conceptual framework for ethical AI development in IT systems. *World Journal of Advanced Research and Reviews*, *21*(3), 408–415. DOI: 10.30574/wjarr.2024.21.3.0735

Lutfi, A., Alqudah, H., Alrawad, M., Alshira'h, A. F., Alshirah, M. H., Almaiah, M. A., & Hassan, M. F. (2023). Green environmental management system to support environmental performance: What factors influence SMEs to adopt green innovations? *Sustainability*, *15*(13), 10645.

Luu, H. S. (2025). Laboratory Data as a Potential Source of Bias in Healthcare Artificial intelligence and machine learning models. *Annals of Laboratory Medicine*, *45*(1), 12–21. PMID: 39444135

Machado, H., Silva, S., & Neiva, L. (2025). Publics' views on ethical challenges of artificial intelligence: A scoping review. *AI and Ethics*, *5*(1), 139–167.

Madavarapu, J. B., Kasula, B. Y., Whig, P., & Kautish, S. (2024). AI-Powered Solutions Advancing UN Sustainable Development Goals: A Case Study in Tackling Humanity's Challenges. In *Digital Technologies to Implement the UN Sustainable Development Goals* (pp. 47–67). Springer Nature Switzerland.

Maguire, D. J., & Longley, P. A. (2005). The Emergence of Geoportals and their Role in Spatial Data Infrastructures. In *Computers, Environment and Urban Systems* (Vol. 29, Issue 1 SPEC.ISS., pp. 3–14). https://doi.org/DOI: 10.1016/j.compenvurbsys.2004.05.012

Malek, J., & Desai, T. N. (2020). A systematic literature review to map literature focus of sustainable manufacturing. *Journal of Cleaner Production*, *256*, 120345.

Malhotra, G., & Ramalingam, M. (2025). Perceived anthropomorphism and purchase intention using artificial intelligence technology: Examining the moderated effect of trust. *Journal of Enterprise Information Management*, *38*(2), 401–423.

Malik, I. A., & Mehraj, D., u Nissa, V., &Wani, A. K. (2025). Unveiling the Dynamics of Sustainable Development: A Holistic Examination of Green Organizational Learning, Innovation, and Performance in Indian SMEs. *Business Strategy & Development*, *8*(1), e70060.

Malkova, Y. (2025). Artificial intelligence and sustainable power. In *The Sustainable Power Grid* (pp. 43–58). Elsevier.

Mangundu, J. (2025). Navigating Artificial Intelligence Governance: Insights from South African Higher Education IT Decision-Makers. *The African Journal of Information Systems*, *17*(1), 1.

Manikandan, S., Kaviya, R. S., Shreeharan, D. H., Subbaiya, R., Vickram, S., Karmegam, N., & Govarthanan, M. (2025). Artificial intelligence-driven sustainability: Enhancing carbon capture for sustainable development goals–A review. *Sustainable Development*, *33*(2), 2004–2029.

Masia, O.A., & Poll, J.A. (2021). A framework for agile project management for the water industry in developing economies. *J. for Global Business Advancement*.

Maurya, S. P., Ohri, A., & Gaur, S. (2022). *Relevance of Spatio-temporal Data Visualization Techniques in Healthcare System*. 59–78. https://doi.org/DOI: 10.1007/978-981-16-9476-9_3

Meadows, D. H. (2008). *Thinking in systems: A primer*. Chelsea Green Publishing.

Meitei, A. J., Rai, P., & Rajkishan, S. S. (2025). Application of AI/ML techniques in achieving SDGs: A bibliometric study. *Environment, Development and Sustainability*, *27*(1), 281–317.

Menon, A., Aishwarya, M. S., Maria Joykutty, A., Av, A. Y., & Av, A. Y. (2021). Data Visualization and Predictive Analysis for Smart Healthcare: Tool for a Hospital. *TENSYMP 2021 - 2021 IEEE Region 10 Symposium*. https://doi.org/DOI: 10.1109/TENSYMP52854.2021.9550822

Mensah, G. B. (2023). AI-Augmented Public Health Administration in sub-Saharan Africa: Addressing Challenges in Ghana's Cyberlaws Regimes for Smooth and Effective Use. *International Journal of Legal Science and Innovation*, *5*(6), 26–54.

Micieta, B., & Binasova, V. (2013). *Defining requirements for energy efficiency in manufacturing*. DAAAM Vienna., DOI: 10.2507/daaam.scibook.2013.54

Mienye, I. D., Sun, Y., & Ileberi, E. (2024). Artificial intelligence and sustainable development in Africa: A comprehensive review. *Machine Learning with Applications*, •••, 100591.

Mishra, R. K., Sharma, M., Kumar, S., & Divyashree. (2024). Leveraging automation for enhanced quality control systems. https://doi.org/DOI: 10.62919/xhie8742

Mishra, P. C., & Giri, A. K. (2018). *Green chemistry*. IGI Global., DOI: 10.4018/978-1-5225-3126-5.ch009

Mogavi, R. H., Deng, C., Kim, J. J., Zhou, P., Kwon, Y. D., Metwally, A. H. S., Tlili, A., Bassanelli, S., Bucchiarone, A., Gujar, S., Nacke, L. E., & Hui, P. (2024). ChatGPT in education: A blessing or a curse? A qualitative study exploring early adopters' utilization and perceptions. *Computers in Human Behavior: Artificial Humans*, *2*(1), 100027. DOI: 10.1016/j.chbah.2023.100027

Mohapatra, A. (2024). Generative AI for predictive maintenance: Predicting equipment failures and optimizing maintenance schedules using AI. [IJSRM]. *International Journal of Scientific Research and Management*, *12*(11), 1648–1672. DOI: 10.18535/ijsrm/v12i11.ec03

Mol, A. P., & Spaargaren, G. (2000). Ecological modernisation theory in debate:A review. *Environmental Politics*, *9*(1), 17–49.

Mukhtar, B., Shad, M. K., Won, L. F., Waqas, A., & Mukhtar, Z. (2023). Role of green technology innovation to promote sustainability performance in Malaysian manufacturing solar PV industry: A conceptual framework. *Platform: A Journal of Management and Humanities, 6*(1), 36-46.

Mukhtar, B., Shad, M. K., & Lai, F. W. (2024). Fostering sustainability performance in the Malaysian manufacturing companies: The role of green technology innovation and innovation capabilities. *Benchmarking*.

Musavi, S. A. S., Sajjad, S., & Sarwari, S. R. (2024). Investigating renewable energy sources. *Nangarhar University International Journal of Biosciences, 03*(ICCC Special), 507–510. https://doi.org/DOI: 10.70436/nuijb.v3i02.278

Mutambara, A. G. O. (2025). *Artificial intelligence: A driver of inclusive development and shared prosperity for the global south*. https://doi.org/DOI: 10.1201/9781003511014

Mutsuddi, I. (2024). *Ethical considerations in the intersection of AI and environmental science*. IGI Global., DOI: 10.4018/979-8-3693-6336-2.ch011

Mwange, C., Mulaku, G. C., & Siriba, D. N. (2018). Reviewing the status of national spatial data infrastructures in Africa. *Survey Review, 50*(360), 191–200. DOI: 10.1080/00396265.2016.1259720

Nandan, S., & Jyoti. (2020). Organizational culture dimensions as drivers of employee engagement for business sustainability: Towards a conceptual framework. In *Sustainable Human Resource Management: Transforming Organizations, Societies and Environment* (pp. 109–132).

Naude, M., Rowe, A. L., Thomas, G., & Nowak, M. (2010). Managing industry-academia partnerships. *International Journal of Management Education, 8*(3), 71–82. DOI: 10.3794/ijme.83.300

Nawab, T., &Shafiq, A. (2024). The Impact of Green Technology Adoption and Dynamic Capabilities on Green Competitive Advantage and Sustainable Development: Moderating Role of Organizational Commitment. *iRASD Journal of Energy & Environment, 5*(1), 24-36.

Nedungadi, P., Surendran, S., Tang, K. Y., & Raman, R. (2024). Big Data and AI Algorithms for Sustainable Development Goals: A Topic Modeling Analysis. *IEEE Access : Practical Innovations, Open Solutions*.

Neema, S., & Gor, P. (2022). Smart waste management using IoT. *International Journal of Scientific Research in Science, Engineering and Technology, 9*(2), 16–21. DOI: 10.32628/ijsrset229529

Nguyen, H. T., Nguyen, T. V., & Tran, T. D. (2020). Artificial intelligence in renewable energy systems. *Energy Reports, 6*, 265–273. DOI: 10.1016/j.egyr.2020.11.156

Ningsih, F. O. (2024). Analyzing the implementation of green industries practice at PT Semen Indonesia (Persero) Tbk. Tuban Plant towards achieving Sustainable Development Goals. *International Journal of Innovative Science and Research Technology*, *9*(5).

Nong, P., Adler-Milstein, J., Apathy, N. C., Holmgren, A. J., & Everson, J. (2025). Current Use And Evaluation Of Artificial Intelligence And Predictive Models In US Hospitals: Article examines uses and evaluation of artificial intelligence and predictive models in US hospitals. *Health Affairs*, *44*(1), 90–98. PMID: 39761454

Noon, C. E., & Hankins, C. T. (2001). Spatial data visualization in healthcare: Supporting a facility location decision via GIS-based market analysis. *Proceedings of the Hawaii International Conference on System Sciences*, 149. https://doi.org/DOI: 10.1109/HICSS.2001.926573

Nzomo, J. K., Kinyua, G. M., & Mwasiaji, E. T. (2023). Green Innovation Strategy as Antecedent of Performance Sustainability Among ISO 14001 Certified Manufacturing Firms in Kenya: Does Competitive Advantage Play a Mediating Role. *International Journal of Education and Research*, *11*(8), 93–108.

Obaideen, K., Albasha, L., Iqbal, U., & Mir, H. (2024). Wireless power transfer: Applications, challenges, barriers, and the role of AI in achieving sustainable development goals-A bibliometric analysis. *Energy Strategy Reviews*, *53*, 101376.

Obradović, V., Todorović, M., & Bushuyev, S. (2018). Sustainability and Agility in Project Management: Contradictory or Complementary? *2018 IEEE 13th International Scientific and Technical Conference on Computer Sciences and Information Technologies (CSIT), 2*, 1-5.

OECD. (2023). *OECD digital education outlook 2023: Towards an effective digital education ecosystem*. OECD Publishing., DOI: 10.1787/9872e201-

Ofosu-Ampong, K. (2024). Artificial intelligence research: A review on dominant themes, methods, frameworks, and future research directions. *Telematics and Informatics Reports*, *14*, 100127. DOI: 10.1016/j.teler.2024.100127

Ogiemwonyi, O., & Eneizan, B. (2024, March). Environmental ethics and green practices in the manufacturing sector: The role of green innovation and environmental policy. In *Natural Resources Forum*. Oxford, UK: Blackwell Publishing Ltd.

Ogunseye, O. O., Ajayi, O. T., Fabusoro, A., Abba, A. O., & Adepoju, B. (2025). Leveraging Artificial Intelligence for Advancing Key Sectors of National Growth and Development. *Asian Journal of Current Research*, *10*(1), 45–55.

Okonkwo, E., Ndu-Anunobi, G. U., & Umeokafor, C. C. (2024). HARNESSING ARTIFICIAL INTELLIGENCE FOR SUSTAINABLE DEVELOPMENT: A PATHWAY TO ACHIEVING SUSTAINABLE DEVELOPMENT GOALS IN AFRICA USING NIGERIA AS A STUDY. *INTERNATIONAL JOURNAL OF PUBLIC ADMINISTRATION AND DEVELOPMENT STUDIES*, *1*(2), 37–58.

Omar, A., Al-shari, A., & Shah, S. H. A., ErkolBayram, G., Zameer Rahman, E., & Valeri, M. (2024). Green manufacturing practices and SMEs' sustainable performance: A moderated mediation mechanisms of green innovation and managerial discretion. *European Business Review*, *36*(4), 588–609.

Onukwulu, E., Dienagha, I., Digitemie, W., & Egbumokei, P. (2021). AI-driven supply chain optimization for enhanced efficiency in the energy sector. *Magna Scientia Advanced Research and Reviews*, *2*(1), 87–108. DOI: 10.30574/msarr.2021.2.1.0060

Ordibazar, A. H., Hussain, O. K., Chakrabortty, R. K., Irannezhad, E., & Saberi, M. (2025). Artificial intelligence applications for supply chain risk management considering interconnectivity, external events exposures and transparency: a systematic literature review. *Modern Supply Chain Research and Applications*, (ahead-of-print).

Ouma, P., Macharia, P. M., Okiro, E., & Alegana, V. (2021). *Methods of Measuring Spatial Accessibility to Health Care in Uganda BT - Practicing Health Geography: The African Context*. Practicing Health Geography.

Ou, S. (2024). Transforming education: The evolving role of artificial intelligence in students' academic performance. *International Journal of Education and Humanities*, *13*(2), 163–173. DOI: 10.54097/cc1x7r95

Papagiannidis, E., Mikalef, P., & Conboy, K. (2025). Responsible artificial intelligence governance: A review and research framework. *The Journal of Strategic Information Systems*, *34*(2), 101885.

Parinsi, W. K., Musa, A. D. L., & Musa, K. S. P. (2025). The Role of AI in Driving Sustainable HRM: A Phenomenological Study on the Use of People Analytics for Corporate Carbon Footprint Reduction. [JUMPER]. *Journal Management & Economics Review*, *2*(6), 191–196.

Patibandla, K. R. (2024). Predictive maintenance in aviation using artificial intelligence. [JAIGS]. *Journal of Artificial Intelligence General Science*, *4*(1), 325–333. DOI: 10.60087/jaigs.v4i1.214

Patra, B. C., & Mishra, D. N. (2024). *Extended producer responsibility (EPR) and e-waste management*. IGI Global., DOI: 10.4018/979-8-3693-1018-2.ch010

Piwowar-Sulej, K., & Iqbal, Q. (2024). The nexus of project management approaches in sustainable development: Innovative behaviors as a mechanism in the Polish financial industry. *International Journal of Managing Projects in Business.*

Piyasena, N. M. P. M., Vithanage, P. A. D. V., & Witharana, S. L. (2023). A Review of Sri Lanka's National Spatial Data Infrastructure (SL-NSDI) with the Aim of Enhancing Its Functionalities. In de Vries, W. T., Rudiarto, I., & Piyasena, N. M. P. M. (Eds.), *Geospatial Science for Smart Land Management: An Asian Context* (1st ed., p. 17). CRC Press., DOI: 10.1201/9781003349518-15

Popoola, O. A., & Popoola, G. O. (2024). Drivers of eco-innovation among manufacturing firms in Nigeria. In *Innovation, entrepreneurship and the informal economy in Sub–Saharan Africa: A sustainable development agenda* (pp. 217–248). Springer Nature Switzerland.

Raihan, A. (2024). Financial technology optimization using artificial intelligence (AI) to accomplish sustainable development goals (SDGs). In *Proceedings of the International Conference on on Digital Finance, Green Innovation, and Sustainable Development.*

Raimi, L., Panait, M., & Sule, R. (2021). Leveraging precision agriculture for sustainable food security in sub-Saharan Africa: A theoretical discourse. *Shifting Patterns of Agricultural Trade: The Protectionism Outbreak and Food Security*, 491-509.

Raman, R., Gunasekar, S., Kaliyaperumal, D., & Nedungadi, P. (2024). Navigating the Nexus of Artificial Intelligence and Renewable Energy for the Advancement of Sustainable Development Goals. *Sustainability*, *16*(21), 9144.

Rashid, A. B., & Kausik, M. A. K. (2024). AI revolutionizing industries worldwide: A comprehensive overview of its diverse applications. *Hybrid Advances*, *7*, 100277. DOI: 10.1016/j.hybadv.2024.100277

Rashid, A., Baloch, N., Rasheed, R., & Ngah, A. H. (2025). Big data analytics-artificial intelligence and sustainable performance through green supply chain practices in manufacturing firms of a developing country. *Journal of Science and Technology Policy Management*, *16*(1), 42–67.

Rashid, N., Jabar, J., Yahya, S., & Shami, S. (2015). Dynamic eco innovation practices: A systematic review of state of the art and future direction for eco innovation study. *Asian Social Science*, *11*(1), 8.

Rath, R. C., Singh, T., Goel, R., & Baral, S. K. (2022). Role of artificial intelligence and machine learning in product design and manufacturing. In *Proceedings of the 2022 IEEE MECon* (pp. 571–575). https://doi.org/DOI: 10.1109/mecon53876.2022.9752455

Regona, M., Yigitcanlar, T., Hon, C., & Teo, M. (2024). Artificial intelligence and sustainable development goals: Systematic literature review of the construction industry. *Sustainable Cities and Society*, •••, 105499.

Reuters. (2023). *Tech companies' indirect emissions rise 150% amid AI infrastructure growth*. https://www.reuters.com/sustainability/climate-energy/tech-giants-indirect-emissions-rose-150-three-years-ai-expands-un-agency-says-2025-06-05/

Richnák, P., & Fidlerová, H. (2022). Impact and potential of sustainable development goals in dimension of the technological revolution industry 4.0 within the analysis of industrial enterprises. *Energies*, *15*(10), 3697.

Richter, V., Katzenbach, C., & Zeng, J. (2025). Negotiating AI (s) futures: Competing imaginaries of AI by stakeholders in the US, China, and Germany. *Journal of Science Communication*, *24*(2), A08.

Robles, P., & Mallinson, D. J. (2025). Artificial intelligence technology, public trust, and effective governance. *The Review of Policy Research*, *42*(1), 11–28.

Rolnick, D., Donti, P. L., Kaack, L. H., Kochanski, K., Lacoste, A., Sankaran, K., & Bengio, Y. (2022). Tackling climate change with machine learning. *ACM Computing Surveys*, *55*(2), 1–96.

Roshanaei, M., Olivares, H., & Lopez, R. (2023). Harnessing AI to foster equity in education: Opportunities, challenges, and emerging strategies. *Journal of Intelligent Learning Systems and Applications*, *15*, 123–143. DOI: 10.4236/jilsa.2023.154009

Ruoxing, C., Jianning, W., Basem, A., Hussein, R. A., Salahshour, S., & Baghaei, S. (2025). Examining the application of strategic management and artificial intelligence, with a focus on artificial neural network modeling to enhance human resource optimization with advertising and brand campaigns. *Engineering Applications of Artificial Intelligence*, *143*, 110029.

Rusmayadi, G., Salawati, U., Haslinah, A., & Judijanto, L. (2023). The effect of investment in green technology and renewable technology adoption on energy efficiency and carbon emissions reduction in Indonesian manufacturing companies. *West Science Interdisciplinary Studies*, *1*(11), 1175–1183.

Russell, S. J., & Norvig, P. (2020). *Artificial intelligence: A modern approach* (4th ed.). Pearson.

Saher, N., Baharom, F., & Romli, R. (2020). Identification of Sustainability Characteristics and Sub-Characteristics as Non-Functional Requirement for Requirement Change Management in Agile.

Sakikhales, M., & Stravoravdis, S. (2017). Using Agile Project Management and BIM for Improved Building Performance.

Samanvitha, C., Dharmendra, H., Nethravathi, N., & Velmurugan, P. R. (2025). Artificial Intelligence for Sustainable Futures: Navigating Social and Environmental Responsibility. In *Advancements in Intelligent Process Automation* (pp. 129-154). IGI Global.

Samarawickrama, M. (2022). AI governance and ethics framework for sustainable AI and sustainability. *arXiv*. https://doi.org//arxiv.2210.08984DOI: 10.48550

Sanchez, T. W., Brenman, M., & Ye, X. (2025). The ethical concerns of artificial intelligence in urban planning. *Journal of the American Planning Association*, *91*(2), 294–307.

Sander, B. (2025). Confronting risks at the intersection of climate change and artificial intelligence: The promise and perils of rights-based approaches. *Netherlands Quarterly of Human Rights*, •••, 09240519251336962.

Saptaputra, E. H., Araffanda, A. S., & Bonafix, N. (2023). Mobile app as digitalisation of waste sorting management. *IOP Conference Series. Earth and Environmental Science*, *1169*(1), 012007. DOI: 10.1088/1755-1315/1169/1/012007

Sargiotis, D. (2024). Fostering ethical and inclusive AI: A human-centric paradigm for social impact. SSRN *Electronic Journal*. https://doi.org/DOI: 10.2139/ssrn.4879372

Sayari, K. T. (2025). Infrastructure and Investment Needs for AI Implementation in Education. In *Teachers' Roles and Perspectives on AI Integration in Schools* (pp. 141–162). IGI Global Scientific Publishing.

Schwaeke, J., Gerlich, C., Nguyen, H. L., Kanbach, D. K., & Gast, J. (2025). Artificial intelligence (AI) for good? Enabling organizational change towards sustainability. *Review of Managerial Science*. Advance online publication. DOI: 10.1007/s11846-025-00840-x

Schwartz, R., Vassilev, A., Greene, K., Perine, L., Burt, A., & Hall, P. (2024). *Towards a standard for identifying and managing bias in artificial intelligence* (NIST Special Publication 1270). National Institute of Standards and Technology. https://nvlpubs.nist.gov/nistpubs/SpecialPublications/NIST.SP.1270.pdf

erbu, R. S., & Mârza, B. . (2024). From Crisis to Opportunity: Embracing Sustainable Development Goals and Artificial Intelligence in the Transformative Innovations World. In *Ukraine's Journey to Recovery, Reform and Post-War Reconstruction: A Blueprint for Security, Resilience and Development* (pp. 49–61). Springer Nature Switzerland.

Sethi, S., & Singh, M. (2024). *Blended Learning and AI in Higher Education: Adapt, Evolve, Thrive*. Cambridge Scholars Publishing.

Shaban, N., Afza, T., Ehsan, S., & Danish, R. Q. (2024). *Leveraging Green Innovation to Foster Sustainable Development through Green Dynamic Capabilities*. Research Journal for Societal Issues.

Shafik, W. (2025). The Darkside of Artificial Intelligence and the Metaverse in Scientific Research and Publishing: Navigating the Academic Standards in the Digital Era. In *Navigating AI and the Metaverse in Scientific Research* (pp. 275–304). IGI Global Scientific Publishing.

Shahvaroughi Farahani, M., & Ghasemi, G. (2024). How artificial intelligence plays a role in achieving sustainable development goals? [situations.]. *Sustainable Economies.*, *2*(3), 66.

Shahzad, M., Qu, Y., Rehman, S. U., & Zafar, A. U. (2022). Adoption of green innovation technology to accelerate sustainable development among manufacturing industry. *Journal of Innovation & Knowledge*, *7*(4), 100231.

Shan, S., Genç, S. Y., Kamran, H. W., & Dincă, G. (2021). Role of green technology innovation and renewable energy in carbon neutrality: A sustainable investigation from Turkey. *Journal of environmental management, 294*, 113004. Fang, Z. (2023). Assessing the impact of renewable energy investment, green technology innovation, and industrialization on sustainable development: A case study of China. *Renewable Energy*.

Simpson, D. (2012). Institutional pressure and waste reduction: The role of investments in waste reduction resources. *International Journal of Production Economics*, *139*(1), 330–339. DOI: 10.1016/j.ijpe.2012.05.020

Singh, A., Kanaujia, A., Singh, V. K., & Vinuesa, R. (2024). Artificial intelligence for Sustainable Development Goals: Bibliometric patterns and concept evolution trajectories. *Sustainable Development*, *32*(1), 724–754.

Singhal, A., Neveditsin, N., Tanveer, H., & Mago, V. (2024). Toward fairness, accountability, transparency, and ethics in AI for social media and health care: Scoping review. *JMIR Medical Informatics*, *12*, e50048. DOI: 10.2196/50048 PMID: 38568737

Singh, N., Gupta, K., & Kapur, B. (2022). Greenwashed word of mouth (GWWOM): A vibrant influence on customer green behaviour. *Journal of Global Responsibility*, *13*(4), 472–487. DOI: 10.1108/JGR-11-2021-0094

Singh, R. K., & Joshi, H. T. (2024). Greening the supply chain: Institutional pressures, data-driven innovations, and the road to circular sustainability. *Business Strategy and the Environment*, *33*(6), 6029–6044.

Siyal, A. W., Chen, H., Shahzad, F., & Bano, S. (2023). Investigating the role of institutional pressures, technology compatibility, and green transformation in driving manufacturing industries toward green development. *Journal of Cleaner Production*, *428*, 139416.

Sjoukema, J. W., Bregt, A., & Crompvoets, J. (2017). Evolving spatial data infrastructures and the role of adaptive governance. *ISPRS International Journal of Geo-Information*, *6*(8). Advance online publication. DOI: 10.3390/ijgi6080254

Sjoukema, J., Bregt, A. K., & Crompvoets, J. (2020). Understanding governance dynamics: The governing system of spatial data infrastructures. *International Journal of Spatial Data Infrastructures Research*, •••, 15.

Song, Y., Zhang, Z., Sahut, J., & Rubin, O. D. (2023). Incentivizing green technology innovation to confront sustainable development. *Technovation*.

Stettina, C. J., & Kroon, E. (2013). Is there an agile handover? An empirical study of documentation and project handover practices across agile software teams. *2013 International Conference on Engineering, Technology and Innovation (ICE) & IEEE International Technology Management Conference*, 1-12.

Stowe, M. (2020). Lean manufacturing principles and their impact on process energy efficiency (pp. 77–137). *River (Weinheim)*. Advance online publication. DOI: 10.1201/9781003150961-3

Stray, V. G., Memon, B., & Paruch, L. (2020). A Systematic Literature Review on Agile Coaching and the Role of the Agile Coach. *International Conference on Product Focused Software Process Improvement*.

Strubell, E., Ganesh, A., & McCallum, A. (2019). Energy and policy considerations for deep learning in NLP. *Proceedings of the 57th Annual Meeting of the Association for Computational Linguistics*, 3645–3650. https://doi.org/DOI: 10.18653/v1/P19-1355

Suki, N., Suki, N. M., Sharif, A., Afshan, S., & Jermsittiparsert, K. (2022). The role of technology innovation and renewable energy in reducing environmental degradation in Malaysia: A step towards sustainable environment. *Renewable Energy*.

Sun, J., Xie, X., Zhou, M., & Yan, L. (2023). How to drive green innovation of manufacturing SMEs under open innovation networks–the role of innovation platforms' relational governance. *Management Decision*.

Sun, Z., Liu, L., Johan, S., & Zhao, L. (2024). FinTech Adoption and Corporate Greenwashing: A Technology Affordance Perspective. *British Journal of Management*.

Tahir, M., Amanat, I., & Awan, S. M. (2024). Ethical considerations and challenges in the integration of artificial intelligence in education: A systematic review. *Journal of Education and Management Studies*, *3*(4). Advance online publication. DOI: 10.69565/jems.v3i4.314

Tan, S. (2023). Harnessing artificial intelligence for innovation in education. In *Learning intelligence: Innovative and digital transformative learning strategies* (pp. 335–363). Springer., DOI: 10.1007/978-981-19-9201-8_8

Tariq, M. U., & Sergio, R. (Eds.). (2025). *Cases on AI-Driven Solutions to Environmental Challenges*. IGI Global, 2025. https://doi.org/DOI: 10.4018/979-8-3693-7483-2

Tariq, M. U. (2025). *AI-Driven Learning and Engagement in Higher Education*. IGI Global., DOI: 10.4018/979-8-3693-4074-5

Tariq, M. U. (2025). Decolonizing Education Systems Through Action Research and Action Learning. In Mapotse, T., Tetteh, E., & Matsekoleng, T. (Eds.), *Enabling Indigenous Knowledge Systems in Action Research and Action Learning* (pp. 107–128). IGI Global Scientific Publishing., DOI: 10.4018/979-8-3693-3542-0.ch006

Tariq, M. U. (2025). Digital Accountability: Revolutionizing Public Sector Transparency and Service Delivery. In Santos Ferreira, A., & Lourenço dos Santos, C. (Eds.), *Enhancing Public Sector Accountability and Services Through Digital Innovation* (pp. 129–154). IGI Global Scientific Publishing., DOI: 10.4018/979-8-3693-9251-5.ch004

Tariq, M. U., & Sergio, R. (Eds.). (2025). *Convergence of AI, Education, and Business for Sustainability*. IGI Global., DOI: 10.4018/979-8-3373-1917-9

Thaler, R. H., & Sunstein, C. R. (2009). *Nudge: Improving decisions about health, wealth, and happiness*. Penguin.

Thi Ngoc Thuyen, T., &NhuBich, L. (2024). Green innovation practices: A case study of Vietnamese manufacturing companies. *Cogent Business & Management*, *11*(1), 2333603.

Tripathi, S., Bachmann, N., Brunner, M., Rizk, Z., & Jodlbauer, H. (2024). Assessing the current landscape of AI and sustainability literature: Identifying key trends, addressing gaps and challenges. *Journal of Big Data, 11*(1). Advance online publication. DOI: 10.1186/s40537-024-00912-x

Trujillo-Cabezas, R. (2025). Exploring the link between foresight and artificial intelligence methods to strengthen collective future-building in contexts of social instability. *foresight, 27*(2), 267-305.

Tu, Y., Lu, L., & Wang, S. (2024). Environmental regulations, GHRM and green innovation of manufacturing enterprises: Evidence from China. *Frontiers in Environmental Science*, *12*, 1308224.

Tu, Y., Wu, P., & Zhang, C. (2023). Assessing the impact of blockchain technology on the overall performance of sustainable supply chains: An analytical perspective. *Environmental Science and Pollution Research International*. PMID: 37858028

Uglev, V. (2023, September). Case Study of Organization of Decision-Making and Feedback Synthesis in Intelligent Tutoring Systems with a Cross-Cutting Approach. In *Novel & Intelligent Digital Systems Conferences* (pp. 114–124). Springer Nature Switzerland.

UNESCO. (2021). Recommendation on the ethics of artificial intelligence. United Nations Educational, Scientific and Cultural Organization. https://unesdoc.unesco.org/ark:/48223/pf0000381137

United Arab Emirates. (2024). *UAE guiding principles on AI policy*. UAE Government. Retrieved from https://ai.gov.ae/wp-content/uploads/2024/10/UAE-Guiding-on-ai-policy-EN-V3.pdf

United Nations. (2015). Transforming our world: The 2030 Agenda for Sustainable Development. https://sdgs.un.org/2030agenda

Vinuesa, R., Azizpour, H., Leite, I., Balaam, M., Dignum, V., Domisch, S., & Nerini, F. F. (2020). The role of artificial intelligence in achieving the Sustainable Development Goals. *Nature Communications*, *11*(1), 233. PMID: 31932590

Vishwakarma, R. K., Patel, H. K., & Sharma, R. (2023). AI and machine learning for production efficiency and sustainable development: A bibliometric analysis. *Frontiers in Sustainability*, *3*, 89–102. DOI: 10.3389/frsus.2023.1508647

Wang, M., & Han, J. (2024).A Study on Promoting Green Production and Sustainable Development of the Manufacturing Industry through Digital Innovation. *Information Systems and Economics, 5*(4).

Wang, S., Wang, F., Zhu, Z., Wang, J., Tran, T., & Du, Z. (2024). Artificial intelligence in education: A systematic literature review. *Expert Systems with Applications, 252*(Part A), 124167. https://doi.org/DOI: 10.1016/j.eswa.2024.124167

Wang, C. (2022). Green Technology Innovation, Energy Consumption Structure and Sustainable Improvement of Enterprise Performance. *Sustainability*.

Wang, J., Liu, Z., Shi, L., & Tan, J. (2022). The Impact of Low-Carbon Pilot City Policy on Corporate Green Technology Innovation in a Sustainable Development Context—Evidence from Chinese Listed Companies. *Sustainability*.

Wang, L., Liu, A., Liu, Z., & Tao, F. (2021). Artificial intelligence in product lifecycle management. *International Journal of Advanced Manufacturing Technology, 114*(3–4), 771–796. DOI: 10.1007/s00170-021-06882-1

Wang, Q., Sun, T., & Li, R. (2025). Does artificial intelligence promote green innovation? An assessment based on direct, indirect, spillover, and heterogeneity effects. *Energy & Environment*, *36*(2), 1005–1037.

Wang, Q., Zhang, F., & Li, R. (2025). Artificial intelligence and sustainable development during urbanization: Perspectives on AI R&D innovation, AI infrastructure, and AI market advantage. *Sustainable Development*, *33*(1), 1136–1156.

Wang, X., Zhou, J., & Maitlo, Q. (2022). Effect of green technology innovation on the upgrading of the manufacturing value chain: Evidence from China. *Frontiers in Environmental Science*, *10*, 994323.

Wang, Z., Gao, Y., Zhou, Y., & Xue, L. (2025). Digital governance and AI: Boosting OFDI's impact on regional innovation performance. *Science & Public Policy*, •••, scae087.

Webster, A. J., Gaitskell, K., Turnbull, I., Cairns, B. J., & Clarke, R. (2021). Characterisation, identification, clustering, and classification of disease. *Scientific Reports*, *11*(1). Advance online publication. DOI: 10.1038/s41598-021-84860-z PMID: 33686097

Wei, X., Jiang, F., Chen, Y., & Hua, W. (2024). Towards green development: The role of intelligent manufacturing in promoting corporate environmental performance. *Energy Economics*, *131*, 107375.

Winkler, H. (2011). Closed-loop production systems—A sustainable supply chain approach. *CIRP Journal of Manufacturing Science and Technology*, *4*(3), 243–246. DOI: 10.1016/j.cirpj.2011.05.001

Womack, J. P., & Jones, D. T. (1997). Lean thinking—Banish waste and create wealth in your corporation. *The Journal of the Operational Research Society*, *48*(11), 1148–1148.

Wu, Z., Zhang, C., & Zhu, X. (2012, May 1). An ant colony algorithm for master production scheduling optimization. *IEEE 2012 CSCWD Conference*. https://doi.org/DOI: 10.1109/cscwd.2012.6221908

Wu, H., Hu, S., & Hu, S. (2022). How digitalization works in promoting corporate sustainable development performance? The mediating role of green technology innovation. *Environmental Science and Pollution Research International*, *30*, 22013–22023. PMID: 36282395

Xu, H., & Wang, Q. (2024). Energy regulatory compliance and corporate social responsibility. *Finance Research Letters*, *67*, 105919. DOI: 10.1016/j.frl.2024.105919

Xu, N., Shahzad, F., & Hu, R. (2025). Unveiling environmental excellence: The confluence of green Industrial Internet of Things, circular economy practices and dynamic capabilities in manufacturing firms. *Journal of Manufacturing Technology Management*, *36*(2), 479–503.

Xu, X., Imran, M., Ayaz, M., & Lohana, S. (2022). The mediating role of green technology innovation with corporate social responsibility, firm financial, and environmental performance: The case of Chinese manufacturing industries. *Sustainability*, *14*(24), 16951.

Yadav, P., Tudela, L. A. M., & Marco-Lajara, B. (2024). The role of AI in assessing and achieving the sustainable development goals (SDGs). In *Issues of Sustainability in AI and New-Age Thematic Investing* (pp. 1–17). IGI Global.

Yan, B., Li, K., Xu, M., Dong, Y., Zhang, Y., Ren, Z., & Cheng, X. (2025). On protecting the data privacy of Large Language Models (LLMs) and LLM agents: A literature review. *High-Confidence Computing*, •••, 100300.

Yang, B. (2024). Enterprise Green Technology Innovation Strategy Based on Environmental Responsibility. *Academic Journal of Business & Management, 6*(1).

Yao, L., & Desalegn, G. (2023). Sustainable practices in global supply chains of Chinese enterprises: Bibliometric approach. *Studia Mundi – Economica, 10*(4), 5–19. https://doi.org/DOI: 10.18531/sme.vol.10.no.4.pp.5-19

Yeolekar-Kadam, B., & J. S., S. (2022). Feasibility Study on Integration of Green Technologies in Prospective Construction Projects: A Case of Vishakhapatnam. *International Journal of Management, Technology, and Social Sciences*.

Yue, H., Wei, Y., Yuan, H., & Li, H. (2025). Revitalizing urban industrial heritage: Enhancing public trust in government through smart city development and open big data analysis using artificial neural network (ANN) modeling. *Cities (London, England), 156*, 105538.

Yu, J., Zhang, C., & Wang, S. (2021). Sparse one-dimensional convolutional neural network-based feature learning for fault detection and diagnosis in multivariable manufacturing processes. *Neural Computing & Applications*. Advance online publication. DOI: 10.1007/s00521-021-06575-6

Zhai, C., Wibowo, S., & Li, L. D. (2024). The effects of over-reliance on AI dialogue systems on students' cognitive abilities: A systematic review. *Smart Learning Environments, 11*(28). Advance online publication. DOI: 10.1186/s40561-024-00316-7

Zhai, X., Chu, X., Chai, C. S., Jong, M. S. Y., Istenic, A., Spector, M., Liu, J. B., Yuan, J., & Li, Y. (2021). A review of artificial intelligence (AI) in education from 2010 to 2020. *Complexity, 2021*, 8812542. Advance online publication. DOI: 10.1155/2021/8812542

Zhang, B., Ma, L., Liu, Z., & Wang, P. (2019). Sustainable Technology Innovation Path Recognition: An Evaluation of Patent Risk of International Trade. *Sustainability*.

Zhang, J., Fan, R., & Shen, F. (2023, December). Introducing Automatic Verification Strategy in Online Study of Computational Science. In *2023 International Conference on Computational Science and Computational Intelligence (CSCI)* (pp. 1708-1713). IEEE.

Zhang, T. J., Zhou, J. Y., Wang, M., Ren, K., Imran, M., & Wang, R. (2022). Cultivation mechanism of green technology innovation in manufacturing enterprises under environmental regulations in China. *Frontiers in Environmental Science, 10*, 926896.

Zhang, T., Ji, W., & Qiu, Y. (2021). A framework of energy-consumption driven discrete manufacturing system. *Sustainable Energy Technologies and Assessments, 47*, 101336. DOI: 10.1016/j.seta.2021.101336

Zhang, W., Ye, S., Mangla, S. K., Emrouznejad, A., & Song, M. (2024). Smart platforming in automotive manufacturing for NetZero: Intelligentization, green technology, and innovation dynamics. *International Journal of Production Economics, 274*, 109289.

Zheng, L., Dong, Y., Chen, J., Li, Y., Li, W., & Su, M. (2022). Impact of Crisis on Sustainable Business Model Innovation—The Role of Technology Innovation. *Sustainability*.

Zhou, B., & Guan, S. (2025). Ethical and Psychological Challenges in Human-AI Romantic Relationships: An Interdisciplinary Critical Study. *Innovative Applications of AI*, *2*(1), 39–45.

Zhuang, M., Concannon, D., & Manley, E. (2022). A Framework for Evaluating Dashboards in Healthcare. *IEEE Transactions on Visualization and Computer Graphics*, *28*(4), 1715–1731. DOI: 10.1109/TVCG.2022.3147154 PMID: 35213306

Zhu, Y., Zhang, H., Siddik, A. B., Zheng, Y., & Sobhani, F. A. (2023). Understanding corporate green competitive advantage through green technology adoption and green dynamic capabilities: Does green product innovation matter? *Systems*, *11*(9), 461.

Ziemba, E. W., Duong, C. D., Ejdys, J., Gonzalez-Perez, M. A., Kazlauskaitė, R., Korzynski, P., & Wach, K. (2024). Leveraging artificial intelligence to meet the sustainable development goals. *Journal of Economics and Management*, *46*, 508–583.

Žužek, T., Gosar, Ž., Kušar, J., & Berlec, T. (2020). Adopting Agile Project Management Practices in Non-Software SMEs: A Case Study of a Slovenian Medium-Sized Manufacturing Company. *Sustainability*.

# About the Contributors

**Cristina Raluca Gh. Popescu**, University of Bucharest, Romania & The Bucharest University of Economic Studies, Romania (popescu_cr@yahoo.com) Bucharest, Romania Bucharest, Romania, Bucharest 0000, RO Dr. Cristina Raluca Gh. Popescu is Full-Professor Habil. at the University of Bucharest, Bucharest, Romania, PhD. Supervisor and Doctoral School Member at The Bucharest University of Economic Studies, Bucharest, Romania, and an award-winning Scientific Researcher. Having more than 24 years of experience, focuses on helping students learn and apply the subjects more effectively, and centers on improving scientific research excellence. Values a special environment where her in-depth knowledge of creative thinking and academic writing can help deliver accurate research results. She is focused on becoming an outstanding researcher, centered on interdisciplinary topics, in a multicultural environment, constantly driven by passion in promoting the Sustainable Development Goals (SDGs). Showing a positive attitude in exploring the endless possibilities of the transformative power of individuals deeply concerned with health and well-being, education, innovation, and responsible production and consumption may be found among the top priorities on her agenda. Her most important skills are: analytical ability and foresight, attention to detail, collaborative spirit, communication skills, creativity, critical thinking, flexibility, intellectual courage, objectivity, persistence, time management, and thirst for knowledge. She is deeply centered on adopting a healthy and balanced lifestyle, thus improving efficiency and productivity in order to be a good and valuable researcher. She is skilled in Business Administration, Economics, Management, Accounting, and Audit. Collaborations: The National Institute for Research and Development in Environmental Protection (I.N.C.D.P.M.), Romania; National Research and Development Institute for Gas Turbines COMOTI, Romania; University of Craiova, Romania; Ministry of Research and Innovation, Romania. She is Member of Chamber of Financial Auditors of Romania (CAFR), Romania as Financial Auditor, and Member of Authority for the Public Oversight of the Statutory

Audit Activity (ASPAAS), Ministry of Public Finance, Romania as Financial Auditor. Single author and coauthor of more than 400 scientific works, with national and international publishers, having national and international coauthors: books, book chapters, articles, congress, conference, and symposium papers. She has more than 3000 citations in national and international publications. Single author and coauthor of numerous scientific works indexed in WorldCat – the world's largest library catalog.

***

**Munir Ahmad** is a seasoned professional in the realm of Spatial Data Infrastructure (SDI), Geo-Information Productions, Information Systems, and Information Governance, boasting over 25 years of dedicated experience in the field. With a PhD in Computer Science, Dr. Ahmad's expertise spans Spatial Data Production, Management, Processing, Analysis, Visualization, and Quality Control. Throughout his career, Dr. Ahmad has been deeply involved in the development and deployment of SDI systems specially in the context of Pakistan, leveraging his proficiency in Spatial Database Design, Web, Mobile & Desktop GIS, and Geo Web Services Architecture. His contributions to Volunteered Geographic Information (VGI) and Open Source Geoportal & Metadata Portal have significantly enriched the geospatial community. As a trainer and researcher, Dr. Ahmad has authored over 50 publications, advancing the industry's knowledge base and fostering innovation in Geo-Tech, Data Governance, and Information Infrastructure, and Emerging Technologies. His commitment to Research and Development (R&D) is evident in his role as a dedicated educator and mentor in the field.

**Raed Atef** is a faculty member, has served as a researcher, and consultant with various organizations. He is actively involved in consulting, research, and training with government agencies, NGOs, and the private sector. He has worked with several universities and has published numerous research papers and studies

**Sushree Behera** is a engineering student at KIIT University.

**Jyoti Dashora**, has a brilliant academic record. She has earned her doctorate degree (Ph.D.) from Faculty of Management Studies, Mohanlal Sukhadia University, Udaipur. She has completed her Master's degree- MBA with specialization in Human Resource Management from ICFAI University, Hyderabad and M.Sc.-Zoology, Mohanlal Sukhadia University, Udaipur Rajasthan. Currently working as Associate Professor, University School of Business, Chandigarh University, Mohali, Punjab. India. She is having 10 years of teaching and research experience. Her keen interest area is Innovative Human resource practices, HR analytics, Business research, Industrial Relation, strategic Human Resource. She has published 32 papers in reputed Journals (including ABDC indexed and SCOPUS indexed Journals and chapters in edited books- Germany publisher –WESER, Wiley publisher (UK), IIP international publisher.. She also presented 28 papers in international and national conferences. She has published 3 books (one authored- National publication, two Edited-Rubicon publication, England and IIP). She has two international innovation patent (Published+ Grant). Recently she has received Best women researcher award of the year. She is a good administrator also as she has worked as Additional Controller of Examination at Sangam University. She is associated with AIMA as a Professional Individual Member (All India Management Association), Delhi.

**Kritika Gupta** is an experienced academician with over 13 years in the education sector. She holds a Ph.D. in Business Management and is currently an Assistant Professor at the University Business School, Chandigarh University. Her research contributions include publications in reputed Q1 journals indexed in SCOPUS and Web of Science. Dr. Gupta is passionate about delivering quality education and advancing academic research, consistently striving to enhance learning outcomes and contribute to the development of knowledge in the field of business management.

**S. Ida Evangeline**, presently working as an Assistant Professor in the Department of Electrical and Electronics Engineering at the Government College of Engineering, Tirunelveli, Tamilnadu, India. She obtained her Bachelor's in Electrical and Electronics Engineering from Manonmaniam Sundaranar University in 2003, and Master's in Power Systems Engineering from Anna University, Chennai, Tamilnadu, India in 2005. She completed her PhD degree in 2023 at Anna University, Chennai, Tamilnadu, India. She has published six research papers in international journals. Her current research interests include optimal power flow, renewable energy, soft computing, machine learning, and deep learning.

**Ilampoornan K** Specialized in High Voltage Engineering, currently he is working as a professor in department of EEE, Bharath Institute of Higher Education and Research

**Hitesh Mohapatra** received the B.E. degree in Information Technology from Biju Patnaik University of Technology (BPUT), Odisha in 2006, and the MTech. Degree in CSE from Odisha University of Technology and Research (OUTR) University, Odisha in 2009. He received his Ph.D. in Computer Science & Engineering in 2021 from Veer Surendra Sai University of Technology (VSSUT), Burla, India. He has contributed 50+ SCI and Scopus indexed research articles. He has authored two books on Software Engineering and C Programming respectively. He has 15 years of teaching experience both in industry and academia. He has served the research community with various capacities like session chair, technical chair, keynote speaker etc. His research interests include wireless sensor network, smart city, smart grid and smart water. Currently he is working as Associate Professor at School of Computer Engineering, KIIT (Deemed to be) University, Bhubaneswar, Odisha, India.

**Suriya Ponnambalam** Specialized in Power system, currently she is working as a Assistant Professor in department of EEE, Bharath Institute of Higher Education and Research

**Muhammad Usman Tariq** has more than 16+ year's experience in industry and academia. He has authored more than 200+ research articles, 110+ case studies, 150+ book chapters and several books other than 4 patents. He is founder and CEO of The Case HQ, a unique repository for courses, narrative and video case studies. Additionally, he is President of Gulf Higher Education (Gulf HE) focused on advancing academic practice. He has been working as a consultant and trainer for industries representing six sigma, quality, health and safety, environmental systems, project management, and information security standards. His work has encompassed sectors in aviation, manufacturing, food, hospitality, education, finance, research, software and transportation. He has diverse and significant experience working with accreditation agencies of ABET, ACBSP, AACSB, WASC, CAA, EFQM and NCEAC. He is a Principal Fellow of Advance HE UK, Senior Fellow of SEDA UK, and Chartered Fellow of CIPD UK other than Senior Member IEEE.

# Index

## A



## B



## C



## D



## E

## T

www.ingramcontent.com/pod-product-compliance
Lightning Source LLC
LaVergne TN
LVHW081523300926
849161LV00006B/1273
* 9 7 9 8 3 3 7 3 7 5 8 4 7 *